WATER IN
DESERT ECOSYSTEMS

US/IBP SYNTHESIS SERIES

This volume is a contribution to the International Biological Program. The United States effort was sponsored by the National Academy of Sciences through the National Committee for the IBP. The lead federal agency in providing support for IBP has been the National Science Foundation.

Views expressed in this volume do not necessarily represent those of the National Academy of Sciences or the National Science Foundation.

Volume

US/IBP SYNTHESIS SERIES | 11

WATER IN DESERT ECOSYSTEMS

Edited by

Daniel D. Evans
University of Arizona

John L. Thames
University of Arizona

Dowden, Hutchinson & Ross, Inc.
Stroudsburg   Pennsylvania

Copyright © 1981 by **The Institute of Ecology**
Library of Congress Catalog Card Number: 79-22432
ISBN: 0-87933-365-0

83 82 81   1 2 3 4 5
Manufactured in the United States of America

Library of Congress Cataloging in Publication Data
Main entry under title:
Water in desert ecosystems.

  (US/IBP synthesis series; 11)
  Includes index.
  1. Desert ecology.   2. Hydrologic cycle.   3. Desert
flora.   I. Evans, Daniel D., 1920–   II. Thames, John
L.   III. Series: U.S./IBP synthesis series; 11.
QH541.5.D4W37   574.5′265   79-22432
ISBN 0-87933-365-0

Distributed world wide by Academic Press,
a subsidiary of Harcourt Brace Jovanovich,
Publishers.

FOREWORD

This book is one of a series of volumes reporting results of research by U.S. scientists participating in the International Biological Program (IBP). As one of the fifty-eight nations taking part in the IBP during the period July 1967 to June 1974, the United States organized a number of large, multidisciplinary studies pertinent to the central IBP theme of the biological basis of productivity and human welfare.

These multidisciplinary studies (Integrated Research Programs), directed toward an understanding of the structure and function of major ecological or human systems, have been a distinctive feature of the U.S. participation in the IBP. Many of the detailed investigations that represent individual contributions to the overall objectives of each Integrated Research Program have been published in the journal literature. The main purpose of this series of books is to accomplish a synthesis of the many contributions for each principal program and thus answer the larger questions pertinent to the structure and function of the major systems that have been studied.

Publications Committee: US/IBP
Gabriel Lasker
Robert B. Platt
Frederick E. Smith
W. Frank Blair, Chairman

PREFACE

This book is one in a series that resulted from the participation of the United States in the International Biological Program (IBP). It deals with hydrologic characteristics of deserts and is based primarily on research conducted as a part of the Desert Biome Program of IBP. The Desert Biome consisted of several sites selected to represent the major desert systems of the western United States. Hydrologic studies were performed at most of the sites, principally by the authors of the various chapters. Many of these studies were designed to support and interact with the biological research of the program conducted primarily in the area of plant and water relations.

The Desert Biome Program, funded through a grant from the National Science Foundation, extended from 1972 to 1977 and was administered by Utah State University. Special recognition is given to Dr. F. H. Wagner, program director for most of the program duration, and to Dr. D. N. Goodall, an early program director. As editors, we wish to extend our sincere appreciation and thanks to each of the authors for his professional efforts in the tedious and time-consuming job of manuscript preparation.

Also, we recognize the valuable contributions of the volume reviewers: Dr. Cyrus McKell, Department of Range Management, Utah State University; Dr. Gerald Stairs, Center for Resource and Environmental Policy Research, Duke University; and Dr. Raymond Turner, U.S. Geological Survey, Tucson, Arizona.

Finally, we gratefully acknowledge the assistance of Dr. Gerald Harwood in editing the manuscript.

Daniel D. Evans
John L. Thames

CONTENTS

LIST OF CONTRIBUTORS

Harry P. Bailey (deceased)
Professor of Geography, Department of Earth Sciences,
University of California at Riverside, Riverside, California 82521

Wayne R. Berkas
Hydrologist, U.S. Geological Survey, WRD, Rolla, Missouri
65401

William B. Bull
Professor of Geosciences, Department of Geosciences,
University of Arizona, Tucson, Arizona 85721

Dwight R. Cable
U.S. Forest Service (retired), 2405 Willa Kenzie Road, Eugene,
Oregon 97401

Gaylon S. Campbell
Associate Professor of Biophysics and Soils, Department of
Agronomy and Soils, Washington State University, Pullman,
Washington 99164

Daniel D. Evans
Professor of Hydrology and Water Resources, Department of
Hydrology and Water Resources, University of Arizona,
Tucson, Arizona 85721

Martin M. Fogel
Professor of Watershed Management, School of Renewable
Natural Resources, University of Arizona, Tucson, Arizona
85721

Lloyd W. Gay
Professor of Watershed Management, School of Renewable
Natural Resources, University of Arizona, Tucson, Arizona
85721

R. J. Hanks
Professor of Soil Science and Biometeorology, Department of
Soil Science and Biometeorology, Utah State University,
Logan, Utah 84322

Grant A. Harris
Professor of Range Management and Forestry, Department of Forestry and Range Management, Washington State University, Pullman, Washington 99164

Louis H. Hekman, Jr.
Assistant Professor of Watershed Management, School of Renewable Natural Resources and Systems Analyst, Center for Quantitative Studies, University of Arizona, Tucson, Arizona 85721

William A. Jury
Associate Professor of Soil Physics, Department of Soil and Environmental Sciences, University of California at Riverside, Riverside, California 92502

John Letey, Jr.
Professor of Soil Physics, Department of Soil and Environmental Sciences, University of California at Riverside, Riverside, California 92502

James A. MacMahon
Professor of Biology, Department of Biology, Utah State University, Logan, Utah 84322

Theodore W. Sammis
Assistant Professor of Agricultural Engineering, Department of Agricultural Engineering, New Mexico State University, Las Cruces, New Mexico 88003

David J. Schimpf
Post Doctoral Research Associate, Department of Biology, Utah State University, Logan, Utah 84322

Lewis H. Stolzy
Professor of Soil Physics, Department of Soil and Environmental Sciences, University of California at Riverside, Riverside, California 92502

John L. Thames
Professor of Watershed Management, School of Renewable Natural Resources, University of Arizona, Tucson, Arizona 85721

WATER IN
DESERT ECOSYSTEMS

1

Desert Systems: An Overview

John L. Thames and *Daniel D. Evans*

DEVELOPMENT PATTERNS

The origins of our modern civilization can be traced back through several millennia to the period when man first learned that it was possible to develop the water resources of warm desert ecosystems. The development of complex irrigation systems in the harsh desert environment stands both as a monument to human ingenuity and as a turning point in history. The advent of irrigated agriculture made the reorganization of nomadic societies into sedentary communities both possible and necessary. The warm desert temperatures, high solar radiation, and mineral-rich soils plus an adequate supply of water allowed the production of food in sufficient abundance to free inhabitants from the onus of existing from one day's food supply to the next. Eventually, and perhaps inevitably, the early civilizations of the arid regions overextended themselves, attaining affluent populations that could not reasonably be supported by their water resources, which were frequently limited, of poor quality, and highly variable.

The peoples of these early civilizations either failed to understand or ignored the tenuous nature of their relationship with the arid environment. Several great civilizations eventually collapsed as their water supplies became inadequate. Prolonged drought, lowering of the water table, salinization, and/or massive siltation were all equally devastating. Succeeding generations rebuilt some of these civilizations, often rediscovering the old methods of water development, but the failures of the subsequent cultures were sometimes more massive than those of their predecessors, and finite water resources were progressively depleted. Frequently these cultures suffered more from man's failure to observe the natural laws of ecological balance than from the capriciousness of nature.

Today this same sequence of events continues to recur to a greater or lesser extent in all arid regions of the world. Many of the old techniques of water development are again being discovered, and many of the errors of ancient times are being repeated as civilizations in arid lands threaten to overextend their finite water resources. The primary difference between the circumstances that prevail today and those that existed in the distant past is one of scale; today's technology can produce benefits and/or failures of a magnitude never before imagined.

In more recent history, most of the world's cultural and industrial development has taken place in geographical areas that have both temperate climate and usually abundant water supplies. Many people and governments have come to regard deserts merely as inhospitable and desolate expanses. But modern man has numerous ties to our planet's arid lands. Emotionally, we have bonds with the desert in both cultural history and religious heritage; economically, we are ever more dependent upon the rich mineral and fossil fuel deposits of the arid lands.

Today many desert areas in the western United States are experiencing rapid growth in population and industry of massive proportions. The developing life-styles in most of these new communities are heavily dependent upon the consumption of both energy and fossil water supplies. It is curious that although we were able to develop a great deal of technology through the ages, we consistently failed to learn from the ecological errors of our predecessors. Today we are capable of understanding the concept of ecological balance, but we seem incapable of internalizing and acting upon the lessons that it can teach us. In nature, ecosystems are based upon a steady-state economy, but human civilization seems to be committed to a growth-oriented system. Ultimately the two are incompatible. Conventional energy and water supplies are finite and may well define the ultimate capacity of our planet for human population. Sooner or later we will reach the point where an inverse relationship will develop between the size of the human population and the quality of life. This relationship will perhaps be first noticed in harsh desert environments where the finite character of the water supply can be more readily appreciated. Whether the necessary understanding and wisdom of action will come in time to prevent our present civilization from following the self-destructive patterns set by our progenitors remains to be seen. In the meantime, the development of the water resources of arid and semiarid lands will increase. An understanding of the intricate roles played by water within various desert environments can help in planning this development so that it does not lead to overextension. It is toward this goal that this book examines some important aspects of the occurrence, behavior, and interaction of water with the biotic and abiotic components of desert ecosystems. The chapters treat several aspects of water—its status, behavior, and influence in desert ecosystems—and primarily reflect the experience gained from the Desert Biome studies in the western desert region of the United States under the International Biological Program.

ARIDITY AND DESERT

As far back as the eleventh century, the word *desert* was used to describe areas that were devoid of human habitation; desolation, more than aridity, was the major connotation of the word. In eighteenth- and nineteenth-century America, the term *desert* was applied to those unsettled lands between the Mississippi River and the Rocky Mountains that were thought to be arid and therefore uninhabitable. Modern dictionaries generally describe deserts as regions of scanty vegetation having little water: "a more or less barren tract incapable of supporting any considerable population without an artificial water supply." Although this definition may be extended to areas of perpetual cold, snow, and, ice and certain oceanic regions as well as the hot, sandy expanses popularized in the various media, most laymen conceive of deserts as areas that do not receive enough rainfall for normal agriculture. This definition is both relative and vague.

Aridity can be defined with greater precision in terms of climate. Much more accurate classifications than those currently existing could be developed if other kinds of data in addition to air temperature were universally available. However, there appears to be no clear distinction between the concepts of aridity and desert. The terms are often used interchangeably, perhaps because most deserts are located within arid systems and share dryness in common, and, similarly to arid systems, are open systems.

Scientists have not appreciably improved on the definitions of these terms. Instead, they have pointed out the complexities of deserts and the inherent difficulties encountered in assigning exact definitions. For example, some areas have abundant groundwater but little precipitation; other regions, such as the Nile Valley, receive water from remote highlands; still other dry areas exist that have sufficient capital to invest in elaborate water resource development projects affording varying degrees of protection from the excessive dryness of their respective climates. On the other hand, areas where annual rainfall may be abundant can experience excessive dryness because of highly permeable soils or periods of drought. The definition of *desert* is further complicated by variability within regions. A desert may have numerous springs and oases or, conversely, a valley situated in an otherwise moist area may lie in the rain shadow of the surrounding mountains and remain dry. Nevertheless, Meigs (1964) notes that some authorities have attempted detailed classifications with terms such as *semiarid, arid, semidesert, desert, true desert,* and *extreme desert,* which are even more relative and qualitative.

Certainly *desert* implies an insufficiency of water, which in turn is related to climate, primarily precipitation and evaporative demand, and which is also influenced on a microscale by geology, soils, and topography. The answer to the question "an insufficiency of water for what purpose?" selects the reference frame; it usually refers to an inability to meet some criterion concerned with fulfillment of the basic human need for growing plants.

DESERT ECOSYSTEMS

The world's desert ecosystems are located within two great arid systems, which almost completely encircle the earth on either side of the equator. The northern system is located between 10 and 50 degrees latitude, and the southern system lies mainly between 20 and 30 degrees latitude. Over 30 percent of the land surface of the earth (including areas within seventy countries, nearly half the nations of the world) is affected by the aridity within these belts. Hydrologically, the belts are open high-pressure systems that develop under the influence of worldwide air circulation patterns; thus, they have no well-defined boundaries. In summer, the systems are displaced toward the equator; consequently, particularly in North America, they are invaded by humid tropical air, which yields high-intensity storms of short duration. The pressure systems drift poleward in winter and are often invaded by frontal storms with characteristic low intensity and long duration.

In a global sense, arid systems are so termed primarily because they receive less precipitation than the world average of 860 mm; this is less than the amount of water that can be potentially evaporated back to the atmosphere.

Numerous climatic indexes have been proposed to characterize the degree of aridity within these systems. Dzerdzeevsklii (1958) listed nineteen indexes that have been modified and proliferated by others. Reitan and Green (1968) observed that most of the indexes and their modifications work about equally well, although some are better suited to particular climate types than others. Classifications based upon soils have been found to be inadequate since in many arid regions there are no true soils but only the materials that have been deposited or exposed without having been appreciably weathered by the environment. In some instances where there are definable soils, their development may have occurred under a different climatic regime. For a similar reason, geomorphological characteristics are unsuitable for defining arid systems, and they are fairly insensitive as reflections of biological characteristics. Vegetative cover can be one of the most effective indicators of aridity because of the close relationship of plants to soil and climate; however, successful interpretation depends upon recognition of the regional patterns of ecologically similar plant associations rather than the presence or absence of single species. Such interpretations have not been made on a global scale.

The classification of warm, arid regions most commonly used is that of Meigs (1953). Meigs used the Thornthwaite (1948) moisture index for determining the portions of the earth's surface that are arid. He then refined the delineation by grouping areas that have similar seasonal distribution of precipitation and similar temperatures for the coldest and warmest months. Three degrees of aridity were thus defined: semiarid, arid, and extremely arid. Boundaries for the three major zones of aridity were established so as to be in substantial agreement with generally accepted temperature limits. The Thornthwaite method was developed empirically using data from humid climates. Although it works well for the conditions under which it was developed, it is well known that the method gives lower estimates of evaporation for arid areas, such as the southwestern United States, than actually occur (see chapter 2). Bailey (1958) developed a precipitation index that assumes the existence of a proportionality between dry bulb and wet bulb temperatures, which would allow humidity to be inferred. The index is $EP = P/1.025^{T \pm x}$, where EP is effective precipitation, P is precipitation, T is temperature, and x is a connection factor that lowers annual temperature for winter rain regimes and increases it for summer rain regimes. Two degrees of aridity are defined by the index: semiarid and arid. Bailey's world map is given in figure 2-4.

The physiographic nature of the various deserts within these arid and semiarid regions may differ widely, but their characteristic lack of water generally results in a reduced amount of vegetative cover. Desert life forms share the common problem of survival in an environment where the availability of water is uncertain, and, in response to this problem, the adaptive similarities among desert plants and animals from the various continents are often striking. Both related and unrelated plant species have developed, through parallel evolutionary processes, comparable forms and structures that permit survival in similar ecological niches. Although remarkable similarities exist among various deserts with respect to the structure and function of their ecosystems, each desert can be distinguished by the associations in its plant and animal communities.

Water in desert ecosystems is in constant motion within the soil system along gradients created by ever-changing differences in potentials. It responds to gravitational forces and the demands of plants and the atmosphere. The water delivered to the system depends upon global patterns of air circulation, which may be modified by local or regional influences. The topography, geology, and soils of the particular locale determine the subsequent distribution of water within the system.

DESERTS OF THE WESTERN UNITED STATES

The desert region of the western United States contains the Great Basin, Mojave, and the northern areas of the Sonoran and Chihuahuan deserts; it extends southward from central and eastern Oregon, through nearly all of Nevada and Utah into southern California, where it borders the eastern slopes of the Sierra Nevada, San Bernardino, and Cuyamoca ranges. Portions of central and eastern Washington on the Columbia plateau form northern satellites to the Great Basin Desert. Eastward, desert extends into southwestern Wyoming, western Colorado, and through most of Arizona into western New Mexico (see figure 2-3).

The greater portion of North America's deserts are located within the basin and range physiographic province that is characterized by numerous mountain ranges of varying size forming biogeographical islands rising from the desert floor; the total area of the basin floors greatly exceeds that of the mountains. The basin and range structure precludes the existence of the vast plains that characterize many of the great deserts of the world. Also unique to the North American deserts is the additional water provided to the basins by runoff originating at higher elevations in the more humid mountain catchment areas. With very few exceptions, the streams originating from the mountain catchments are ephemeral. These sandy and often highly permeable water courses are dry most of the time and generally run only short distances, frequently anastomosing as they traverse the desert bajadas and basin floors. Following the course of least resistance, many of the streams dissipate their occasional water flows through sandy channel beds to groundwater or discharge into local basins within the desert. Water losses to seepage and evaporation are so high in desert streams that little of the flow reaches terminal basins or larger river systems.

The mountains and hills of the basin and range province are sharply defined massive folds or uplifts or formations of volcanic material that rise from the desert valley floors in rocky hills, cliffs, or escarpments. Generally desert mountains are surrounded by bajadas or gentle slopes of alluvium, which fan and intergrade with moderately level basin floors. The orographic effects of the mountain islands create a higher frequency of fluvial processes, greater rates of runoff, erosion, and sedimentation. The interrelationships and effects of these processes on land-form building processes are described in chapter 3.

The sequence of soils in the mountain and basin country typically follows a repeating pattern of lithosols on the mountains, medium- to coarse-texture soils on alluvial fans and terraces, and alluvial, solonchak, or solonetz soils in the bottoms. In general, the soils of the mountains and hills are shallow and coarse textured with little moisture-holding capacity. The alluvial fans of the bajadas are also coarse textured but much deeper. Infiltration rates are relatively high on the alluvial fans. Consequently the materials can store considerable water for later release to plants and, in some areas, to ground water aquifers. Infiltration into the soils of the basins is not rapid, and the downward movement of water is often impeded by indurated calcium carbonate layers and, more infrequently, by silicified hardpans.

Desert basin soils are low in organic matter content and generally have hard surfaces with little or no protective cover or litter. Surface crusting is also common. Exceedingly high temperatures occur in the upper three to six inches of soil due to the high solar radiation, which is unimpeded by cloud cover (see chapter 4). Because of the resulting high evaporation rates, the surfaces are almost always dry, even within a few days after a rain. As one would expect from the harsh surface environment, the population of microfauna and flora that would help maintain soil porosity at the surface is considerably less than that of more humid areas, particularly within the large expanses between the widely spaced plants of the desert. Similarly plant roots are sparse near the soil surface, and arthropod numbers are low. Burrowing animals, whose activities help maintain soil permeability, are largely restricted to areas beneath shrubs and cacti.

Raindrop compaction of the unprotected surface of the bare interspaces between plants is pronounced. Since the compacting action of raindrops is a function of their terminal velocity, the intense summer rains have an especially severe effect on surface compaction. In addition, many of the soils have a thin surface film of readily dispersible clay colloids, which may swell to form an impervious barrier to the entry of water, even when the water remains ponded on the surface for extended periods. Soils containing appreciable amounts of exchangeable sodium are also common and produce even greater dispersion and sealing effects.

Desert pavements are common, but their role in desert hydrology has not been well established. Many of the pavements were formed by the erosion of finely grained materials from the soil's surface. Pavements do protect the soil surface from splash erosion by raindrops and create a surface roughness that quite possibly detains surface runoff. In areas where a vesicular layer is formed beneath the pavement, infiltration might be enhanced. However, regardless of the existence of pavements, sheet flow of surface water on desert soils is a common phenomenon and, when concentrated in channels, produces violent flash flooding.

Precipitation in the western desert region is greatly influenced by such factors as the distance from the ocean, the formation of dry, stable air masses, a paucity of storm systems, and the absence of mechanisms that regularly cause significant atmospheric convergence, instability, and lifting. The climatic effects of orographic barriers are greatest near the northern boundaries of the desert region where winter rains are considerably reduced. This barrier effect extends southward into Baja California, but it becomes masked by the decreasing frequency of winter cyclones. Alteration in wind belt patterns during summer brings moisture from the Gulf of Mexico and distributes it westward across Mexico and northward into the southwestern United States, including the Arizona-California border region and part of Baja California. This moist air produces scattered summer convection storms in the desert and is important in the differentiation between the Sonoran and Mojave deserts; the former receives considerably more precipitation and supports a more luxuriant growth of vegetation. The southwestern desert regions receive most of their rainfall in the summer while the northern and western regions have a winter maximum; the Arizona deserts enjoy some precipitation in both seasons.

VEGETATION OF NORTH AMERICAN DESERTS

Although the deserts of North America cover a vast expanse of land, they have certain features in common. Prominent among these are low precipitation of erratic frequency and quantity and very high diurnal and seasonal temperature variation, which affect both soil and air. Strong winds and low humidity are also common to the desert environment. Succulents and other dominant plants of these desert regions are well adapted to these conditions. The Great Basin, Mojave, Sonoran, and Chihuahuan deserts are distinguished primarily by regional environmental differences of climate and terrain and by their characteristic plant species. The vegetation of the desert regions of the western United States is of two general types, sagebrush (*Artemisia* spp.) and saltbushes (*Atriplex* spp.) in the northern portion and mixed shrubs and succulents in the southern portion. Creosote bush (*Larrea divaricata*) communities provide the dominant cover of the southern deserts, particularly in the basins between mountain ranges; however, the varied topography and greater fluvial activity on the alluvial bajadas give rise to mixed stands of vegetation including large shrubs, notably mesquite (*Prosopis*) and palo verde (*Cercidum* sp.), and a variety of succulents. The two most widespread communities in the northern Great Basin Desert are those dominated by sagebrush and saltbrush.

The Great Basin Desert consists of wide valleys at elevations approximating 4,000 feet separated by numerous mountain ranges, which often exceed 8,000 feet. Its climate is distinct from those of the Sonoran, Mojave, and Chihuahuan deserts largely by virtue of its being considerably cooler; here, the frost-free period is quite short and killing frosts are possible at any time during the year. The Great Basin Desert has been termed a "cold" desert by Oosting (1956). Here the dominant vegetative forms tend to be shrubby chenopods and composites, which are distinct from the scrub plants found in the southern deserts. Oosting has described two major communities in the Great Basin Desert, having few dominants. The first is an association of shrubs dominated by various species of *Artemisia* in the northern portions of the desert. Throughout the southern portion of the Great Basin Desert is the shadscale association, with shadscale (*Atriplex confertifolia*) and bud sage (*Artemisia* sp.) as major species. The two communities are often associated, but saltbush more frequently occurs at lower elevations and on saline soils or those with alkaline tendencies. The communities often appear in pure stands whose boundaries are determined by changes in soil type. Other plant species found within these communities differ according to salt concentrations and other soil conditions.

The Mojave Desert lies almost entirely within the state of California and is physiographically similar to the Great Basin except that its elevations are generally lower (between 1,000 and 4,000 feet); it usually receives less than five inches of rain, compared to four to twelve inches in the Great Basin. Mojave desert summers are hot and dry (except for occasional cloudbursts); most of the rainfall occurs during winter storms. Generally the environment of the Mojave is similar to, although more extreme than, that of the Great Basin. Oosting (1956) notes that this is borne out by the presence of similar plant species, the distribution of which is controlled by soil conditions such as texture and salinity. However, the presence of certain characteristic species such as the Joshua tree (*Yucca brevifolia*), found at higher elevations (3,000 to 4,000 feet), and the absence of *Artemisias* justifies the vegetational distinction from the Great Basin desert. At lower elevations, where precipitation is reduced, creosote bush is found in association with *Franseria* sp. These two plants are dominants at the lower elevations and occupy perhaps 70 percent of the total area of the Mojave Desert.

The Sonoran Desert is highly variable both physiographically and botanically and contains large areas of sand dunes and plains. Precipitation is uncertain and varies from two to four inches near the Gulf of California to more than ten inches in parts of Arizona. Temperatures in the Sonoran Desert are frequently quite high. At lower elevations and on the plains, *Larrea-Artemisia* associations dominate as in the Mojave Desert. Ocotillo (*Fouquieria splendens*) is common. Drainage tends to streambeds and rivers rather than playas and lakes, and species such as *Prosopsis, Cercidium,* and *Olyneya* are common along riverbeds. In Arizona and northern Sonora, the Sonoran Desert occurs at elevations of 1,000 to 3,000 feet where a great variety of life forms is found. Palo verde is dominant and is associated with many columnar and arborescent cacti, including the saguaro (*Carnegiea gigantea*) and various species of *Opuntia*.

The Chihuahuan Desert extends southeastward from southern New Mexico and western Texas into Mexico. Much of it lies between 4,000 and 6,000 feet; precipitation varies from three to twelve inches, occurring mostly in the summer. Temperatures in the Chihuahuan Desert tend to be slightly lower than in the Sonoran Desert, and frosts are not uncommon. Oosting (1956) notes that plant communities of the Chihuahuan Desert tend to be somewhat less complex than in the Sonoran Desert. Shrubs and semishrubs predominate in association with various stem succulents. Ocotillo (of wide occurrence), creosote bush, and mesquite are the only major species of both the Chihuahuan and the Sonoran deserts. Additional species are locally important and may be conspicuous due to their large size; these include large semi-succulents, such as yucca, *Nolina,* and *Dasylirion,* and leaf succulents such as *Agave*.

WATER IN DESERT ECOSYSTEMS

Perhaps more is known of precipitation in the deserts of the western United States than other large desert regions of the world, particularly the sparsely populated deserts of the developing countries. However, our knowledge of the degree of aridity or dryness of the U.S. deserts is no greater than exists for the rest of the world. This is due not so much to a lack of meteorological records as to a lack of methods for expressing dryness. Historically such expressions have attempted to establish relationships between supply (precipitation) and demand (potential evapotranspiration). The problem lies in expressing demand. Three methods of doing this have been: direct measurement of water loss from evaporation pans or lysimeters; empirical relationships developed between observed water loss from irrigated crops, lakes, or watersheds and commonly available climatological data; and theoretical relationships attempting to describe the transfer of moisture at the surface of the earth, which fall into two approaches. In one the energy balance at the earth's surface is determined, and the portion of the heat that goes into evaporation is computed. The other approach attempts to measure the turbulent transfer of water vapor from the earth's surface by measuring the vapor pressure gradient at the surface and computing the transport by turbulent diffusion. These methods are discussed in detail in chapter 8.

It is questionable if actual evapotranspiration ever approaches the potential demand under natural desert conditions except perhaps in colder seasons during and immediately after substantial and prolonged precipitation. However, if deserts are to be developed for production, a critical factor must be the establishment of a balance between water supply and need. This requires a precise definition of aridity. Methods for defining evaporative demand are discussed in detail in chapter 8.

In the deserts of the western United States, as in all other desert regions, the character of the plant and animal species and their associations has been forged by the stresses of extreme climatic variability. In Tucson, Arizona, for example, there can be three months or more between significant rainfall events 5 percent of the time. Rain may not occur within a period of up to five months 2 percent of the time. These rare but inevitable occurrences, compounded by high temperature and radiation loads, have resulted in the physiological, morphological, and symbiotic strategies employed by the hardy and resourceful desert biota to avoid, evade, or moderate the effects of the harsh desert environment. For example, the inverted cone shape of many desert shrubs acts much as a funnel to concentrate meager rainfall events, converting them by stem flow into meaningful amounts at the base of the plant. Other examples of plant adaptability are given in chapter 7.

One of the more interesting mechanisms of adaptability is the apparent ability of some desert plants to withdraw water from soils at pressures much greater than those that can be accurately measured (see chapter 6). Vapor movement in the soil, which has little or no importance in humid systems, may allow some desert plant species, particularly the lower forms, to survive and even thrive in the absence of liquid flow. An example can be found in the algal colonies growing beneath crystalline rocks, which transmit some light. The importance of these lower forms is discussed in chapter 4. The large diurnal temperature extremes of western deserts provide the driving force that may be a basic factor in sustaining desert life. Vapor transfer in desert soils is discussed in chapter 9.

It is something of a paradox that the tough desert ecosystems are often termed fragile. But they are fragile only to the extent that the activities of man impose different extremes to which the native biota cannot adapt. Desertification by man's activities is being decried the world over. The process is not limited to areas more productive of human needs, for almost without exception the deserts of the earth themselves have been and are being desertified, many to the point where they fit the predictions of Ezekiel, who warned that the highly developed Mesopotamia would become a "desolation, a dry land, a place wherein no man dwelleth."

HYDROLOGIC MODELING

Despite more than a century of quantitative study of hydrologic processes, a comprehensive model of a complete system in nature has yet to be developed. Deterministic modeling of hydrologic subsystems has advanced greatly during the last two decades; but unfortunately, the more closely a deterministic model approximates a real world process, the greater must be its complexity and the number of parameters considered. Thus opportunities for both instrumental and sampling errors are increased in complex models, and many of them cannot be determined, either directly or independently. The problem becomes further compounded when attempts are made to link several processes in order to simulate the behavior of a system. Accordingly it is a common practice to determine parameters empirically by calibrating the model to some actual world system. The resultant transferability of the model then depends upon the degree of accuracy with which the selected system represents the real situation.

Complex models have the advantage of increasing the understanding of a system. By means of sensitivity analyses, the magnitude of the influence of a model's components can be appreciated. Models that are designed to answer specific questions must be greatly simplified, but their potential applicability can be exceedingly diverse. For example, Darcy's law was devised as a simple and direct means by which questions on the design of a water filter system for Dijon, France, could be answered. It has in turn, however, provided a basis for hundreds of additional models that have produced better understanding and more exact quantification of a number of processes that are operative in the movement of water through soils.

Water movement through saturated soils can generally be reasonably quantified. In desert soils, however, the predominant movement of water occurs as an unsteady, unsaturated flow. Models have been developed for this unsaturated liquid flow in two-dimensional systems (see chapter 11), but modeling the simultaneous movement of water in both liquid and gaseous phases in nonhomogenous systems remains a goal for the future, as does the formidable task of devising a satisfactory model of a three-dimensional system.

The modeling of the overland flow of water from precipitation, as currently done, involves the assumption of sheet flow, a common phenonenon observed in desert systems during and after intense rains. Such models use either kinematic routing or a system of routing flow between and adjacent to facets of a drainage area while maintaining continuity of flow. Usually storm hydrographs developed from these routings compare well with actual desert stream hydrographs.

Modeling of water flow in plant systems is still in its infancy. The phenomenon itself is not well understood because it involves both physical and physiological processes and is further compounded by flow across various boundaries of plant root and foliage systems. For purposes of modeling, plants are often considered to be passive systems governed by the changing potentials between soil and atmosphere (see chapter 7).

Groundwater models have been used in practical applications for some time and are frequently considered as systems that are independent of the surface. In fact, groundwater systems in desert regions are not often greatly affected by natural hydrologic processes occurring near the desert surface. Recharge in desert systems takes place primarily through permeable reaches of ephemeral channels, through geologic structures higher up on the bajadas, or through more humid mountain catchments. Groundwater is sometimes an important factor in the makeup of the biota of localized areas of desert ecosystems; examples are found in oases and in phreatophytic communities along major desert stream channels. The primary emphasis of the Desert Biome portion of the International Biological Program has been placed upon phenomena in the life zones of desert ecosystems.

Considerable progress has been made in modeling rainfall as a stochastic process (see chapter 10) although the problem of spatial distribution remains. A logical approach to hydrological modeling of a desert system is to combine stochastic models of precipitation input with deterministic models of soil water movement and overland flow (see also the discussion in chapter 5). Simulations made over a long period with such a model would provide a probabilistic output of evapotranspiration, soil water status, and runoff; this type of modeling and simulation is presented in chapter 12.

Although numerous advances have been made, the complete quantification of water in desert ecosystems has a long way to go. Much has been learned, but much more remains to be learned. The remaining problems are not simple; they involve both exceedingly complex physical and physiological processes and sensitive areas of our social, political, and economic structure. Solutions will not be easy and may never be complete, but they are worthy of endeavor by the best minds who will seek technical solutions and will also attempt to achieve a rational and lasting pattern of development that is compatible with the natural functioning of desert ecosystems.

REFERENCES

Bailey, H. P. 1958. A simple moisture index based upon a primary law of evaporation. *Geograf. Ann.* **3–4**:196–215.

Dzerdzeevskii, B. L. 1958. On some climatological problems and microclimatological studies of arid and semi-arid lands in the U.S.S.R., pp. 315–325. In *Climatology and Microclimatology,* v. 11. Proc. Canberra Symp. UNESCO, Paris.

Meigs, P. 1953. World distribution of arid and semi-arid homoclimates, pp. 203–210. In Arid zone programme, v. 1, *Reviews of Research on Arid Zone Hydrology.* UNESCO, Paris.

Meigs, P. 1964. Classification and occurrence of Mediterranean and dry climates. In Arid zone research, *Land Use in Semi-arid Mediterranean Cli-*

mates, v. 26. UNESCO, Paris.

Oosting, H. J. 1956. *The Study of Plant Community: An Introduction to Plant Ecology,* 2d ed. W. H. Freeman and Co., San Francisco.

Reitan, C. H., and C. R. Green. 1968. Appraisal of research on the weather and climate of seven environments. In Arid zone research, *Land Use in Semi-arid Mediterranean Climates.* UNESCO, Paris.

Thornthwaite, C. W. 1948. An approach toward a rational classification of climate. *Geogr. Rev.* **38:**55–94.

2
Climatic Features of Deserts

Harry P. Bailey

A substantial proportion of the earth's land surface is arid. According to James (1959) 17.3 percent of continental area must be so classified, and nearly a tenth of that figure must be attributed to the dry lands of North America. Planimetry of arid areas (figure 2-1) gives comparable proportions. Mexico and the United States share aridity in nearly equal areas, but in neither country are large areas subject to the extreme aridity that affects part of North Africa and Southwest Asia. In a world context, the dry lands of the United States are located in higher latitudes and stand at higher altitudes than is typical of many other arid regions of the world.

Aridity can be accounted for largely, although not entirely, in climatic terms. It is the distinctive property of an arid climate that terrain subjected to the influence of aridity will lose all or nearly all water gained through precipitation to evaporation losses. Although evaporation cannot dispose of precipitation as it occurs, in dry climates it can be considered a continuous process that overtakes the episodic occurrence of rainfall within a matter of days or weeks, thus allowing no moisture surplus to accumulate as surface waters that perennially flow to the sea. The major rivers found in desert regions owe their existence to bordering humid regions that export moisture surplus by rivers that may cross deserts, but only at the expense of diminished flow.

The atmospheric process common to all dry regions is that of descending air (Leighly, 1953). In the subtropics, such descent is part of large-scale planetary circulation and is seen on weather charts by the prevailing presence of atmospheric pressure greater than that in surrounding parts of the globe. Sinking motion of air is also aided by the presence of cool surfaces, as noted in the cool sea-surface temperatures found in the eastern parts of the oceanic gyres in subtropical latitudes (Lydolph, 1957). In contrast, the western sections of the same gyres feature much warmer sea-surface temperatures, thus allowing air to rise in convective columns deep enough to initiate the precipitation process before encountering high-level subsidence. This difference is the principal reason for the existence of humid climates on east coasts of continents that have dry climates on west coasts.

Air descent is also caused by the interaction of airstreams with rough terrain, a condition found in many coastal regions with bordering mountains. The upgliding motion of air on windward slopes leads to enhancement of precipitation, whereas lee slopes are dry in the presence of descending air. If the mountains are very high, as in the Andes and Himalayas, or are arranged in ridges parallel to the coast, a rain-shadow desert is created of regional scope

13

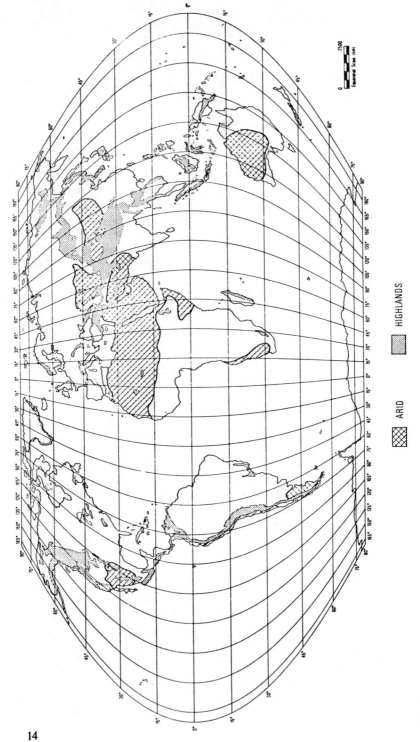

FIGURE 2-1. *Arid regions of the world, delimited by the Bailey moisture index* $(S = 2.5)$.

ARID   HIGHLANDS

rather than of local nature in the lee of the mountains. Such is the case in the United States, where moist air from the Pacific first encounters coastal mountains and then the still higher Sierran-Cascadian chain.

In the United States, in fact, all factors pertinent to aridity apply to some degree. In the Southwest, high pressure prevails much of the year; only occasionally in the winter half of the year does the atmosphere develop structures that bring substantial precipitation. In the Southwest, summer is even more placid than the winter season, although wandering streams of tropical air bring scattered showers to the interior (Leighly, 1956). Certainly the northern sections of the intermountain region—that lying between the mountains of the Pacific border and the Rocky Mountains in midcontinent—would be much better watered if they were not hemmed in by highland chains to the east as well as to the west.

Sufficient increase of latitude or altitude terminates aridity, as is expressed by the forested summits of the highest mountains of even the driest state, Nevada, and by the lack of true desert along the international boundary with Canada. However, the varied terrain of the intermountain region supplies many combinations of circumstances that serve as climatic controls over the aridity factor. Hence, the lowest and flattest sections of the Columbia Basin are arid even though they are north of the forty-sixth parallel. A thousand miles to the south, aridity is far more widespread, as might be expected from the increasing gradient of heat and decreasing gradient of precipitation, but slopes above 1,500 meters in altitude lose the aspect of true aridity, and high mountains, as found in Nevada, are generally forested.

To examine precipitation-evaporation relations, the distribution of precipitation must be compared with that of evaporation from lakes and reservoirs (figures 2-2 and 2-3). However, the distribution of precipitation is known with greater accuracy than is true of evaporation, which is measured at points much less numerous than those representing rain gauges. Despite that discrepancy, it can be safely concluded that losses to standing water through evaporation are greater than gains from precipitation throughout the intermountain region except on those highlands restricted to altitudes greater than 2,000 meters.

Evapotranspiration, when measured from soil and vegetation, is less than that measured from standing water, particularly as measured from evaporation pans. Since this is so, the flow of the Colorado River can be explained. In terms of depth of runoff, averaged over its entire basin area, the Colorado River is not impressive: 1.1 inches (2.8 cm) (Miller et al., 1963). Great Basin drainage is similar in depth, but geomorphic history of that region has not allowed formation of an integrated drainage system that can deliver its waters to the sea.

DEFINITION OF ARIDITY

In a region with terrain as complex as that of the western United States, it is difficult to delineate with conviction the limit (boundary) of the arid province or to depict variations in intensity of aridity within the dry zone. The difficulty lies in the fact that aridity is controlled not by precipitation alone (which is fairly well known) but also by the factors that control evaporation (which are

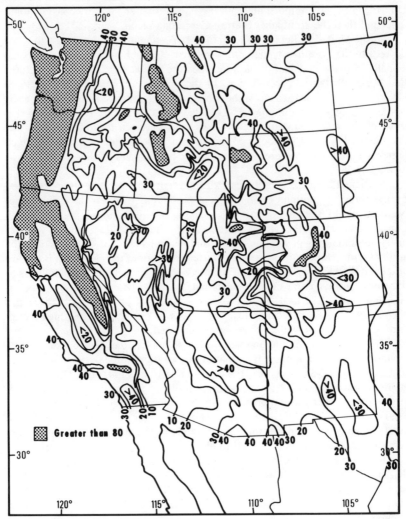

FIGURE 2-2. *Mean annual precipitation (cm) in the western United States (after Bryson and Hare, 1974).*

less well known). Moisture indexes have been generally determined by equations that take the following form:

$$\text{Moisture index} = k \; \frac{\text{Moisture gain, or precipitation}}{\text{Moisture loss, or evaporation}} \qquad (2.1)$$

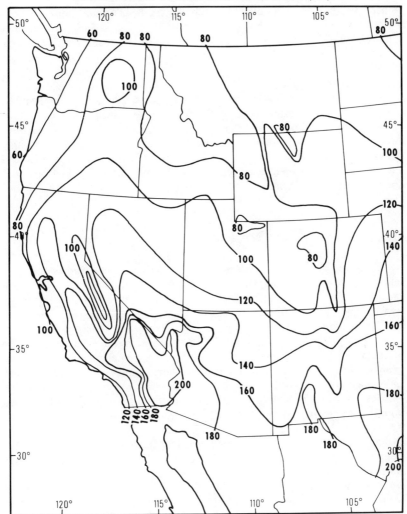

MEAN ANNUAL EVAPORATION FROM LAKES (cm)

FIGURE 2-3. *Mean annual evaporation from lakes (cm) in the western United States (after Bryson and Hare, 1974).*

In such an equation, the proportionality constant k serves to adjust the moisture index to a scale dictated by convenience, precipitation is usually given as a depth (or its heat equivalent, LE, where L is the latent heat of vaporization), and moisture loss is given as a depth (or the heat available for evaporation as supplied by a radiation term such as net radiation, R). It is not necessary in forming an index for all terms to refer to the same physical units, but all terms must move numerically as if they referred to consistent units. Hence, moisture loss in equation 2.1 has often been stated indirectly by a temperature term or a vapor-pressure deficit for the sake of convenience (Thornthwaite, 1943). However, the validity of so doing rests entirely upon the accuracy with which such substitutions can be converted to actual or potential evaporation.

From the form of equation 2.1, it is obvious that the moisture index is in the form of a ratio and thus is dependent only upon the comparative magnitude of precipitation and evaporation, not their absolute magnitude. Thus, a low-budget moisture regime with minimal evaporation may create a more mesic environment than one with more precipitation and high evaporation. As evaporation is inhibited in cold climates, aridity tends to disappear as latitude and altitude increase, as mentioned previously with respect to the distribution of aridity in the United States.

MEASUREMENT OF EVAPORATION

From the viewpoint of instrumentation for climatic calculation of evaporation, systems of measurement can be divided into mass-transfer systems or radiation-balance systems (U.S. Geological Survey, 1952). By the mass-transfer approach, the upward transport of water vapor is sensed by the difference in humidity between two or more psychrometers mounted on a mast, which also carries anemometers. The great sensitivity of evaporation to the turbulent nature of daytime air movement requires an elaborate equation for approximation of real air motion; it is in the shortcomings of both measurement and theory of the wind field that the mass-transfer approach incurs errors.

The radiation-balance approach compares the amount of heat and light from the sky hemisphere with that emanating from the terrestrial hemisphere (net radiation). Measurement of the difference is indicative of the amount of heat consumed in the evaporation process. That heat term is then converted to a depth of water. With the radiation-balance method, it is necessary to determine heat flows from the surface to the air and to the subsoil by conduction and also to determine the amount of heat entering the system through advection if accuracy is to be obtained comparable to that of the mass-transfer analysis. Unfortunately the conductive and advective terms are difficult to measure, so the radiation-balance method is really a heat-balance determination of complex nature.

Penman (1956) has supplied an empirical method of calculating evaporation from instruments at a single level, a method preferred by researchers in agriculture as a practical alternative to the more elaborate installations required by mass-transfer and radiation-balance analyses. For regional studies, however, even the Penman equation demands wind, humidity, and radiation measurements that cannot be supplied for a sufficient number of places. Hence, geographers and others interested in regional assessments have been forced to accept temperature as a basis for estimating evaporation.

SIMULATION OF EVAPORATION FROM TEMPERATURE

The best-known method of calculating evaporation from temperature is that of Thornthwaite (1945), who derived regression equations from selected sites where both evaporation and temperature were known by measurement. Thornthwaite's equations fit his data well but lose accuracy when applied to regions differing in climatic properties from those of his data base. Hence, warm subtropical climates have conditioned his equations to suit the cloud cover, humidity, and wind conditions of the southeastern United States. In the Southwest, those equations understandably underestimate evaporation. In cold climates, by contrast, his equations have been conditioned by the dry, sunny summer climate of elevated basins of the intermountain region. To calculate sufficient evaporation for a dry, sunny summer combined with a cold winter, an overriding term was necessary to make summer evaporation the more efficient the colder the winter. However, the override overcorrects in the very cold conditions of subpolar and subalpine environments, where the calculated evaporation is much too great to account for the stream systems that obtain from those environments (Bailey and Johnson, 1972).

For those reasons, the Thornthwaite system of water balance is not employed in this study. In its place, evaporation is simulated from temperature by a method suggested by Bailey (1958) that rests upon stipulation in advance of a reasonable humidity environment in which temperature acts as the independent variable. The term 1.025^t was used to calculate the depression of the wet-bulb thermometer (in °F) representative of an environment in which the relative humidity averaged around 70 percent. The depression of the wet-bulb thermometer is related to evaporation through the psychrometric constant:

$$\text{Psychrometric constant} = \frac{\text{Vapor pressure deficit}}{(\text{Wet-bulb depression})\rho}, \qquad (2.2)$$

where the vapor pressure deficit is the difference between the vapor pressure of the evaporating surface at the wet-bulb temperature, and the vapor pressure of ambient air; ρ is atmospheric pressure (Smithsonian Institution, 1958).

The significance of vapor-pressure deficit in equation 2.2 was established by Dalton in the last century, who found experimentally that evaporation was proportional to the product of the vapor-pressure deficit (as defined above) and wind speed (Dalton, 1802). To incorporate the Bailey temperature term in a moisture index suited to metric data, his monthly moisture index(s) becomes:

$$s = 0.018 \left(\frac{P}{1.045^t} \right), \qquad (2.3)$$

where P and T refer to monthly precipitation (mm) and temperature (°C), respectively.

An annual moisture index (S) is then formed by summation of monthly indices or can be approximated by direct calculation:

$$S = 0.018 \ (P/1.045^{T + x}), \tag{2.4}$$

where P and T refer to annual precipitation (mm) and temperature (°C), respectively, and x is a correction to T supplied by nomogram or calculation.

Comparison of the moisture schemes of Bailey and Thornthwaite shows many differences to the advantage of the former. Less cumbrous in use, the Bailey moisture index avoids signal defects to the Thornthwaite index: bias toward aridity in winter-rain climates (the lower Sacramento Valley of California is classed as arid by Thornthwaite, despite the presence of a prosperous rain-fed agriculture and stream-sculptured landscape), bias toward aridity in cold climates (which are represented in alpine and subalpine portions of the intermountain region), and lack of flexibility in adjusting the moisture index to complex terrain where lapse rate corrections are essential.

To convert the temperature term of equation 2.3 to a calculation of evaporation, it is necessary to recognize the conditions under which s represents the evaporating power of the climate:

$$s = s_u = 0.018 \ (p/1.045^t), \tag{2.5}$$

where s_u is the moisture index if precipitation p equals evaporation (N_1 at temperature t).

With monthly data, s_u attains a numerical value around 0.5; mechanics of the Bailey moisture index suggest refinement to 0.531. Monthly evaporation, which is conceived under the constraints of the argument to represent water need (N_1), is then calculated by equation 2.6:

$$N_1 = 0.531 \ \left(\frac{1.045^t}{0.018} \right) = 29.5 \ (1.045^t), \tag{2.6}$$

where N_1 is monthly evaporation in mm, and t is monthly temperature in °C.

If the limitations of accuracy of a temperature-driven calculation of evaporation are accepted for the moment, the performance characteristics of equation 2.6 can be summarized:

1. Monthly evaporation ranges from 29.5 mm at a temperature of 0°C to 266.5 mm at 50°C.
2. Evaporation increases exponentially with temperature increase at the rate of 4.5 percent for each Celsius degree.
3. Such a rate of increase, if other things were equal, would take place in air with relative humidity averaging (over a twenty-four-hour day) 77 to 78 percent in the temperature range 0 to 10°C, but dropping to less than 60 percent at temperatures in excess of 40°C.
4. For climatic data in the United States, N_1 is about 90 percent of potential evapotranspiration (PET) as calculated by Thornthwaite. Note, however, that monthly temperatures below 0°C calculate zero evaporation by Thornthwaite's equations, while zero evaporation is approached only asymptotically by equation 2.6 (see point 1 above).

Comments on these characteristics must include note of the fact that equation 2.6 unrealistically calls for evaporation at subfreezing temperature conditions, although the amounts are low. Relative to point 3, it must be expected that the equation will overestimate evaporation if ambient air is moister than that subsumed. Conversely a negative error will develop in ambient air drier than that subsumed.

Most readers will be concerned by point 4, indicating that N_1 is but 90 percent of PET. Several considerations recommend the utility of N_1 however:

1. For time-averaged data as long as a month, monthly precipitation sufficient to equal N_1 ordinarily contains periods of rain sufficiently intense to exceed the infiltration capacity of the soil. Hence, runoff greater than zero can be expected with rainfall equal to N_1; it will increase, of course, as precipitation rises above that level.

2. In dry climates, at least, it is unrealistic to calculate PET on the basis of ambient temperatures that are developed in fact over a dry landscape. If enough water were introduced to induce PET, temperatures would lower in consequence of attendant evaporation, and "actual" evaporation in that case might fall closer to N_1 than to PET.

3. Rain-fed agriculture reaches its dry margin in the cultivation of the small grains (wheat, barley, and millet, for example). In such practice it is not necessary to receive rainfall in amounts equal to PET. Dry periods during the growth period are normal and expected; the water need of such crops is therefore below the amounts called for by a full, green vegetation cover. Inspection of data up to this point indicates that precipitation equal to or exceeding N_1 for as few as three consecutive months is sufficient inducement to establish grain crops.

With these considerations in mind, it is now possible to return to the moisture provinces of the western United States through discussion of the analyses provided by equations 2.3 and 2.4.

DISTRIBUTION OF THE MOISTURE PROVINCES
OF THE WESTERN UNITED STATES

When the Bailey moisture index was first published in 1958, the suggestion was made that moisture provinces be defined according to the critical values of S (the moisture index in annual form) that are shown in table 2-1.

The numerical series provided in table 2-1 under S are in geometric progression, arranged so that the extremes fall in geographically reasonable locations; thus the arid zone agrees in distribution with the regions of interior drainage and, in the case of the wet category, in agreement with forest types generally viewed as rain forests. The number of subdivisions between those extremes is arbitrary and could be viewed as infinite if advantage is to be taken of the capability of the equations to provide a continuous numerical series. The

TABLE 2-1. *Limits of Five Moisture Provinces*

S	Province	Realm
	Arid (E)	
2.5		
	Semiarid (D)	Dry
4.7		
6.4	Subhumid (C)	
8.7		
	Humid (B)	Humid
16.2		
	Wet (A)	

midpoint of the series falls on 6.4, which supplies the separation between the dry and humid realms of the earth.

Viewed on a monthly basis, normal seasonal variations of precipitation and temperature create variations in the moistness of climate through the year. Climates that calculate an annual moisture index around $S = 2.5$ may not be comparable when subjected to seasonal analysis. A desert-margin locality becomes more mesic in character if at least a short season dependably combines sufficient heat and moisture to initiate the germination of annual plants and to provide a seasonal increment of growth to perennials. However, data search has not yet revealed places of $S \sim 2.5$ with three or more months' rainfall in excess of the amounts called for by N_1 (equation 2.6). Therefore, the basis for season-long runoff does not materialize in deserts, a failure that extends as well to the moisture required for a continuous grass cover or its economic equivalent, a grain crop.

These remarks apply to the margins of arid regions, which comprise their rainiest portions. By far, the greater part of the arid realm receives so little rain that soils are wetted to but a shallow depth, and then only infrequently. Although rain showers of considerable intensity are not unknown in arid regions, the duration and frequency of heavy precipitation is such that their effects are scattered and transitory. Most students believe that heavy rains, rare as they are, elevate the statistic of the arithmetic mean to an unrealistically high level and that median rainfall is much more representative in arid regions. In the driest portions of eastern California and southern Nevada, median monthly precipitation is only 25 percent of mean monthly amounts (Colorado State University Experiment Station 1971). Only in the northern and elevated parts of the intermountain region does median precipitation become as much as 75 percent of the mean, on a monthly basis.

The moisture provinces of the western United States (figure 2-4), prepared from equation 2.3, must be regarded in the light of the characteristics that have been discussed up to this point. The arid category is bounded by the annual moisture index of $S = 2.5$, and that of the semiarid province by $S = 4.7$. Moisture categories A, B, and C have not been distinguished one from the other. All three are located only in the humid coastal province and in elevated regions of the continental interior. The latter are highly generalized in figure

2-4, but prominent rainy islands are formed by the highlands of north-central Arizona and of northeastern Nevada. Small humid islands also appear in conjunction with the Chiricahua Mountains of southeastern Arizona, the Coconino and Kaibab plateau flanking the Grand Canyon in northern Arizona, and the Sangre de Cristo range of New Mexico. Large aprons of humid climate cover the highland borders of the intermountain region, and a prominent salient of humid climate extends through northeast and central Oregon from the northern

MOISTURE PROVINCES OF THE WESTERN UNITED STATES

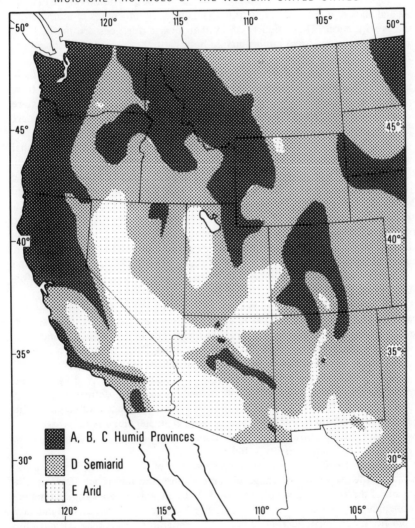

FIGURE 2-4. *Moisture provinces of the western United States according to the Bailey moisture index.*

Rockies. That salient includes the Wallowa and Blue mountains and the drainage divide of the upper John Day River of northern Oregon.

Arid climate, in contrast, is an attribute of interior location and low altitude. A climatic equivalent, too fine in detail to be shown in figure 2-4, exists in relation to the complex topography of the intermountain region, a topographic complex seen only in smoothed form on the climatic map. Despite generalization, small outposts of aridity appear beyond the main body of arid climate in California, Nevada, and Arizona. Among them are the upper Rio Grande and Colorado valleys, the basin occupied by the Great Salt Lake, and minor outliers shown in the Columbia Basin and in northern Wyoming.

Figures 2-6, 2-7, and 2-8, prepared for several of the stations given in table 2-2 and shown in figure 2-5, illustrate the elementary attributes of temperature and precipitation. These figures show that local differences are marked and thus become of practical importance in both natural and economic considerations.

Figure 2-6 is divided into four quadrants such that each axis is shared in common except for the temperature axis, which separates quadrant 3 from quadrant 4. All data points originate from records in which the annual moisture index is <2.5; all places are considered to be arid. Their locational data are given in table 2-2 and are mapped in figure 2-5.

In quadrant 1 the data points are scattered with respect to mean annual range of temperature (X axis) and the seasonal concentration of precipitation (Y axis). The latter property is defined numerically as the percentage of the year's precipitation that falls in the winter half-year (October–March in the Northern Hemisphere). The data points show clearly that California has by far the highest concentration of winter rain, whereas summer rain is characteristic of Texas, New Mexico, and Colorado. Intervening states generally show nearly equal amounts of precipitation in summer and winter. Seasonal differences of temperature vary little among the several states, but Colorado and Utah show wider swings of temperature than is true of the arid parts of California, Texas, and Arizona.

In quadrant 2, the X axis is a scale of mean annual precipitation in millimeters. The data points are scattered at random, but the wettest places, with yearly precipitation around 300 mm, are located in Texas, Arizona, and New Mexico, whereas California has the driest localities. The scatter with respect to winter concentration of precipitation is identical to that in quadrant 1.

In quadrant 3, the scatter in precipitation amount is arrayed against the mean temperature of the wet season (a temperature term defined in remarks about figure 2-7). It is noteworthy that the warmest places differ greatly in precipitation—from less than 60 mm to more than 300 mm annually—whereas wet-season temperatures differ fewer than 10°C, and rainfall occurs only in a restricted range, approximately 160 mm annually.

Quadrant 4 shows the most compact scatter of the four. The X axis of the graph is the mean annual range of temperature (the difference between the means of the warmest and coldest months). The Y axis is mean annual temperature applying to points from 5 to 25°C. The X axis displays points that indicate from twenty to thirty degrees of seasonal temperature difference. Despite the lack of dispersion of the points, profound thermal differences exist within the data scatter. Figure 2-7 assists in the interpretation of the several quadrants.

REPRESENTATIVE CLIMATIC STATIONS

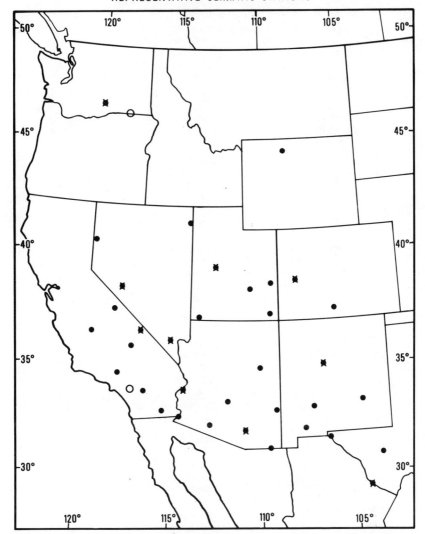

FIGURE 2-5. *Representative climatic stations of the western United States.* •
indicates data shown in figures 2-6 and 2-7; ✖ *indicates data shown in figures
2-6, 2-7, and 2-8; and* ○ *indicates data shown in figure 2-9 only.*

In quadrant 3 are plotted lines of stipulated annual moisture index, identified by the numerals emplaced in the lines: $S = 1$, $S = 2.5$, $S = 4.7$. Data
points lying in the sector of the graph with $S < 1$ represent hyperarid localities.
Death Valley ($S = 0.3$) is the driest locality both in terms of annual precipitation (45 mm) and moisture index. The wettest locality (Balmorhea Exp Pan,
Texas) in terms of precipitation (322 mm) is so warm that its moisture rating is

TABLE 2-2. *List of Weather Stations*

Map index number	Station name	Elevation (meters)	Latitude	Longitude
		Arizona		
1	Ajo	537	32° 22′	112° 52′
2	Camelback	380	33 29	111 58
3	Douglas Smelter	1,210	31 21	109 35
4	Holbrook	1,545	34 54	110 10
5[a]	Parker	129	34 08	114 17
6[a]	Tucson AP	787	32 07	110 56
7	Yuma AP	60	32 40	114 36
8	Clifton	1,056	33 03	109 17
		California		
9	Bishop AP	1,252	37 22	118 26
10	Brawley 2 SW	−30	32 59	115 32
11[a]	Death Valley	−71	36 27	116 52
12	Hanford	73	36 19	119 40
13	Palmdale	809	34 35	118 07
14	Palm Springs	125	33 49	116 33
15	Trona	516	35 46	117 23
16[b]	Riverside	250	33 57	117 24
		Colorado		
17	Alamosa AP	2,296	37 27	105 52
18[a]	Delta lE	1,562	38 45	108 03
		Nevada		
19[a]	Las Vegas AP	658	36 05	115 10
20[a]	Mina	1,387	38 23	118 06
21	Montello	1,486	41 16	114 12
22	Sand Pass	1,188	40 19	119 48
		New Mexico		
23[a]	Albuquerque AP	1,618	35 03	106 37
24	Elephant Butte Dam	1,394	33 09	107 11
25	Roswell AP	1,102	33 24	104 32
26	Deming	1,320	32 16	107 45
		Texas		
27	Balmorhea Exp Pan	982	31 00	104 41
28	El Paso AP	1,194	31 48	106 24
29[a]	Presidio	786	29 33	104 24
		Utah		
30	Bluff	1,315	37 17	109 33
31[a]	Deseret	1,383	39 17	112 41
32	Hanksville FAA AP	1,358	38 25	110 42
33	St. George PH	822	37 06	113 34

TABLE 2-2. *continued*

Map index number	Station name	Elevation (meters)	Latitude	Longitude
		Washington		
34[a]	Sunnyside	227	46 20	120 00
35[b]	Walla Walla	289	46 02	118 20

a. Data shown in figures 2-6, 2-7, and 2-8.
b. Data shown in figure 2-9.

$S = 2.4$ and falls in the arid category despite its relatively high precipitation. In contrast, Palmdale, California, with but 225 mm is sufficiently cool that its moisture rating rises slightly above the arid limit: $S = 2.56$. The climatic record for Palmdale generates the only data point lying on the humid side of the line for $S = 2.5$.

Obviously temperature is an effective modifier of precipitation in the calculation of the moisture index adopted for this discussion. It is therefore appropriate to interpolate the definition of the term *wet-season temperature* that distinguishes Balmorhea from Palmdale as being much the warmer of the two even though Balmorhea is only slightly warmer in terms of mean annual temperature (T). For Balmorhea Exp Pan, T is 18.4 and $T + x$ (wet-season temperature) is 20.1. For Palmdale, T is 16.4 and $T + x$ is 10.1.

The reason for the elevation of the wet-season temperature at Balmorhea above its mean annual temperature lies in the seasonal distribution of precipitation, which is received mainly in summer in western Texas. The opposite is true at Palmdale, where 87.0 percent of all precipitation occurs in the winter half-year. The calculation of the term $T + x$ has been derived in this study by initial use of equation 2.3, from which monthly indexes have been calculated and summed to give the annual moisture index S. Thus, equation 2.4 can be rearranged for solution of the term $T + x$:

$$T + x = \frac{ln\ [(0.018P)/S]}{ln\ 1.045} . \tag{2.7}$$

The wet-season temperature shown in quadrant 3 is the temperature $(T + x)$ that satisfies the basic equation for the annual moisture index (equation 2.4) when all terms except temperature are known. By plotting data points in quadrant 3 with respect to wet-season temperature, correct alignment is secured in relation to moisture index lines plotted in the same quadrant, thus assuring consistency in both tabular and graphical data presentations.

The basis for altering mean annual temperatures up or down is also given by the lines plotted in quadrant 1, where the correction x is defined by lines ranging from a positive correction of ten degrees to a negative correction of ten degrees. The sign and magnitude of the correction are functions of the arguments of the graph: mean annual range of temperature and winter concentra-

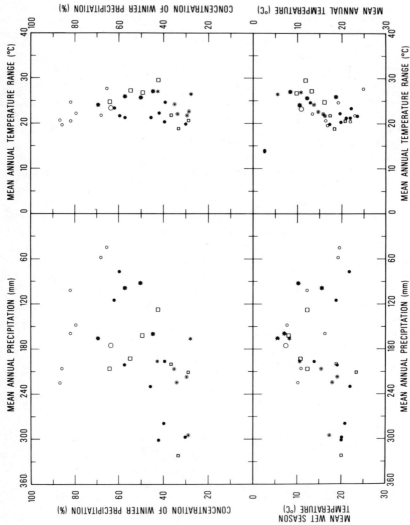

FIGURE 2-6. *Scatter diagrams according to five climatic elements with data identified by state.*

28

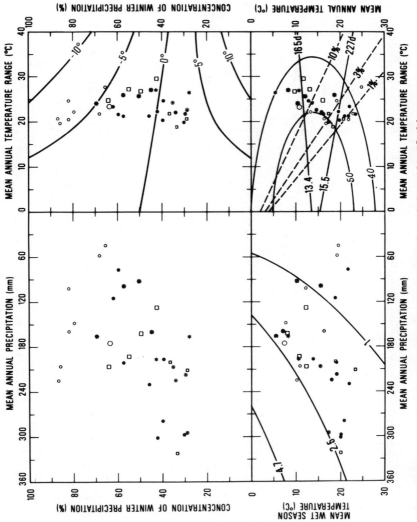

FIGURE 2-7. *Scatter diagrams with analytical lines and data identified by state.*

29

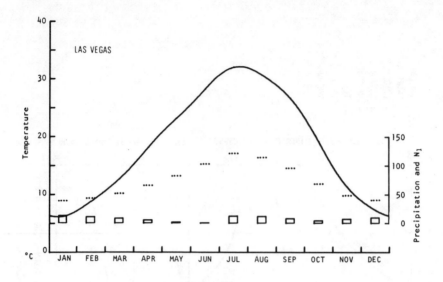

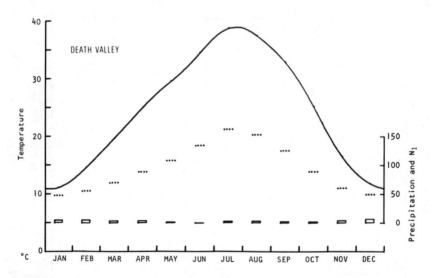

FIGURE 2-8. *Graphs of temperature, precipitation, and water need of ten arid localities: Las Vegas, Death Valley, Tucson, Parker, Presidio, Albuquerque, Delta, Deseret, Mina, and Sunnyside.*

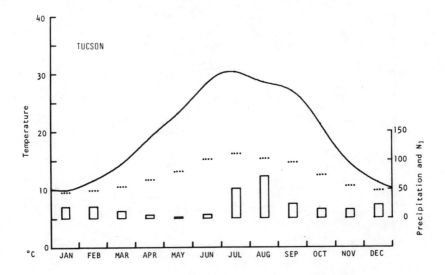

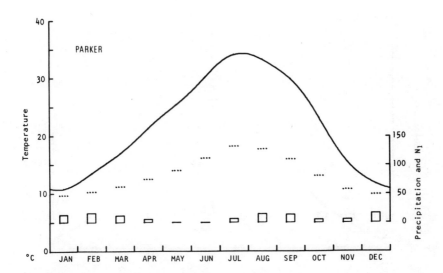

FIGURE 2-8. *continued*

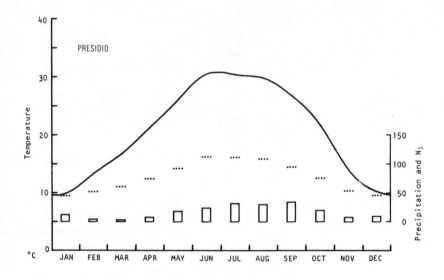

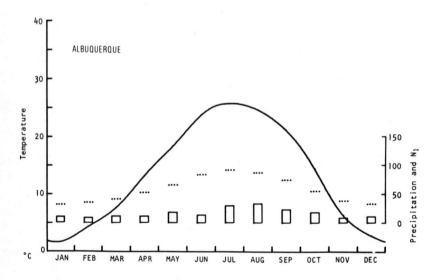

FIGURE 2-8. *continued*

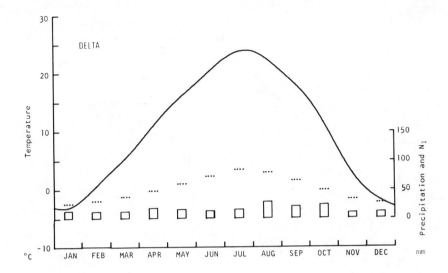

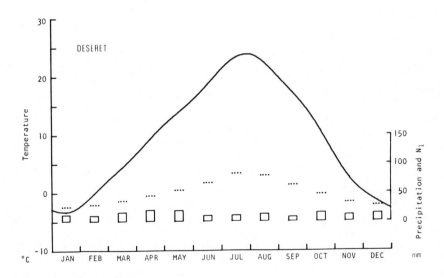

FIGURE 2-8.   *continued*

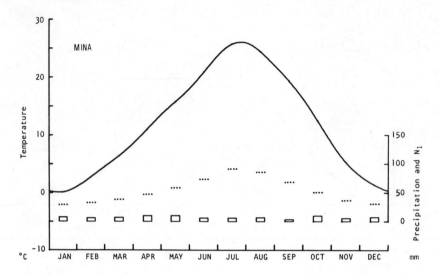

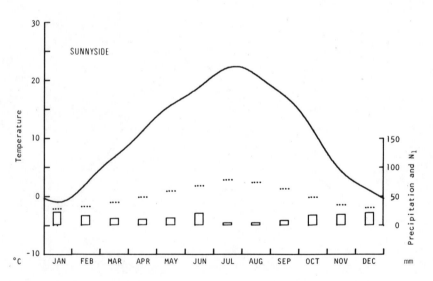

FIGURE 2-8.   *continued*

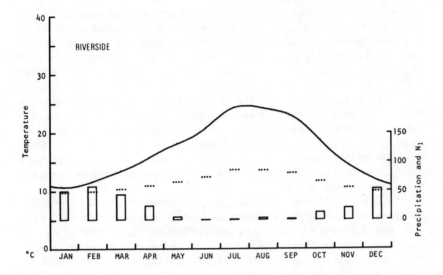

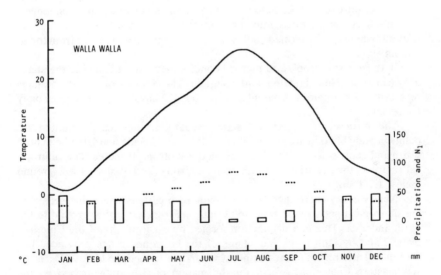

FIGURE 2-9. *Graphs of temperature, precipitation, and water need for Riverside, California, and Walla Walla, Washington.*

tion of precipitation. The correction is not affected by absolute magnitudes of either mean annual temperature or precipitation. It follows that places with a high concentration of precipitation in winter are corrected downward in temperature, thus allowing precipitation to be more effective. The same relation is established by the alignment of the moisture index lines in quadrant 3, relative to the data points.

In the United States, the upper limit of annual rainfall occurring in the presence of cool wet-season temperatures falls along boundary values close to 180 mm. Under a condition of warm summer-rain regimes, the upper allowable limit of precipitation lies above 300 mm annually. Most data points, of course, represent localities far distant from the edge of the desert and so develop a more distinct arid aspect. Five of the thirty-two data points lie in the hyperarid sector of the quadrant.

Quadrant 4 of figure 2-7 shows several families of analytical lines that distinguish thermal differences within the arid climates of the United States.

Lines Indicating Warmth and Duration of Summer (Bailey, 1960). Two such lines appear on the diagram, identified on the left by the numerals 13.4 and 15.5°C and on the right as 165d and 227d. Interpreted, the upper line stands for the isotherm of 13.4°C, marking the beginning and ending of a summer period 165 days in duration. The sector of the graph above that line has a summer period that is cooler and of shorter duration than that just specified. The lower line indicates a summer period in which a 227-day period commences and ends at a temperature of 15.5°C. Below that line, summer is still warmer and longer. The graph is thus divided into three sectors, with respect to the lines of warmth, which can be termed cool, warm, and subtropical, reading from top to bottom.

In those terms, cool, arid thermal conditions are to be found in the states of Washington, Nevada, Utah, and Colorado. The coldest point on the graph is represented by Alamosa, Colorado, where but 122 days lie above a mean daily temperature of 12.0°C.

The warm sector applies to all states except Washington and Colorado. All points in New Mexico are so classified. Data from Nevada and Utah lie in both warm and cool sectors but fail to show in the subtropical sector. The subtropical sector is thus confined to California, Arizona, and Texas on low ground (below 1,100 m).

Nearly everywhere there is a pronounced break in terrain that separates the subtropical parts of Arizona and California from the higher ground to the north and east. This is a disjunction formed by escarpments of the Colorado plateau and by fault-block mountains of the basin and range province. The subtropical arid region of the southern lowlands is termed the Mojave Desert in southeastern California, except for the margin of that state formed by the Colorado River and adjacent low-lying basins. There and in the lowlands of southern Arizona east of the Colorado River, the term Sonoran has been applied to the region by virtue of greater warmth and a summer-rain period bringing more moisture at that time of the year than is usual in the Mojave. Distinctive floral elements distinguish the two subtropical desert regions.

Lines Indicating Annual Frequency of Subfreezing Hours (%) (Bailey, 1966). The high desert areas of Nevada and Utah are also distinctive in vegetation;

collectively they form the Great Basin Desert type. Thermally they are distinctly cooler in all seasons than the subtropical deserts. The pattern of frost-frequency lines in quadrant 4 of figure 2-7 is evocative of winter conditions. The warmest parts of the subtropical deserts lie close to the frequency line of 1 percent (indicating that about 1 percent of annual hours of the year are sub-freezing—less than 100 hours in total), but all data points for Nevada and Utah show implied frost frequencies of 3 to 10 percent and more.

Lines Indicating Temperateness of Climate (Lack of Thermal Extremes) (Bailey, 1964). The difference between summer and winter extremes is indicated by the scale of mean annual temperature range. The graph in that respect shows that California and the warm parts of Arizona and Texas are most equable, whereas the greatest seasonal ranges of temperature are developed in Utah. However, with respect to the fixed mean of 14°C, the magnitude of seasonal extremes is ascertained by comparison of the data points with the two ellipses enumerated as *40* and *50,* indexes that define variances of 200 and 93, respectively. Variance in this case refers to the departure of hourly temperatures around 14°C (Bailey, 1964). So judged, Death Valley (the lowest open circle in the diagram) is the least temperate of the localities sampled, and the most temperate are found in California in the San Joaquin Valley and western Mojave, relatively close to the Pacific Ocean, and also in southern Arizona at the altitude of Douglas.

Temperateness as a factor in plant-climate relations has been set forth as an indicator of the richness with which plants overlap in geographic range. The higher the temperateness, the greater the ability of unlike species to coexist (Axelrod, 1967). In terms of agriculture, flexibility in crop choice and calendar would seem to increase with temperateness.

Figure 2-8 illustrates seasonal progressions of temperature and precipitation for arid parts of the United States. The graphs show the annual course of mean daily temperature, plotted day by day from six components of harmonic analysis for the normal period of 1931–1960. The precipitation bars represent mean monthly precipitation averaged over the same period of time (thirty years). The horizontal pattern of four dots shown above the precipitation bars is the amount of water need (N_1) calculated from equation 2.6. In all instances water need exceeds precipitation.

Death Valley represents the arid extreme of the North American continent; it is both extremely arid and extremely hot in summer. As such, it is neither typical of the Mojave nor the Sonoran desert types, for it is warmer than the former and drier than the latter. Las Vegas is located at the northeastern boundary of the Mojave. To the south and east, the climate is warmer, and it features a greater proportion of the year's precipitation in summer, as seen in Parker (at the dry margin of the Sonoran Desert) and Tucson (typically Sonoran in character). At Tucson, precipitation is substantial in summer and it supports a relatively rich arboreal population of succulents in contrast to the low sparse shrubs of the Mojave region of southern California. A dip in temperature in August is seen in the curve for Tucson, an effect of the cloud cover and evaporative consumption of heat that accompanies summer rain. Albuquerque, with an altitude above 1,600 meters, displays a lowered temperature curve; heavy frosts of winter remove from it a Sonoran climatic character. Albuquerque is thus transitional to the Great Basin climatic patterns illustrated by Delta, Deseret, and Mina. Presidio, in west Texas, is more representative of the Chihuahan Desert region of Mexico than the arid parts of the intermountain region. This is so chiefly by virtue of heavy concentration of precipitation in summer, but the coldest weather at Presidio is more severe than that experienced in the Chihuahan plateau.

Delta and Deseret are set apart from the preceding localities by the dip of their temperature curves into the subfreezing range, so that winter precipitation occurs in conjunction with subfreezing temperatures. The resultant snow cover is generally shallow and intermittent but may attain depths as great as 100 cm on valley floors and is much greater on high mountain slopes. Mina represents a somewhat warmer environment but exhibits the general characteristics of Great Basin climate and vegetation.

Sunnyside, in the Columbia Basin, is scarcely to be distinguished from the Great Basin localities on the basis of climate. It does not share in the late summer rains that are typical of the Sonoran and Great Basin deserts, however, and is the cloudiest locality of all in midwinter. Snow, 2.5 cm or more in depth, occurs on an average of seven days but seldom forms a continuous cover and is less of a factor in winter weather of the Sunnyside region than is the case on the much higher ground of the Great Basin.

VARIABILITY FACTORS

Day-to-day weather changes create significant departures from normal. The departures involve all aspects of the heat and moisture balance of the atmosphere and are persistent enough in some cases so that weeks or months may display anomalous characteristics.

Precipitation variability is usefully expressed by the statistic of the coefficient of variation (the ratio of the standard deviation to the mean). The coefficient of variation of annual precipitation is greatest in the United States in the lower Colorado River Valley, where it exceeds 50 percent. More typical of the arid parts of California, Nevada, and Arizona are coefficients of variation lying between 30 and 50 percent. Along the northern margin of the arid parts of the United States, the coefficient drops to 25 percent. For New Mexico and Texas, a value of 40 percent is typical of dry sites (Bryson and Hare, 1974). In contrast, the rainy eastern part of the United States has a coefficient of variation for annual precipitation as low as 15 to 20 percent. Clearly, rainfall amounts become less dependable from year to year the drier the climate, an unfortunate characteristic in view of the greater press upon water resources of developed arid regions.

Temperature variability is usually expressed by statistics giving the frequency of high and low temperatures. Days with maxima above 90°F (32.2°C) and minima below 32°F (0°C) appear in many summaries and atlases (U.S. Department of the Interior, 1970). On the low ground of the Mojave and Sonoran desert regions, maxima above 32°C occur on from 100 to 150 days annually, depending largely upon altitude of the site. The same altitude factor keeps the region relatively warm in winter also, when from 10 to 60 days start in the subfreezing range. Beyond and above the terrain break setting off the subtropical desert areas from the Great Basin, heat extremes are decreased, and cold extremes are increased. Only the lowest and warmest parts of the Great Basin experience more than 60 summer days with maxima above 32°C, but minima below freezing are generally noted for 150 to 180 days. Arid parts of New Mexico and Texas are intermediate in the comparison of temperature extremes of the Great Basin with those of the Mojave and Sonoran regions.

Thermal stratification of the atmosphere is strongly developed on calm winter nights in the Great Basin. Thus a consideration of the vertical profile of temperature is mandatory in the study of microclimates of the region. No attempt has been planned here to present the data and theory that describe profile structures, but they have been important in some site studies. The ecology of ground-dwelling organisms also requires recognition of superheating effects under summer conditions of insolation. At ground level, obviously, thermal extremes are much more severe than is apparent by examining instrument shelter data.

In arid regions, lack of water undoubtedly represents the most effective extreme of all climatic factors. In comparison to more mesic parts of the world, shortage of water is a perennial condition, and it is expressed as such by the gap between the precipitation available and water need, as calculated for N_1, PET, or some normative definition of water shortage. For example, if it is stipulated that at least 25 mm (1 inch) of precipitation is needed within a two-week period to avoid drought, there are twenty-six such periods in the arid part of the United States; for them the entire year consists of drought (Visher, 1954). This is true of no other part of the United States.

Even within the arid region, some seasons and years are short of water relative to that normal for the locality. Spectra of drought periods are not a usual source of summarization. The most useful calculation made to date concerning the occurrence of wet and dry spells in the western United States has been made through application of a first-order Markov chain to daily precipitation probabilities averaged week by week throughout the year (Colorado State University Experiment Station, 1971). Along the lower Colorado River at Blythe (near Parker), the probability that a dry day (one with less than 0.25 mm of precipitation) will be followed by another dry day remains high throughout the year. The week beginning December 21 is the rainiest as indicated by a probability of 91 percent of a dry/dry sequence. All other weeks at Blythe have higher probabilities of a sequence of two dry days. The entire month of June lists that probability as greater than 99.5 percent. In contrast, at Tucson the probability for two successive dry days drops to 69 percent for the week beginning August 2.

The tables referred to have been derived from a thirty-year period (1931–1960) and establish useful expectancies of rainfall occurrence over any chosen period of time. They do not prepare one for the fact, however, that Bagdad (in the Mojave Desert) went without measurable precipitation over a period of 767 days (October 1912–November 1914), and, on the other hand, that Death Valley has received monthly rainfall in amounts ≥ 38 mm (1.50 inches) on six occasions, between 1911 and 1960 even though the long-term mean is but 45 mm annually.

One must conclude that inadequate, erratic rainfall combined with long, warm summers provide ingredients that are the essence of the harshness of the arid climate. Not all factors that contribute to this harshness have been described here, such as intense solar heating and occasional high winds. By widening the scope of atmospheric properties in climatic studies, the arid climate can be defined in more realistic terms. Conventional aspects of climate, nevertheless, convey much of the totality that is in fact the essence of aridity. This is indicated by the comparison of graphs in figure 2-8 with those of figure 2-9, where Riverside, California, and Walla Walla, Washington, display a moisture surplus in winter months. Both localities, little more than 100 km from arid valleys, maintain successful crops on the basis of dry farming.

REFERENCES

Axelrod, D. 1967. Quaternary extinctions of large mammals. *Univ. Calif. Publ. Geol. Sci.* **74**:8–9.

Bailey, H. P. 1958. A simple moisture index based upon a primary law of evaporation. *Geograf. Ann.* **3–4**:196–215.

Bailey, H. P. 1960. A method of determining the warmth and temperateness of climate. *Geograf. Ann.* **1**:1–16.

Bailey, H. P. 1964. Toward a unified concept of the temperate climate. *Geogr. Rev.* **54**:516–545.

Bailey, H. P. 1966. The mean annual range and standard deviation as measures of dispersion of temperature around the annual mean. *Geograf. Ann.* **48A**:183–194.

Bailey, H. P., and C. Johnson. 1972. Potential evapotranspiration in relation to annual waves of temperature, pp. 4–12. In Thornthwaite Memorial Volume 1, Papers on Evapotranspiration and the Climatic Water Balance. *Publ. Climatol.* **25**:1–57.

Bryson, R. A., and F. K. Hare, eds. 1974. *Climates of North America.* Elsevier, New York.

Colorado State University Experiment Station. 1971. Probability of sequences of wet and dry days for 11 western states and Texas. *Tech. Bull. 117,* 303 pp.

Dalton, J. 1802. Experimental essays on the constitution of mixed gases on the force of steam or vapour from water and other liquids in different temperatures, both in a Torricellian vacuum and in air; on evaporation and the expansion of gases by heat. *Manchester Lit. Philos. Soc. Mem.* **5**:525–602.

James, P. E. 1959. *A Geography of Man,* 2d ed. Ginn and Co., Boston, 656 pp.

Leighly, J. 1953. Dry climates: their nature and distribution, pp. 3–18. In *Desert Research,* Proc. Internat. Symp. Jerusalem, May 7–14, 1952. Research Council of Israel in cooperation with UNESCO.

Leighly, J. 1956. Weather and climate, pp. 25–37. In C. M. Zierrer (ed.), *California and the Southwest.* Wiley, New York, 376 pp.

Lydolph, P. 1957. A comparative analysis of the dry western littorals. *Ann. Assoc. Am. Geogr.* **47**:213–230.

Miller, D. W., J. J. Geraghty, and R. S. Collins. 1963. *Water Atlas of the*

United States. Water Information Center, Port Washington, N.Y., 40 plates.

Penman, H. L. 1956. Estimating evaporation. *Trans. Am. Geophys. Union* **37**:43–50.

Sellers, W. D., and R. S. Hill, eds. 1974. *Arizona Climate, 1931–1972*, 2d ed. Univ. Arizona Press, Tucson, Ariz., 616 pp.

Smithsonian Institution. 1958. *Smithsonian Meteorological Tables*. Washington, D.C., 527 pp.

Thornthwaite, C. W. 1943. Problems in the classification of climates. *Geogr. Rev.* **33**:233–255.

Thornthwaite, C. W. 1945. Report of the committee on transpiration and evaporation, 1943–44. *Am. Geophys. Union Trans. 1944*, pp. 686–693.

U.S. Department of the Interior. 1970. *The National Atlas of the United States of America*. Govt. Printing Off., Washington, D.C., 417 pp.

U.S. Geological Survey. 1952. Water-loss investigations. Volume 1—Lake Hefner studies technical report. *Geol. Survey Circ. 299,* 153 pp.

Visher, S. S. 1954. *Climatic Atlas of the United States*. Harvard Univ. Press, Cambridge, Mass., 403 pp.

The interested reader will find in research libraries many specialized studies on topics that pertain to the arid sections of the United States. Other chapters in this book refer to such material, including the site and validation projects of the US/IPB Desert Biome, and to many other sources. Meteorological literature in the various journals and monographs of the American Meteorological Society are particularly informative. Climatic studies of individual states are not undertaken often by climatologists, but the work compiled by Sellers and Hill (1974) on Arizona is an impressive exception.

3

Soils, Geology, and Hydrology of Deserts

William B. Bull

Many discussions about deserts concern water, and the very scarceness of water is a common way of defining deserts. About one-fourth of the earth's land surface can be classed as deserts according to Meigs (1953). Although desert regions are most commonly defined as being areas of low rainfall, many other factors, such as temperature, humidity, and insolation, can be used to define them. Polar deserts have been defined by Smiley and Zumberge (1974) as being glacier-free terrestrial areas with less than 250 mm of precipitation annually and with a mean temperature for the warmest month of the year of less than 10°C. This section will attempt to synthesize some important aspects regarding the behavior of water in the hot deserts of the world, including the deserts of the western United States described in chapter 1. The pervasive influence of water will be used as a theme for this section and to provide coherence between the discussions of the interactions of climate, geology, biology, and hydrology through time.

The material presented emphasizes a geomorphological viewpoint; thus, most topics are treated as hydrologic, open systems. This format allows discussion of the behavior of water in regard to the soils (see chapters 5 through 9 and 11) and vegetation (see chapters 4, 7, 8, and 9) of deserts. A systems approach is applicable for insight into problems involving time spans that range in magnitude from geologic proportions to the brief periods being considered by those who are concerned about the impact of human activities on the fragile desert environment.

DESERT GEOMORPHIC SYSTEMS

The instability of some geomorphic systems in deserts underscores the need for understanding feedback mechanisms and thresholds. The chief threshold considered here is the one that separates the erosional and depositional modes of streams operation: the threshold of critical power. Of course, streams are controlled by the discharge of water and sediment from the hill-slope subsystem. Therefore the general sequence for discussion is to evaluate changes in the hill-slope subsystem, then to introduce the concept of the critical-power threshold, and finally to examine the behavior of streams. But first we should consider the components—the variables—that are important to the understanding of the complex behavior of water on the hills and streams of desert regions.

Although water, among the noneolian processes, has a pervasive influence on land forms, its interrelations with soils, plants, and geology are different for each hill and stream. Consider the chief variables of a fluvial geomorphic system. Some of the independent variables include rock type and structure, climate, basin level at the mouth of the drainage basin, drainage-basin area, and time. Dependent variables subject to feedback mechanisms (listed in order of increasing dependency) include total relief of drainage basin, hill-slope morphology, drainage net and valley morphology, soil-profile development and weathering, vegetation, sediment yield, stream-channel slope and patterns, and water and sediment discharge from the basin (modified from Bull, 1975). These variables represent many of the factors that affect the behavior of water. Some are independent of each other, but others are highly dependent on both the independent and dependent variables. Some variables such as rock type and structure are not related to water at all. Others are the product of interaction between variables. For example, total relief is controlled by both crustal tectonic movements and the erosiveness of fluvial processes through time. Base level—the altitude to which a stream, or a reach of a stream, tends to downcut—is an important control on the slopes of desert streams and may be affected by the processes of tectonism, erosion, and deposition. Some of the many dependent variables may be considered as being highly interdependent with other dependent and the independent variables. Although hill-slope morphology is largely a function of independent variables, it is also subject to feedback mechanisms from the other dependent variables. Soil-profile development and weathering is a highly important category because these processes affect the type and density of vegetation and are responsible for the production of fluvial sediment from geologic materials. (The behavior of water in deserts, as it affects plant communities, is the subject of the discussions in chapters 4, 7, 8, and 9.) From a hydrologic viewpoint, the pervasive influence of plants is highly sensitive to changes in the independent variable of climate (chapter 2); therefore, it is responsible in large part for the trends in geomorphic processes of both the hill-slope and stream subsystems. The variable of sediment yield, together with water yielded from the hill slopes, largely determines the stream-channel slopes and patterns. Finally, the discharge of water and sediment from a basin, as reflected in hydrographs or measurements of sediment discharge, may be regarded as the output of all the preceding interactions.

Time is also an important variable. Different workers will approach research in deserts according to the time spans of most interest to them. A geologist interested in the time needed to erode desert mountain ranges will use time spans of more than 10^6 years. A geomorphologist interested in the impact of climatic changes on fluvial systems will try to understand those processes that involve time spans of 10^1 to 10^3 years. An engineer interested in stream discharge would use a time span of 10^{-2} years and would consider sediment yield and any additional variables as being independent for the time span that is of interest to him.

Figure 3-1 shows the basic components of arid fluvial systems. These represent the basic categories for my discussion of the behavior of water in

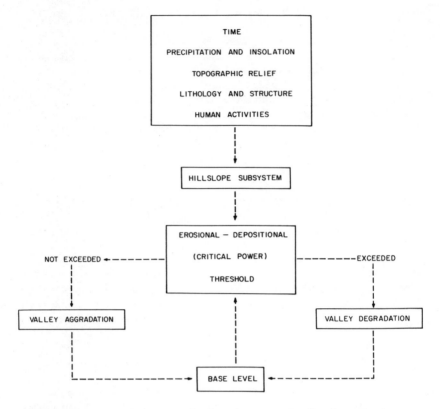

FIGURE 3-1. *Basic elements of a fluvial system. Feedback mechanisms are indicated by the dashed lines and arrows (from Bull, 1979; copyright © 1979 by the Geological Society of America).*

deserts. Included in the variables at the top of the flowchart are the activities of humans. Humans are in a unique position. They may deliberately act as an independent variable and upset the delicate balance within fluvial systems, or they may be considered as helpless dependent variables that suffer the consequences of desert floods. The interactions among the variables of the hill-slope subsystem determine the input to the stream subsystem and therefore determine whether the threshold between stream erosion and deposition is exceeded. Both valley aggradation and valley degradation change the altitude of any given point of the stream, and these changes in base level may affect stream energy gradients and consequently the threshold of critical power. Aggradation and degradation also initiate feedback mechanisms that affect the hill-slope subsystem (figure 3-1).

THE HILL-SLOPE SUBSYSTEM

The change to Holocene climates in the hot deserts can be generalized by stating that precipitation decreased and temperature increased. Such trends in

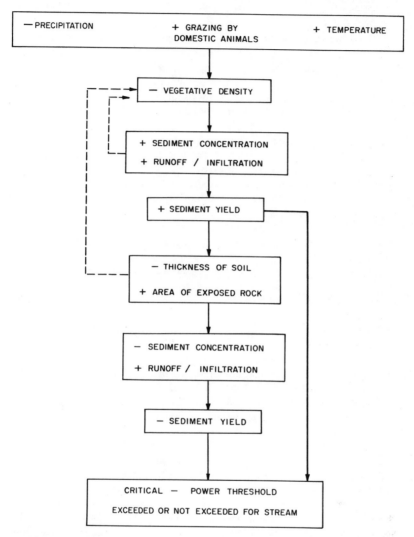

FIGURE 3-2.   *Increases (+) and decreases (−) in elements of a hypothetical arid hillslope subsystem. Self-enhancing feedback mechanisms are shown by dashed lines and arrows (from Bull, 1979; copyright © 1979 by the Geological Society of America).*

climate have an effect on vegetation density that is similar to those of overgrazing. Figure 3-2 outlines some of the consequences of these changes for a typical hill-slope subsystem in a hot desert and where a resistant bedrock substrata weathers into soil for sparse vegetation to grow in. The changes in the independent variables that cause the decrease in vegetative density also initiate other changes that affect the behavior of water within the hill-slope subsystem. Reduction of vegetation density exposes more soil to raindrop impact, which results in decreased infiltration rates. The resulting increase in runoff of water, for a given rainfall event, will have a higher sediment concentration than before the decrease in vegetation density. The decrease in soil moisture establishes a self-enhancing feedback mechanism that tends to decrease vegation density further. Because this feedback mechanism is self-enhancing instead of self-arresting, the operation of the hill-slope subsystem is driven further from equilibrium (steady state) conditions. Increases in both volume of water and concentration of sediment for a precipitation event of a given amount and intensity lead to increases in the amount of sediment yielded from a unit area for a given length of time. In this regard, it is important to recognize that sediment yield is a function of both water runoff and sediment concentration—the Langbein-Schumn rule discussed by Wilson (1973). The continuing increases in sediment yield result in a situation where the rates of hill-slope erosion exceed the rates of soil formation. There are concurrent decreases in soil thickness and increases in the areas of the exposed bedrock substrata. Such decreases in soil thickness act as a second self-enhancing mechanism that tends to decrease vegetative density even further. The sediment concentration of hill-slope runoff decreases because of the increases in areas of exposed bedrock. For a slope that is a composite of soil and outcrops, the result is further decreases in overall infiltration rate and increases in the amount of water runoff. The net effect is for flashier runoffs where erosion of the remaining soil is concentrated at the soil-outcrop interfaces. A third self-enhancing feedback is established that further tends to decrease the thickness of soil and increase the area of outcrops. Thus, the behavior of the hill-slope subsystem tends to progressively decrease vegetative density and soil thickness. Although water runoff increases, the amount of sediment available for erosion is substantially less, and the net result is a decrease in sediment yield compared to that which occurs after the initial decreases in the vegetative density.

The situation of climatic change or human activities that tend to decrease vegetative density was deliberately selected as an illustration for figure 3-2 rather than the converse. Major climatic changes to drier and/or warmer climates occurred about 8,000 to 12,000 years ago in most of the hot deserts of the world. The lag times of the ensuing responses outlined by the flowchart of figure 3-2 varied considerably as functions of soil thickness and depth of weathering at the time of climatic desiccation and with such additional factors as sediment size, hill-slope steepness and length, and types of vegetation. The relative strength of the suite of feedback mechanisms is much greater for some hill slopes than others, but the overall trend has been for increasingly rocky hill slopes with progressively thinner soils that support less vegetation. Such changes are not merely of academic curiosity to hydrologists and ecologists. They represent a conceptual framework of changing and interacting variables that are useful as an historical background for those interested in the studies of present-day soils, plant communities, and streams that are the subjects of most of the chapters of this book.

An example of the marked changes that have occurred on the hill slopes of hot deserts is shown in figure 3-3. Nahal Yael is a small research watershed in southern Israel (Schick and Sharon, 1974) that is about 4 km northwest of Elat and has a mean annual rainfall of about 32 mm. Nearly all of this rain falls

FIGURE 3-3. Contrasts in the smoothness of outcrops on a hilltop of Elat granite, Nahal Yael, southern Israel (from Bull and Schick, 1979; copyright © 1979 by Academic Press, Inc.).

between October and April. Some years have virtually no rain. The winters are mild, and summer daytime temperatures commonly exceed 40°C. The hillslope shown in figure 3-3 is underlain by coarse-grained, jointed, and sheared pink porphyritic Elat granite. An outstanding characteristic of the bare slopes is the marked contrast in smoothness of outcrops. Rough exposures are coated with desert varnish (coatings of manganese and iron oxides), are little weathered, and ring when struck with a hammer. Smooth bedrock surfaces occur immediately adjacent to rough surfaces even when there is no visible change in mineralogy or fracture density. The smooth slopes are not coated with desert varnish and are crumbly.

The two types of granite outcrops are the result of different weathering environments on the same rock type. Rough outcrops occur on topographic highs and in stream channels. Joint and shear planes promote the differential weathering of the granite where they are exposed to raindrop impact, sheet flow, and stream flow. Chemical weathering is slow in such a microenvironment, and the rock retains desert varnish except where subjected to abrasion by stream flow. Smooth exposures occur in topographic lows and under alluvium and remnants of alluvium. The coarse-grained nature of the granite promotes rapid weathering of smooth surfaces where a cover of colluvium provides a moist microenvironment after prolonged rains.

Although the hill slopes are presently bare, the weathering contrasts are clear evidence that many of the slopes were previously mantled with grussy colluvium. The different weathering modes of the Elat granite allow mapping of the former extent of the colluvial mantle (Bull and Schick, in press). The weathering contrasts show clearly on aerial photographs and indicate that about two-thirds of the granitic hill slopes had thin colluvium, which has since been stripped.

The hill-slope of figure 3-3 represents an extreme endpoint of the behavior of water as outlined by the flowchart of figure 3-2. Granite is particularly sensitive to the impact of climatic change because of the small amounts of rainfall needed to generate runoff on outcrops and the easily transported size range of the particles produced by weathering processes. Outcrops of Elat granite generate runoff after only 2–3 mm of rain, and rainfalls of 8–10 mm are sufficient to erode the grus (monomineralic grains weathered from granite), thereby increasing the bedrock area that contributes to runoff in subsequent rainfall events. The reestablishment of the colluvial mantle on the granitic hill slopes of Nahal Yael would require the stabilizing presence of vegetation to create the conditions favorable for deposition rather than erosion of grus. This would require a climate sufficiently wetter and/or cooler to eliminate the extended droughts that kill most hill-slope vegetation.

The response of the same climatic change had different effects on the other rock types of the Nahal Yael watershed. Also present is a sheared complex of mafic rocks that consist of deeply weathered biotite-plagioclase amphibilite, hornblende-plagioclase schist, and gabbro. Much of Nahal Yael is underlain by metasedimentary rocks, such as biotite-quartz schist, muscovite-biotite schist, and biotite-plagioclase schist. The hill slopes underlain by amphibolite responded to the climatic change in a manner similar to the granite, but the amphibolite was much more deeply weathered, and the colluvial mantle was only partially stripped. Least stripping of colluvium occurred on schist hill slopes, partially because schist outcrops require more rain to generate runoff and partially because angular blocks of schist require larger flows to initiate transport, compared to the other slope lithologies. About 3 mm in three minutes of precipitation are required to initiate runoff at the amphibolitic outcrops; 4–8 mm of rainfall are needed to initiate runoff on those slopes underlain by metasedimentary rocks (Yair and Klein, 1973). Although the sparse vegetation is largely restricted to the stream courses and the hill slopes are largely devoid of vegetation at present, past distributions and types of plants also must have been controlled in large part by the variations in bedrock parent material for the soils.

THE THRESHOLD OF CRITICAL POWER

Both figures 3-1 and 3-2 include an important threshold that separates the modes of operation of the stream subsystem; Bull (in press) calls this the threshold of critical power.

Streams may be regarded as sediment-transporting machines and may be analyzed in terms of the availability of stream power to do work (Bagnold, 1973, 1977). Where stream power is more than sufficient to transport sediment load, scour of alluvium and perhaps bedrock may occur. Where stream power is insufficient, part of the saltating bed load will be deposited as the stream bed aggrades. Bagnold describes the kinetic power along a stream channel as γQS, where γ is the absolute density mass per volume, Q is discharge, and S is a gravity gradient. The total power supplied per unit area of stream bed ω is

$$\omega = \gamma QS/\text{width}. \tag{3.1}$$

The threshold of critical power is merely a ratio of those factors affecting stream power that tend to promote sediment transport (stream power) as compared to those that tend to promote sediment deposition (critical power):

$$\frac{\text{stream power}}{\text{critical power}} = 1.0 \tag{3.2}$$

Critical power is the stream power needed to transport the average sediment load supplied to a reach of a stream. Critical power may change rapidly in response to changes in amount and size of sediment and hydraulic roughness as determined by flow characteristics and roughness elements of the channel and vegetation. The stream power available to transport sediment is the other component of the threshold; it can be estimated by measurements of discharge and stream gradient. Many stream-flow parameters respond to changes in water and sediment discharge, but the stream power was selected as one component of the critical-power threshold because sediment transport is highly sensitive to changes in slope and discharge. Both stream and critical power change with time. Changes in stream power during short time spans generally are the result of changes in discharge. Rates of change of slope tend to be more conservative. Critical power changes with amount and size of sediment derived from the hill-slope subsystem and with changes in hydraulic roughness. Like the useful concept of hydraulic roughness, critical power cannot be measured directly in the field. Despite this apparent drawback, the ratio definition of the threshold is substantially more versatile than erosion-deposition thresholds, which are stated merely in terms of available channel slope.

The threshold of critical power can be applied to the flowchart of figure 3-2 to provide useful elaborations about the behavior of water in the fluvial systems of arid regions. Each of the boxes pertaining to the sediment yield in figure 3-2 connects with the box for the critical-power threshold. The general lack of remnants of Pleistocene alluvial fills in the valleys of small, rocky desert watersheds in the American Southwest and in the Middle East indicates that prior to the Pleistocene-Holocene climatic change, streams either were downcutting (an equation 3.2 ratio of more than 1.0) or approximated the threshold (a value of 1.0). The changes in the input variables for the stream subsystem shown at the top of figure 3-2 resulted in increases of sediment yield that were in excess of the increase in water discharge to carry the sediment load. Critical power increased more rapidly than stream power, resulting in streams' being unable to carry the sediment load imposed upon them and causing valley alluviation. The opposite would be true during times of decreasing sediment yield as outlined at the bottom of figure 3-2.

Fill terraces, such as those in the Nahal Yael watershed, are ubiquitous in the mountain valleys of the arid parts of the Mojave and Sonoran deserts of Arizona and California. The terraces are remnants of valley fills that were 6 m to 30 m thick, but nearly all the streams now are downcutting into bedrock. These fluvial systems have been changing as a result of climatic change and the types of changes are described by the flowchart of figure 3-2. The single major perturbation of Pleistocene-Holocene climatic change resulted in consecutive valley alluviation and downcutting as self-enhancing feedback mechanisms changed stream and critical power. Because the stream subsystems of these watersheds changed modes of operation twice in response to a single perturbation, they may be regarded as an excellent example of what Schumm (1973) has referred to as complex response of fluvial systems. Along some streams, more valley alluviation occurred in the headwaters rather than farther downstream, resulting in stream gradients that were as much as 25 percent steeper than either the present stream gradients or the gradients that were present prior to the valley alluviation. Other streams have terraces that parallel the present gradients. The initial increases in sediment yield caused the critical-power threshold to be exceeded, despite increases of stream power due to increased stream gradients. The time of change from net aggradation to net degradation represents a brief threshold before decreases in sediment yield decreased critical power sufficient to switch the mode of system operation to erosion. Although the changes in stream gradient caused large changes in stream power, the changes in critical power resulting from changes in size and amount of sediment were even larger and occurred more rapidly.

RESPONSES OF PEDOGENIC AND VEGETATIONAL SUBSYSTEMS
TO CLIMATIC CHANGE IN HOT DESERTS

Changes in the pedogenic and vegetational subsystems of fill terraces are equally profound. The rocky soil profiles of the Sinai peninsula and the southern Negev Desert of Israel have great variety. Many geomorphic surfaces that are only a few meters above the present stream channels have dark desert pavements and calcic soil horizons consisting chiefly of minor amounts of calcium carbonate illuviated at depths of only 2 to 10 cm. Both the lack of pedogenic clay and the shallow depth of carbonate alluviation accord with what one would expect from the limited amounts and frequencies of soil wetting in the present arid climate. Furthermore such soils have never gone through a period of frequent and deep wetting. Other terraces that are only a few meters higher along the same stream courses have bright reddish-brown argillic B horizons that are more than 30 cm thick and are underlain by well-developed calcic horizons more than 0.5 m thick. The presence of argillic horizons and the much greater depths of the tops of the calcic horizons indicate that the higher alluvial geomorphic surfaces not only are older but also have passed through a period of wetter climate than have the lower surfaces with only thin soils.

Similar contrasts in pedogenic features of geomorphic surfaces are typical of the lower Colorado River region of the United States. Although this region receives more annual precipitation (50–100 mm as compared to 20–50 mm for much of the Sinai), the late Quaternary soils are readily classified into arid and semiarid modes of pedogenic processes. The arid mode in parent materials composed of alluvium derived from granitic rocks, schist, and gneiss consists of desert pavement with weathered rocks that have a brown desert varnish. Argillic horizons are lacking, but discontinuous pebble coatings less than 0.5 mm thick occur to depths of 10 to 20 cm and locally as deep as 30 cm. The semiarid mode of pedogenic processes is represented by desert pavements with highly weathered and split rocks that have a brownish-black desert varnish. Beneath the desert pavements are bright reddish-brown argillic horizons to depths of 20 cm below the surfaces and locally to depths of more than 0.5 m. Beneath the argillic horizon is a well-developed calcic horizon that typically is 0.5 to 1 m thick. Continuous pebble coatings and some interpebble fillings indicate a stage II calcic horizon development (Gile, Peterson, and Grossman, 1966).

The plant communities of the lower Colorado River region also reflect the arid and semiarid modes of late Quaternary climate. In the Whipple Mountains of southeastern California, one can find fresh-appearing juniper stems and leaves in small caves and crevices at altitudes of only 350 m, and pinon pine can be found in caves at altitudes of 500 m. Such plants are fossils because neither juniper nor pinon currently occurs anywhere in the Whipple Mountains, which extend to altitudes of more than 1,200 m.

The plants were collected and stored by pack rats (*Neotoma* sp.) for both food and shelter. Van Devender (1973, 1977) used these abundant sources of plant fossils to date the times of climatic change by radiocarbon methods. He concluded that starting about 8,000 years ago, annual precipitation in western

Arizona decreased about 50 percent, that most of the decrease occurred during the winter rainy season, and that the mean annual temperature increased about 3°C. Although such conclusions should be regarded as crude estimates, they do provide a measure (for one region) of the amounts and types of changes in the independent variable of climate that have resulted in the types of changes in the geomorphic systems outlined in figure 3-2.

STREAM SUBSYSTEM

Additional facets regarding the behavior of water in desert ecosystems may be illustrated by considering time spans of only a few years and fluvial systems that receive 100 to 400 mm in annual precipitation. The responses to grazing (or short climatic variations) are most pronounced in semiarid systems underlain by fine-grained, easily eroded materials, where changes in sediment loads and hydraulic roughness are large during time spans of 10^1 to 10^2 years.

Many of the arroyos of the western United States represent situations of continuous entrenchment of once-discontinuous ephemeral streams (Hack 1942; Schumm and Hadley, 1957; Packard, 1974). Discontinuous ephemeral streams flow through vegetated valley floors underlain by sand, silt, and clay and undergo changes in channel pattern that are repeated in the downstream direction. Stream channels start at headcuts in areas of sheet flow on channel alluvial fans, but these headcut channels progressively decrease in depth downstream until flow spreads out on the next small channel alluvial fan. Both valley alluviation and channel downcutting may be occurring simultaneously in adjacent reaches of the same stream.

Deposition of a new increment of fan deposits on the surface of the valley fill results in both steep and gentle reaches. In reach A of figure 3-4, the mode of operation is to alluviate the valley floor through increases in flow width, infiltration, and vegetation entrapment of sediment, all of which act as self-enhancing feedbacks that promote additional alluviation. In reach B of figure 3-4, the hypothetical valley-floor surface is inherently unstable because the slope is steeper than the overall slope of the valley. Entrenchment of the channel into the alluvium may occur, particularly at high discharges. The formation of channels tends to concentrate stream flow and establishes self-enhancing feedbacks that tend to destroy the patch of alluvium. Thus local aggradation may result in reaches that either exceed or are less than the critical-power threshold and where the relative rates of change of processes and land forms are dependent on two offsetting, self-enhancing feedback mechanisms. Feedback mechanisms tend to perpetuate two distinct modes of operation of discontinuous ephemeral stream systems. Figure 3-5 shows that the critical-power threshold separates two modes of operation. Where the threshold is exceeded for a stream (such as reach A of figure 3-4), decreases in the density of vegetation and in the flow width of channels and increases in flow depth and velocity within the channels tend to act as self-enhancing feedback mechanisms to perpetuate the downcutting mode. The effects of these factors tend to be offset by increases in sediment load and decreases in slope. Most entrenching streams downcut rapidly, approximate threshold conditions

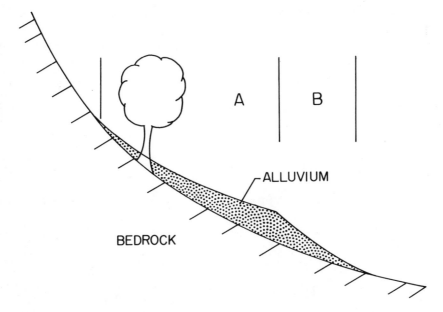

FIGURE 3-4. *Diagrammatic sketch of a stream profile showing adjacent alluvial reaches that are more gentle* (A) *and steeper* (B) *than the pre-existing bedrock channel (from Bull, 1979; copyright © 1979 by the Geological Society of America).*

for a while, and then backfill or renew downcutting in response to either new changes in the independent variables or to complex responses (Schumm, 1973) of the system. The valley aggradation mode shown at the left side of figure 3-5 has changes in dependent variables that are opposite to those of downcutting mode. For either mode, changes in base level directly affect the threshold of critical power.

An example of the sensitivity of such streams to the impact of human activities is provided by the Dead Mesquite Wash study area (Packard, 1974) near Tucson, Arizona. A discontinuous ephemeral stream locally supports a lush growth of trees, bushes, and grass. Where stream flow spreads out on channel fans that are the sites of valley aggradation, vegetation reduces the velocity of stream flow, thereby causing deposition of additional clayey soil and prolonged infiltration of stream flow. Grazing, fire, or encroachment by headcuts in the adjacent downstream reach may cause the critical-power threshold to be exceeded and thereby establish an opposite suite of self-enhancing feedback mechanisms. Such changes are particularly pronounced in clay-rich soils because the initiation of any minor channel greatly decreases the residence time of ephemeral sheet flow and the infiltration of water needed to support the vegetation. Within decades, lush growth such as that shown in figure 3-6 is transformed into badlands studded with bleached tree trunks such as those shown in figure 3-7.

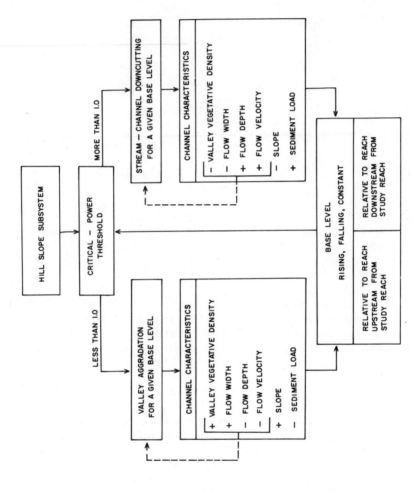

FIGURE 3-5. *Increases (+) and decreases (−) in elements of a hypothetical semiarid stream subsystem. Self-enhancing feedback mechanisms are shown by dashed lines and arrows (from Bull, 1979; copyright © 1979 by the Geological Society of America).*

FIGURE 3-6. *Threshold relations for a discontinuous ephemeral stream, Dead Mesquite Wash study site, Arizona. Shown here is a densely vegetated reach at critical-power threshold (from Bull, 1979; copyright © 1979 by the Geological Society of America).*

CONCLUSIONS ABOUT THE BEHAVIOR OF WATER IN DESERT ECOSYSTEMS

Fluvial geomorphic systems in hot arid and semiarid regions are complex. The interdependency of geomorphic, pedogenic, and vegetational subsystems creates extreme variations in the rates and magnitudes of geomorphic processes. Although a tendency toward equilibrium conditions exists in streams, the attainment of equilibrium conditions for long periods of time is unlikely for many reaches of streams. Changes in independent variables such as climate, total relief as affected by tectonic movements, erosion and deposition, the erodibility of soils and surficial materials, and the impact of human activities create conditions conducive to change instead of equilibrium in fluvial systems. In order to approach a new equilibrium, most fluvial systems respond to

FIGURE 3-7. *Threshold relations for a discontinuous ephemeral stream, Dead Mesquite Wash study site, Arizona. Shown here is a barren reach adjacent to that shown in figure 3-6. The critical-power threshold has been exceeded for this reach (from Bull, 1979; copyright © 1979 by the Geological Society of America).*

various changes, with individual time lags, in the independent variables. Furthermore, where self-enhancing instead of self-regulating feedback mechanisms are present, there may be a distinct tendency for increasingly great departures from equilibrium conditions.

The threshold of critical power occupies a key position in the complex interactions between the hill-slope and stream subsystems and is affected by feedback mechanisms and complex responses operating in either subsystem. Recognition of how far removed a stream is from the critical-power threshold should aid in better understanding how man interacts with his environment. When considering environmental impacts on desert ecosystems, the following considerations should be made:

Are the present trends for a given reach of a stream tending toward erosion or deposition?

How close is a reach of a stream to the critical-power threshold?

What effect will a proposed change in human activity have on the hill-slope and stream subsystem?

What will be the impact of the human activity on critical power and stream power?

Will feedback mechanisms be created that will tend to promote or alleviate the channel entrenchment?

This chapter has discussed several markedly different aspects of the behavior of water in desert ecosystems. The impact of climatic change on the rocky hill slopes of the hot deserts has fostered feedback mechanisms that have made the hills progressively more barren of vegetation and soil. Channel downcutting has followed valley aggradation as an example of a complex response to a single perturbation. It would be virtually hopeless for humans to attempt to reverse the modes of operation of these stream subsystems in view of the strength of the feedback mechanisms and the magnitude of the initial perturbation. However, the mode can be reversed for many southwestern streams that are ephemeral and discontinuous. Fine-grained sediment is trapped by vegetation and promotes favorable feedback mechanisms of added soil and moisture to promote vegetative growth further. These are areas of widespread grazing by cattle and sheep, so it would seem to be important that humans be able to identify those reaches of discontinuous ephemeral streams that are close to the critical-power threshold. Experience has shown that even densely vegetated areas may cross the threshold as vegetative cover is reduced and destructive feedback mechanisms are initiated.

REFERENCES

Bagnold, R. A. 1973. The nature of saltation and of bed-load transport in water. *Proc. Roy. Soc. (London),* Ser. A, **323:**473–504.

Bagnold, R. A. 1977. Bedload transport by natural rivers. *Water Resour. Res.* **13:**303–312.

Bull, W. B. 1975. Allometric change of landforms. *Bull. Geol. Soc. Am.* **86:**1489–1498.

Bull, W. B. 1979. Threshold of critical power in streams. *Bull. Geol. Soc. Am.* **90:**453–464.

Bull, W. S., and A. P. Schick. 1979. Impact of climatic change on an arid watershed: Nahal Yael, southern Israel. *Quaternary Res.* **11:**153–171.

Gile, L. H., F. F. Peterson, and R. B. Grossman. 1966. Morphologic and genetic sequences of carbonate accumulation in desert soils. *Soil Sci.* **101:**347–360.

Hack, J. T. 1942. *The Changing Physical Environment of the Hopi Indians.* Peabody Mus. Nat. Hist. Paper 35.

Meigs, P. 1953. World distribution of arid and semiarid homoclimates, pp.

203–210. In Arid zone programme, v. 1, *Reviews of Research on Arid Zone Hydrology*. UNESCO, Paris.

Packard, F. A. 1974. *The Hydraulic Geometry of a Discontinuous Ephemeral Stream on a Bajada near Tucson, Arizona*. Ph.D. dissertation. Univ. Arizona, 127 pp.

Schick, A. P., and D. Sharon. 1974. *The Geomorphology and Climatology of Arid Watersheds*. U.S. Army European Res. Off. Tech. Rept. DA JA-72-C-3874, 161 pp.

Schumm, S. A. 1973. Geomorphic thresholds and complex response of drainage systems, pp. 229–310. In M. Morisawa (ed.), *Fluvial Geomorphology*, Proc. 4th Ann. Geomorph. Symp. Ser., Binghamton, New York.

Schumm, S. A., and R. F. Hadley. 1957. Arroyos and the semiarid cycle of erosion. *Am. J. Sci.* **255**:161–174.

Smiley, T. L., and Z. H. Zumberge. 1974. *Polar Deserts and Modern Man*. Univ. Arizona Press, 173 pp.

Wilson, L. 1973. Variations in mean annual sediment yield as a function of mean annual precipitation. *Am. J. Sci.* **273**:335–349.

Van Devender, T. R. 1973. *Late Pleistocene Plants and Animals of the Sonoran Desert: A Survey of Ancient Packrat Middens in Southwestern Arizona*. Ph.D. dissertation. Univ. Arizona, 179 pp.

Van Devender, T. R. 1977. Holocene woodlands in the southwestern deserts. *Science* **198**:189–192.

Yair, A., and M. Klein. 1973. The influence of surface properties on flow and erosion processes on debris-covered slopes in an arid area. *Catena* **1**:1–18.

4

Morphological and Physiological Characteristics of Desert Plants

Grant A. Harris and *Gaylon S. Campbell*

A great variety of plant life grows on the lands and in the seas of the earth's biosphere. In this rich flora are found plant varieties having specialized physiology and morphology adapting them to survival in almost all of the biosphere's adverse habitats.

Desert environments present some of the most unfavorable conditions for life found in the natural habitats of the earth. Water is universally essential to the biochemical processes of all organisms, and on dry sites it is generally the controlling factor of biomass production. Deserts are deserts because they have a low precipitation to evaporation ratio, generally less than 0.20 (Livingston and Shreve, 1921). Average annual precipitation ranges from about 10 to 25 mm in the driest areas to 250 mm in semiarid regions. Extreme variations in amount and season are common. Furthermore, a large proportion of the precipitation received may be lost through surface runoff, leaving upland sites dry but recharging aquifers in drainages.

Restricted water availability also indirectly influences other biotic and abiotic factors of the ecosystem, compounding and intensifying the difficulties of plant survival. For example, restricted plant growth adds little in the way of surface litter or humus to ameliorate the poor insulating qualities of mineral soil. Clear daytime skies (associated with low precipitation) transmit most of the available solar radiation directly to the earth's surface. Desert soils have minimum water available for conversion of this energy into latent heat through evapotranspiration. Consequently temperatures of soil and contiguous atmosphere often become excessively high, and relative humidity is low. On the other hand, energy loss via long-wave radiation is at a maximum because of predominantly clear nighttime skies. Thus sensible heat levels become extreme, with a wide range of diurnal temperatures common.

Water plays a significant role in soil profile development and maturity, as well as in shaping drainage pathways through local and regional topography. Not only do typical desert soils have minimal morphologic development, but they frequently contain concentrations of salts normally absent in regions of higher precipitation. Calcium carbonate concentrations are common at variable depths below the surface, sometimes forming hardpans. Saline and alkaline soils may develop where such phenomena as perched water tables, playa lakes,

59

and other manifestations of imperfect drainage and high rates of evaporation occur. (For additional discussion of the physical characteristics of desert ecosystems, see chapter 3.)

At some seasons and in some places, water may be plentiful in the desert. Following winter snow melt and spring rains in the cool deserts or summer storms in the warm deserts, as well as deep in the water table of drainageways, water may be equally as available as in mesic ecosystems. But plants are stressed in desert habitats when growing conditions change quickly from favorable to very unfavorable. Mortality of mesic plants is high under these conditions.

It is generally agreed that plants now growing in deserts and displaying effective adaptations to xeric environments have evolved from mesophytic ancestors. Such plants have physiologic and morphologic adaptations that allow them to survive under conditions of severe water stress, as well as under conditions of energy, nutrient, and space availability found in deserts, all or part of which are too severe for the survival of their mesophytic ancestors.

Many species of desert plants belong to phylogenetic groups commonly found growing in and well adapted to mesic habitats. However, they continue to maintain sufficient morphologic characteristics to be recognized as belonging to the same taxonomic classes. The regular appearance of similar adaptations in unrelated plant species developed in deserts of different parts of the world suggests that these adaptations have widespread survival value. Daubenmire (1959) warns that human logic should not be relied upon to evaluate the survival value of morphologic adaptations, which should be the subject of physiologic experimentation. Morphologic features can only be assumed to be of significance as far as they actually influence the physiology of a plant. Unfortunately experimentation has often not been carried far enough to allow precise statements of these relationships, due in part to the complexity of the problem and in part to limited attention by research scientists. This review will reflect such limitations.

This chapter examines a few of the more obvious characteristics of desert plants that adapt them to their environments. (Additional detail can be found in chapter 7.) Primary emphasis is given to plants of the deserts of western North America, but the same general principles apply to desert plants throughout the world.

Several classifications of desert plants, based on strategies of survival, have appeared in the literature. However, the diversity of adaptations found in multicombinations, with many occurring across recognized phylogenetic boundaries, has added to the difficulty of developing a fully satisfactory classification scheme. Schantz (1927) published a widely used classification based on xerophytic adaptations that allow plants to evade, escape, endure, or resist drought. Differentiations among *evade* and *escape* or *endure* and *resist* are neither clear-cut nor always useful. Raunkiaer (1934) developed a classification based on the location of perennating buds during periods of dormancy in relation to protection afforded by the soil surface. His classes (phanerophytes, chamaephytes, hemicryptophytes, geophytes, and therophytes) are uncommon in American literature and only partially account for the breadth of adaptations found. Lange et al. (1975) used two categories (arido active and arido passive) to describe plants that grow and reproduce during the driest, hottest periods or that pass through this season in a dormant phase. Others have also been proposed, but none seems to categorize the diversity of adaptations better than these commonly used groupings: lichens, annuals, herbaceous perennials, shrubs, succulents, and trees.

LICHENS

Lichens are an important part of the vegetation in deserts but are often overlooked in discussion of desert plants. Soil formation is one of their important functions. Lichens grow on bare rock or soil surfaces, usually in the direct sun, where drought and temperature stresses are extreme. Still these plants are able to carry on photosynthesis and other normal life functions even in the hottest seasons. Lichens have no roots and so must depend exclusively on water and nutrients absorbed by the thalus from rain, dew, nitrogen dissolved in rain, minerals in direct contact, dust, and so forth.

Lichens are composed of an algal component and a fungal component living together in a symbiotic, or perhaps a controlled parasitic, relationship. This combination is itself an adaptation to xeric environments. Tracer studies with radioactive carbon dioxide have demonstrated that the algal component provides photosynthates for both, and it is thought that the fungal component provides nitrogenous materials and a moist environment for algal life processes.

These plants often live on sites where water received as precipitation is inadequate to account for the observed increase in biomass. On some sites lichens would be moistened directly by rain only enough for metabolic activity to proceed during a few days each year. Some other source of water is needed to account for their success.

Lange et al. (1975) have shown that photosynthesis proceeds in lichens at very low water potentials, even approaching −290 bars. They believe that vapor condensation, or the presence of air with a high water vapor pressure, is sufficient to activate metabolic processes. These conditions of moisture availability are not unusual in the desert during the early morning. They also demonstrated that lichens can endure strong desiccation and high temperatures brought on at midday by extreme solar radiation for several successive days without apparent injury. In one demonstration, they subjected a lichen thalus to extreme heat and desiccation continuously for a year in the laboratory. When moistened, it returned immediately to 100 percent of its original photosynthetic capacity. This ability demonstrates an unusual physiologic adaptation to desert environments. Even minor desiccation brings on irreversible biochemical degradation in the cells of most plant species tissues.

ANNUALS

Annual grasses and forbs are a conspicuous part of desert vegetation, particularly during periods of seasonally abundant precipitation or relatively high soil moisture derived from snow melt. Normally closed perennial plant communities of the desert become open to invasion by annuals during brief periods of excess soil moisture. To be successful in the desert, an annual plant must promptly respond to favorable growing conditions, reproduce itself abundantly, and return to a dormant state (seed) awaiting the next opportunity. The most successful annuals do this best.

Although there are exceptions, annual plants of the desert generally resemble mesic rather than xeric plants in morphology and function. Leaves are succulent, broad and simple in shape, and have relatively thin coverings of epidermal cells. Large numbers of stomates are openly exposed to the atmosphere to expedite exchange of moisture and carbon dioxide in photosynthesis (figure 4-1). The C_4 photosynthesis pathway is common among warm desert annuals and is an important adaptation to short growing seasons (Solbrig and Orians, 1977).* Roots are typically shallow, fibrous, and lacking in storage organs or heavily suberized exterior cellular structures.

Summer precipitation patterns, typically found in the warm deserts of the southwestern United States, encourage summer annual types of plant growth. Precipitation in this region is highly variable between years, sometimes increasing phenomenally in the local area or even over a broad section of the desert. During these relatively rare occasions, mesic site conditions prevail temporarily, and a multitude of annuals respond, giving the desert an appearance of a flower garden. Seeds that have lain dormant, perhaps for several years, quickly germinate. The plants grow profusely, produce a new crop of seeds, and disappear with the reestablishment of a normal desertic environment. Adaptation of annuals in the southern desert requires prompt response to irregularly occurring favorable growth periods, rapid completion of the reproductive process, and production of massive numbers of durable propagules that can survive long periods of unfavorable environment.

In the cool deserts (Great Basin, Columbia Basin, Wyoming High Plains, and related mountain valley and foothills of the northwest), fall-winter-spring (nongrowing seasons) precipitation patterns predominate. Under these conditions, winter annuals are best adapted. They are capable of germinating rapidly in the cool, moist environments provided by normal fall weather. Most annuals in this region are adapted to survival in the deep cold of winter, entering a semidormant state during which a limited amount of growth may occur even under a cover of snow. Root tips of some species continue growth at depths where the soil is not frozen, even on the coldest days (Harris, 1967). Cheatgrass (*Bromus tectorum L.*) and medusahead (*Taeniatherum asperum* (Simonkai) Nevski), two widely distributed introduced winter annuals, grow and reproduce even when held at a temperature of 2°C (Harris and Wilson, 1970). During brief periods in the winter when usual cold temperatures are relaxed, growth is promptly renewed. Warm spring temperatures, coupled with favor-

---

*C_4 designates a group of species for which the first product of the dark reaction in photosynthesis is a four-carbon sugar. The more common photosynthesis pathway is C_3, in which the first product is a three-carbon sugar. At optimum temperature and high irradiance, photosynthetic rate and dry matter produced per unit of water used can be twice as high in C_4 as in C_3 species (Black, 1973).

able soil moisture conditions resulting from snow melt and seasonal precipitation, bring on rapid phenological development to maturity. Death of the mature plant ensues when summer temperatures and surface soil moisture conditions become critical. Life is maintained through the environmental stress periods of summer in the dormant seed phase. The annual cycle is completed when the seed germinates in the fall.

During unusual and infrequent storms in the northern desert, summer rains may be of sufficient frequency and amount to hold some winter annuals, such as cheatgrass, alive into midsummer to produce a second set of inflorescenses, or sometimes into fall, allowing the plants to live through a second winter and spring (Harris, 1967). This phenomenon may also occur where the stand is thinned by some catastrophe, resulting in reduced evapotranspirational stress on the soil water supply and leaving enough soil water remaining to provide for the summer needs of the reduced number of survivors. While this is not a significant feature in overall biomass production, it is of academic interest that winter annuals may become biennial (or even perennial) if certain limiting factors are ameliorated.

With all annuals there is an ever-present danger that germination may be triggered by precipitation from a storm of short duration and the resulting highly vulnerable seedling crop killed in a subsequent hot, dry period. Germination of seeds of most annuals is inhibited by biochemical controls so they are delayed in germination until this danger period has passed. Hulbert (1955) showed that cheatgrass seed germination in the laboratory was inhibited by immaturity, high temperatures, and high light intensity. Nelson and Wilson (1969) found that medusahead seed produced in dry areas required aging for maximum germination.

Annuals commonly exhibit rapid germination of seeds, rapid extension of primary root systems, and high vigor in seedlings. Medusahead seeds have been observed to show initial hypocotyl growth nine hours after being placed on a germination medium. Primary root growth in this species was more than double the rate of growth of roots in vigorous perennial grass species (Harris and Wilson, 1970). These adaptations are of the first order of significance in the initial establishment of plants under highly variable soil moisture conditions. High seed germination percentage is the usual response in annuals.

Annuals have very low structural carbon requirements for maintaining leaves, roots, and other plant parts when compared to perennials. Annual plant structures are normally functional but once, and then they die and disintegrate. It is not necessary that plants be heavily protected against drought and excessive temperature because they grow only in relatively favorable seasons. Roots and leaves of cheatgrass provide an excellent example of this adaptation (compare figs. 4-1 and 4-2 with figs. 4-3 and 4-4). Thus root contact with the soil and photosynthetic exposure to radiant energy per unit of structural photosynthate produced is maximized by annuals.

Many annual plants, such as wheat, rice, and corn, are of high economic importance in our social system. Most of these commercial species are not adapted to desert ecosystem environments and require irrigation for optimum production.

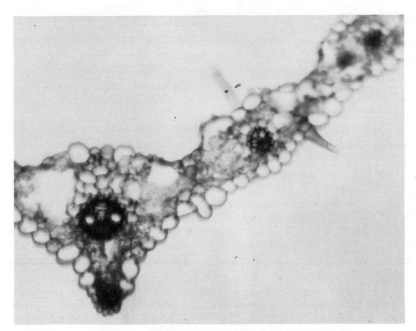

FIGURE 4-1. *Leaf cross-section of* Bromus tectorum *(annual grass) showing mesophytic type structure, including unrolled condition, thin-walled epidermis, and exposed stomates (approx. 182X).*

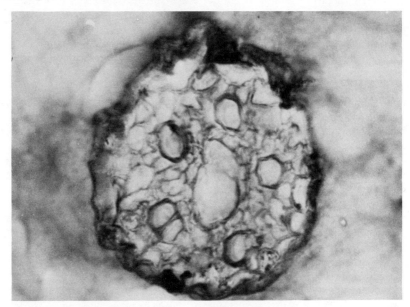

FIGURE 4-2. *Root cross-section of* Bromus tectorum *(annual grass). Cells are thin-walled and root diameter is relatively small (approx. 455X).*

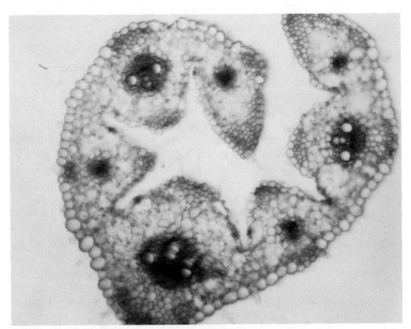

FIGURE 4-3. *Leaf cross-section of* Agropyron spicatum *(perennial grass). Stomates are mostly located in grooves on interior involuted surface. Leaf blades are open in moist conditions, involuted in dry conditions (approx. 120X).*

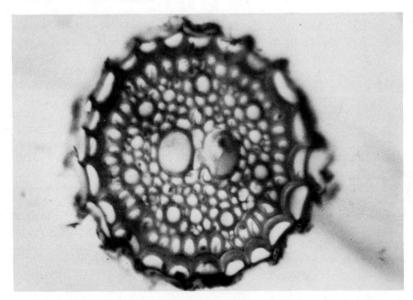

FIGURE 4-4. *Root cross-section in* Agropyron spicatum *(perennial grass). Note heavy cell wall structure, particularly in the exterior (endodermis) section (approx. 160X).*

HERBACEOUS PERENNIALS

The perennial habit has important adaptive value in desert environments. Established plants are able to enter the recurring favorable growing seasons with structural growing parts in place, prepared to begin life processes almost immediately. Many of the previously accumulated resources and structures are preserved for the next period of growth. By its presence on the site, a perennial exercises a degree of continuous control over the piece of landscape it occupies. Invaders are usually at a disadvantage because they must establish seedlings in the presence of established individuals, which collectively form a closed community. In desert ecosystems where water is the limiting factor, established perennial root systems ordinarily remove soil moisture ahead of emerging seedling roots, either annual or perennial. Rooting in most herbaceous perennials is restricted to depths of one or two meters where available moisture is annually depleted, leaving the plants without soil moisture for part of the year.

Perennial herbaceous plants are adapted to desert environments by virtue of their ability to become dormant when drought stress interrupts physiologic growth processes. During a period of excessive drought stress, the leaves and stems may die, but life is preserved in perennating buds and in roots. Perennating buds survive at the soil surface under the protection of heavy bud scales, dead stem bases, and litter accumulation. With the return of favorable growing conditions, these buds produce new growth, leading to leaf, stem, and seed production, as well as restoration of starch reserves in the roots. Inactive roots may die during serious water stress, sloughing off root hairs and thin-walled root sections that are normally subject to water loss in dry soils. Major root trunks and branches are protected by heavily suberized endodermis or other equivalent structures (figure 4-3).

All perennials store food reserves (various polysaccharides) in their roots and stem bases. Many have specialized organs—corms, bulbs, rootstalks, and tubers—for this purpose. Food reserves are necessary for replacing photosynthesizing organs that were shed in the process of adjusting to drought prior to dormancy.

Rooting habits also influence the spatial distribution of perennial plants over the desert floor. Herbaceous perennials of the desert are almost universally caespitose, with crowns spaced far apart, leaving bare surface soil between plants. These apparently bare spaces usually are occupied below the surface by the extended root systems of peripheral individuals. Excavated root systems of bluebunch wheatgrass (*Agropyron spicatum* (Pursh) Scribn. and Smith) demonstrate this growth pattern (Harris, 1967). Roots of this species grow out laterally for as much as 30 cm and then turn downward to exert a degree of control over a block of soil with a curtain of roots (figure 4-5).

DESERT SHRUBS

Desert shrubs and half-shrubs dominate most desert ecosystems and give them their characteristic desertic appearance (figures 4-6 and 4-7). Shrubs dis-

FIGURE 4-5. *Exposed roots of a one-year old* Agropyron spicatum *plant (perennial grass). Note roots spreading horizontally from caespitose crown, to control soil resources in the adjacent space. Seedlings of other plants have difficulty becoming established in competition with these already established roots.*

play their stems, leaves, and perennating buds above the ground level, where they are exposed to extremes of solar radiation, temperature, low relative humidity, and wind. This growth form presumably has both positive and negative values for survival but requires various adaptations to offset at least partially the disadvantages inherent in the erect life form.

The apparent advantage of the erect life form lies in maintaining a framework available for displaying photosynthetic tissue during recurrent periods of available moisture. Theoretically at least, with stems and leaves in place, less new structural material, and hence less delay, is required to complete reproductive phases when favorable conditions return. Disadvantages arise from the large energy cost to the plant of building, maintaining, and protecting these living structures.

FIGURE 4-6. *Big sagebrush* (Artemisia tridentata) *is an important shrub, typical of the cool desert. This plant continues to grow and produce seed during the driest part of the year.*

FIGURE 4-7. *Shadscale* (Atriplex confertifolia) *is a salt and alkali tolerant desert shrub.*

Maintenance of a framework for displaying photosynthetic tissue requires the desert shrub to maintain its water balance in a basically different way from the desert annual or herbaceous perennial. Herbaceous species generally have high diffusive conductances and control water loss by adjustments to transpiring area. Shrubs, on the other hand, tend to maintain at least a certain minimum transpiring (and photosynthesizing) area and adjust transpiration through decreasing stomatal conductance.

A number of studies on desert shrubs indicate a correlation between stomatal conductance and available water. Campbell and Harris (1977) have shown that sagebrush (*Artemisia tridentata* Nutt.) stomatal conductances during a dry summer were less than one-tenth those during a wet summer. Daily adjustments in stomatal conductance of some warm desert shrubs are shown in figure 4-8. The deep-rooted mesquite (*Prosopis juliflora* (Swartz) DC) and creosote bush (*Larrea tridentata* (DC.) Colville) maintain high conductances throughout the day, suggesting that they have relatively free access to stored soil water. Other desert species have high conductance early in the day, but when the water from soil storage that was recharged during the previous night is exhausted, they must close stomates to maintain water balance. Yucca, a CAM plant, closes stomates early in the day and has conductances lower than any of the shrubs.*

There are many apparent morphologic, anatomic, phenologic, and physiologic adaptations evident in the array of variations found in desert shrubs. These plants usually combine survival strategies in a variety of ways for success.

Creosote bush is a good example of a drought-resistant, warm-desert shrub (Runyon 1934, 1936; Chew and Chew, 1965). This species, found over large areas of the Mojave, Sonoran, and Chihuahuan deserts, develops both lateral roots and a tap root in deep soil, which draw upon surface soil moisture brought by light rains and also deep-stored moisture beyond the reach of roots of herbaceous species. Winter leaves, along with some twigs, abscise in summer and are replaced by smaller, more drought-resistant leaves, thus reducing the transpiring surface. These summer leaves have small, thick-walled cells and are adapted to survive heavy water losses. They can survive a reduction in water content to less than 50 percent of their dry weight and an internal saturation deficit of at least 77 percent. Even at these levels of desiccation, some metabolic activity continues, and recovery of normal water content occurs promptly after a rainstorm. In this example, physiologic adaptation to cell water loss appears to have survival value. Also the observable morphologic adaptation of dropping winter leaves and replacing them with smaller and fewer summer leaves appears to be a significant adaptation to drought.

Big sagebrush is the most characteristic shrub of the cool desert region. It covers millions of hectares of valley bottoms and foothills in the intermountain regions of the West. This shrub continues semiactive growth through the summer after most associated understory plants are dormant and yet matures seed

---

*Crassulacean acid metabolism (CAM) is a third photosynthetic pathway in which CO_2 is stored at night to be used the following day for photosynthesis. Thus stomates are open mainly at night, resulting in water use efficiencies (ratio of dry matter produced to water used) ten times larger than in C_3 species (Black, 1973).

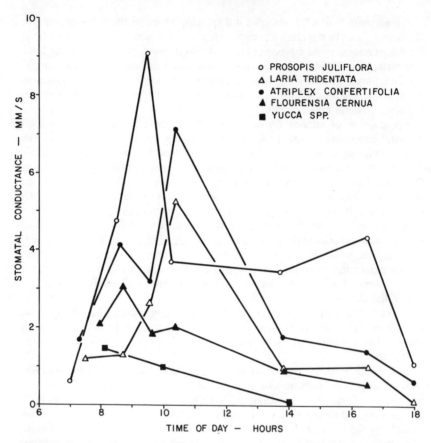

FIGURE 4-8. *Daily variation in stomatal conductance of some warm desert species. Measurements were made at the Journada Experimental Range near Las Cruces, New Mexico, September 18, 1973 using a steady state diffusion porometer (Campbell, 1975). Points are individual measurements.*

in the late fall. Large spring leaves are dropped following a period of rapid growth in the spring and are replaced by a smaller set of summer leaves after the advent of hot weather and the exhaustion of soil moisture. Big sagebrush has both shallow and deep root systems (Sturges, 1977). This two-level root system draws upon subsurface soil water in the spring and deep water during the dry summer months.

Desert shrubs also exhibit many other adaptations. Some completely drop their leaves during stress periods (*Fouquieria splendens* Engelm.). Others have stems provided with stomates and chlorophyll (*Ephedra* spp.). Sclerophyllus leaves found on oak and pinion of the desert appear to resist drought. Other apparent leaf adaptations include sunken stomates covered by trichomes; thick waxy cuticles; edges folded, involuted, or revoluted; and dense pubescence to provide shade and reduce surface air movement.

HALOPHYTIC DESERT SHRUBS

Some parts of desert landscapes commonly have soil of high salt content. Where evaporation greatly exceeds precipitation, as in deserts, there is usually an accumulation of salts in the surface soils. In other situations, the floors of brackish seas of past geologic ages have been raised through diastrophism to become the hills and plateaus of today's desert landscapes. The amount and kinds of salts from deposits or accumulations strongly influence the composition and density of vegetation that is present.

Adaptation to saline and alkaline soils appears to be largely a physiologic adjustment. Most plants otherwise able to grow in a given environment can tolerate small quantities of salt in the soil solution; however, as concentrations increase, fewer and fewer species are found growing, until at some upper limit the soil surface is bare of vegetation.

In many instances salt and alkali tolerance is more important in plant adaptation to site than other factors. For example, some salt-tolerant species (particularly on wet sites) are found in both the warm and cool deserts.

Plants grow best on salty soils during the rainy season, when concentration of surface salts is reduced by leaching them below the root zone by percolation. Seedlings of most nontolerant species germinate poorly on salty soils. High salt concentrations not only increase the osmotic concentration of soil solutions, thus increasing the difficulty of water uptake, but also have a phytotoxic influence on biochemical functions of plant cells, the intensity depending on the specific ions present as well as on the tolerance of particular plant species, (Goodin and Mozafar, 1972).

Tolerant species have the ability to lower the osmotic potential of cell contents to compensate for highly saline soil solutions. Some can pass salt off in water of guttation or through specialized glands or cells adapted for this purpose. Some shrubs concentrate salts under their crowns by drawing the salt into leaves, excreting it onto leaf surfaces, and dropping leaves to the ground through normal leaf fall. Salt is also washed from attached leaves onto the soil during rainstorms.

SUCCULENTS

Succulent plants of the desert (figure 4-9) are adapted to absorb quickly and store water from small amounts of precipitation, enabling them to continue near-normal physiologic functions through the driest seasons. The most common American plants in this group belong to the cactus family, but some are found in Liliaceae, Euphorbiaceae, and other families.

Succulents have shallow root systems arrayed near the soil surface. Root hairs of succulents are thought to dry up during periods of moisture stress to reduce the possibility of reverse water movement from plant to dry soil. The thick cuticle covering the plant body resists evaporational losses. Photosynthesis is by the CAM pathway so that stomates open at night, keeping water loss to a minimum. There is some evidence that these plants recycle and balance the products of photosynthesis against the products of metabolism

FIGURE 4-9.   *Succulent plants (cactus and yucca spp.) of the warm desert. These plants conserve water from infrequent storms.*

without serious loss of any of them. Growth of succulents is very slow under adverse conditions. However, this does not appear to be a serious disadvantage because flowers and seeds are produced without much new growth.

Succulents have water potentials that are much higher than those typical of other desert species, even though they may be without water for long periods of time. Soule and Lowe (1970) measured osmotic potentials of giant Sahuaro cactus (*Cereus giganteus* Engel.) ranging from −4.6 bars at maximum hydration (January) to −8 bars at minimum hydration (September). Typical minimum water potentials for other desert species are an order of magnitude or more lower than these values (chapter 7).

ADAPTATIONS TO RESIST GRAZING USE

Deserts of the world are traditionally used primarily for grazing. In contrast, the highest economic use of arable lands is usually determined to be intensive agriculture, with livestock kept to use crop residue. Deserts are not suited to intensive agricultural cropping unless they are irrigated, but they are well suited to the practice of nomadic or managed livestock husbandry.

Cropping of plants generally removes transpiring tissues, thus reducing the water stress on the remaining plant and assisting in survival. On the other hand, cropping also removes photosynthetic tissue and structural material critical to plant life functions. Heavy and repeated cropping of plants may be highly destructive, particularly during the active growing period when plant parts are most nutritious and palatable to grazing animals. Such intensive grazing frequently removes the most valuable grazing species and gives a competitive advantage to less palatable plants. Species that are adapted to resist or avoid grazing use will also be able to persist and gradually increase in abundance.

Annual plants often grow in such profusion over a short period that it is not possible for animal populations to remove significant proportions of the seed crop. Once seed is produced, little damage can be sustained by removal of the dead and dying mature plants. Where grazing of annuals is excessive, unpalatable or low stature annuals are best adapted and may be expected to assume dominance in the plant community.

In contrast with annuals, perennial herbaceous and shrubby plants are susceptible to serious injury if excessively grazed. If destroyed by overuse, they are replaced by noxious species that are low in palatability, poisonous, protected by thorns or spines, or in other ways adapted to resist or avoid grazing use. Under continuing heavy use, even these species can be destroyed by the processes of desertification and replaced by annual species.

CONCLUSION

Xerophytic plants have presumably evolved from measophytic ancestors in adjusting to xeric environments. These adaptations include many morphologic and physiologic features such as specialized leaf, stem and root structures, life form, phenology, photosynthetic pathways, heat tolerance, salt tolerance, resistance to cell sap desiccation, timely leaf abscission, and others. Desert plants may be classified as lichens, annuals, herbaceous perennials, shrubs, succulents, and trees. The regular appearance of similar adaptations in unrelated kinds of plants suggests that these adaptations have significant survival value.

REFERENCES

Black, C. C. 1973. Photosynthetic carbon fixation in relation to net CO_2 uptake. *Ann. Rev. Plant Physiol.* **24**:253–286.

Campbell, G. S. 1975. Steady state diffusion porometers, pp. 20–23. In E. T. Kanemasu (ed.), *Measurement of Stomatal Aperture and Diffusive Resistance,* Bull. 809, Washington Agric. Res. Center, Washington State Univ., Pullman, Wash.

Campbell, G. S., and G. A. Harris. 1977. Water relations and water use patterns for *Artemisia tridentata* Nutt. in wet and dry years. *Ecology* **58**:652–659.

Chew, R. M., and A. E. Chew. 1965. The primary productivity of a desert shrub (*Larrea tridentata*) community. *Ecol. Monogr.* **35**:355–375.

Daubenmire, R. F. 1959. *Plants and Environment.* Wiley, New York.

Goodin, J. R., and A. Mozafar. 1972. Physiology of salinity stress, pp. 255–259. In C. M. McKell et al. (eds.), *Useful Wildland Shrubs—Their Biology and Utilization.* USFS Gen. Tech. Rept. INT-1.

Harris, G. A. 1967. Some competitive relationships between *Agropyron spicatum* and *Bromus tectorum. Ecol. Monogr.* **37**:89–111.

Harris, G. A., and A. M. Wilson. 1970. Competition for moisture among seedlings of annual and perennial grasses as influenced by root elongation at low temperature. *Ecology* **52**:530–534.

Harris, G. A., and C. J. Goebel. 1976. *Factors of Plant Competition in Seeding Pacific Northwest Bunchgrass Ranges.* Agric. Res. Center, Washington State Univ., Pullman, Wash., 21 pp.

Hulbert, L. C. 1955. Ecological studies of *Bromus tectorum* and other annual bromegrasses. *Ecol. Monogr.* **25**:181–213.

Lange, O. L., E. D. Schulze, L. Kappeu, U. Basehbom, and M. Evanari. 1975. Adaptations of desert lichens to drought and extreme temperature, pp. 20–37. In N. F. Hadley (ed.), *Environmental Physiology of Desert Ecosystems,* Dowden, Hutchinson and Ross, Inc., Stroudsburg, Pa.

Livingston, B. E., and F. Shreve. 1921. *The Distribution of Vegetation in the United States as Related to Climatic Conditions.* Carnegie Inst. Washington Publ. No. 284.

Nelson, J. R., and A. M. Wilson. 1969. Influence of age and awn removal on dormancy of medusahead seeds. *J. Range Manage.* **22**:289–290.

Raunkiaer, C. 1934. *The Life Forms of Plants and Statistical Plant Geography.* Clarendon Press, Oxford.

Runyon, E. H. 1934. The organization of the creosote bush with respect to drought. *Ecology* **15**:128–138.

Runyon, E. H. 1936. Ratio of water content to dry weight in leaves of the creosote bush. *Bot. Gaz.* **97**:518–553.

Shantz, H. L. 1927. Drought resistance and soil moisture. *Ecology* **8**:145–157.

Solbrig, O. T., and G. H. Orians. 1977. The adaptive characteristics of desert plants. *Am. Sci.* **65**:412–421.

Soule, O. H., and C. H. Lowe. 1970. Osmotic characteristics of tissue fluids of the sahuaro giant cactus (*Cereus giganteus* Engelm.). *Ann. Missouri Bot. Garden* **57**:265–351.

Sturges, D. L. 1977. Soil water withdrawal and root characteristics of big sagebrush. *Am. Midl. Nat.* **98**:257–274.

5

Modeling Soil-Water-Plant-Atmosphere Systems of Deserts

Gaylon S. Campbell and *Grant A. Harris*

A model is a simplified verbal, graphic, or mathematical representation of a complicated system. The soil-plant-atmosphere system of deserts is extremely difficult to describe in detail, but a reasonably accurate description of the behavior and interactions of its components is attainable through combinations of equations describing the various physical and biological processes that occur in the desert. The collection of equations that describes all fluxes and storages of mass and energy within the desert system may be regarded as a model of the soil-plant-atmosphere system of the desert.

In order for a model to be useful, it should be simple enough to be understood by those using it and reasonably easy to use. At the same time, it should describe the most important aspects of the behavior of the system. These two requirements are, to some extent, mutually exclusive. The real talent of the modeler comes in knowing what is important enough to include and what is insignificant enough to be left out. The choice is not an absolute one since effects that are negligible for general descriptions are sometimes quite important for specific studies. At least two criteria can be used to determine significance of a given component of a model. The first is the size of a component compared to other components or to the total quality of energy or mass in the system. If a total mass or energy balance for a system is able to account for, say, 90 percent or more of the inputs, losses, and storages, the model could probably be considered successful.

A second criterion for determining significance of components might be the size of a component in comparison with plant or animal needs at a particular time. For example, thermally induced vapor flow in desert soil is probably insignificant in magnitude compared with other components of the water budget, but it can materially affect the water budget of some species during certain times of the year (see chapter 6).

Other considerations of importance to the modeler are the choices of time and space scales for the model. For many purposes, it is sufficient to treat the soil-plant-atmosphere system as one-dimensional, but in desert systems where plants are often widely spaced (chapter 3), a detailed description of the system would require consideration of horizontal temperature and moisture gradients. With respect to time scales, one may be interested in annual production or water use, but because of nonlinear relationships between input and output variables, annual or even daily averages of input variables may not be sufficient to permit the model to give accurate results.

The discussions in this chapter will not deal with general desert models but will outline certain aspects of water and energy budgets in deserts. Detailed descriptions of specific models will be given in later chapters. The space scale for this analysis will vary in size from single plants to entire plant communities; the time scale will include both instantaneous observations and annual averages. An attempt will be made to show essentially all inputs, losses, and storages of heat and water in the desert soil-plant-atmosphere system. The discussion will be centered on estimates of those components that are most important to the energy and water balance of the desert in terms of percentage of the annual total rather than in terms of the budget at a particular time or place. Typical sizes of components in desert systems will also be indicated.

THE ENERGY BUDGET

The energy budget for a desert gives all of the inputs, storages, and losses of energy for the desert surface. Figure 5-1 diagrams such a budget. The boxes represent places where energy is stored within the system. Arrows represent both fluxes of energy to or from the various components of the system and resistances to transport. In many cases, the fluxes of energy from one system component to another are proportional to the concentration difference between storage compartments and inversely proportional to the resistance in the flow path. Transport of four forms of energy is indicated in the figure. Sensible heat is transported by convection and conduction within the soil and canopy and from the canopy and soil to the atmosphere. Latent heat is transported from the plant and soil to the atmosphere and within the soil by water evaporation and condensation. Radiant energy is transported to the canopy and soil as short- and long-wave radiation. Long-wave radiation transports energy within the canopy, between the canopy and the atmosphere, between the ground and atmosphere, and between the ground and the canopy. Chemical energy is stored by photosynthesis, transported by translocation within the plant, and converted into heat by respiration.

Short-Wave Radiation

The radiant flux density normal to the solar beam, above the earth's atmosphere, is about 1,400 watts per square meter (W/m^2). the atmosphere attenuates the beam and scatters energy from it, so the direct solar irradiance at the earth's surface is less than this value. The reduction is partially compensated by reflected and scattered sky and cloud radiation. The irradiance at the earth's surface, normal to the solar beam, can therefore approach 1,400 W/m^2 (in some cases, with reflections, it may exceed this value). The irradiance on a horizontal surface is 1,400 W/m^2 only when the sun is directly over the surface. The horizontal irradiance during the day is less than the perpendicular ir-

TABLE 5-1. *Average Annual Solar Irradiance on a Horizontal*
Surface Outside the Earth's Atmosphere, and Probable
Extremes in Average Annual Absorbed Radiation for
Deserts at Various Latitudes

Latitude	Extraterrestrial irradiance (W/m²)	Maximum absorbed short wave (W/m²)	Minimum absorbed short wave (W/m²)
0	415	255	177
10	409	252	175
20	392	241	168
30	365	224	156
40	328	202	140

radiance, ranging from zero at night to 1,000 to 1,200 W/m² on clear days near midday.

Table 5-1 shows the average annual extraterrestrial irradiance for four latitudes along with estimated maximum and minimum annual net short-wave irradiance. The estimates were made assuming a surface albedo of 0.25. The maximum values were calculated assuming a ratio of measured to extraterrestrial radiation of 0.82. This value represents the long-term average for Inyokern, California, and according to Sellers (1965), is the highest ratio measured anywhere. The minimum estimate was calculated assuming a ratio of 0.6, the average ratio for the earth (Sellers, 1965), on the assumption that deserts would tend to have ratios above the average. Table 5-1 indicates that the average energy input for a desert from solar radiation is around 200 W/m².

Short-wave radiation is stored as photosynthate, absorbed by the canopy, transmitted by the canopy, and absorbed directly by the ground (figure 5-1). The amount of radiation absorbed by the canopy is directly proportional to the surface cover. Methods for estimating this are given by Ross (1975) and Fuchs (1972), among others. Crude estimates, which are often adequate, can be made by inspection. The short-wave radiation absorbed by the soil is the total minus that absorbed by the canopy.

The amount of energy stored as photosynthate can be estimated from simple assumptions. A rapidly growing barley crop may fix as much as 45 g CO_2 m^{-2} day^{-1} (Biscoe et al., 1975), about half of which is respired. The average rate of energy storage for such a crop would be less than 6 W/m². Maximum canopy photosynthesis in deserts is considerably lower than that for barley because of low plant densities, and average rates of energy storage would therefore be much lower than 6 W/m². The components in the stored chemical energy portion of figure 5-1 therefore represent considerably less than 1 percent of the energy budget and will not be considered further.

Long-Wave Radiation

The long-wave emittance of a surface is a function of the surface temperature and emissivity. Most natural surfaces have emissivities near unity (Mon-

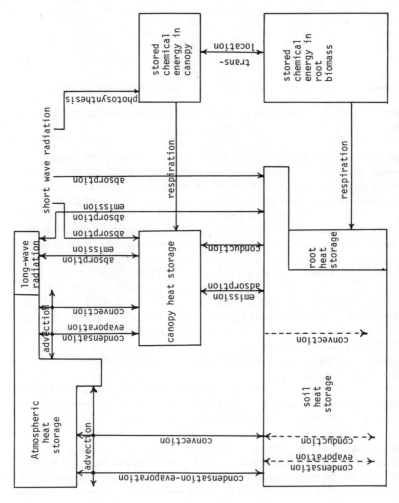

FIGURE 5-1. *Energy storage and exchange in a soil-plant-atmosphere system*

TABLE 5-2.   *Ground and Minimum Sky Emittance and Net Radiation for an Isothermal (Sky Temperature Equal to Ground Temperature) Clear Sky Condition as a Function of Temperature*

Temperature (°C)	Ground emittance (W/m²)	Minimum sky emittance (W/m²)	Net isothermal radiation (W/m²)
0	316	228	−88
10	364	280	−84
20	419	344	−75
30	479	417	−62
40	545	501	−44

teith, 1973), but the atmosphere has an emissivity that varies with temperature from a value near 1 at high temperatures to a low of around 0.7 at 0°C (Campbell, 1977). Table 5-2 shows surface and clear sky emittance as a function of temperature, assuming the surface emissivity is unity.

The net isothermal long-wave radiation is also shown in table 5-2. This represents the net radiation for a surface at air temperature under a clear sky. During the day, under a clear sky, surface temperature is higher than air temperature, and at night it is lower than air temperature. Net long-wave radiation therefore ranges from values near zero (for overcast days or nights with very strong surface cooling) to perhaps double the net isothermal values. On the average, the net isothermal long wave may approximate the actual net long-wave radiation. Thus, one-third to one-half of the average net short-wave radiation is dissipated via the net long-wave route. Instantaneous daytime values are, of course, much lower, probably not exceeding 20 percent of the instantaneous net short-wave radiation.

Evaporation

When water evaporates from a surface, the latent heat of vaporization is carried with the vapor. Evaporation therefore represents heat as well as mass transfer. The latent heat of evaporation is 2.45 megajoules per kilogram (MJ/kg) at 20°C, and although it varies slightly with temperature, the variation is not significant for order of magnitude calculations. Evaporation of 1 mm of water (1 kg/m²) from the ground surface requires 2.45 MJ/m² of energy. Peak potential evaporation rates in the desert may reach 1 mm/hr (chapter 8), so peak latent heat loss rates would be on the order of 700 W/m², roughly equal to the peak net radiation. When large areas are wet, peak latent heat transfer rates are not likely to exceed net radiation, but advection of heat from surrounding dry areas to wet areas can cause latent heat transfer to exceed net radiation when only a small area is wet.

Average annual evapotranspiration in the desert is roughly equal to the annual precipitation. For every millimeter of annual evaporation, the average rate of latent heat transfer is 0.08 W/m², so a desert with 100 mm of precipitation would have an annual latent heat loss of 8 W/m². For 300 mm of precipitation, the latent heat loss would be 24 W/m². Average annual latent heat loss therefore accounts for less than 10 percent of the absorbed short-wave radiation supplied to the surface.

Latent heat transfer to the surface occurs during dew fall. The total quantity of dew deposited is a small fraction of total evaporation, and evaporation is a small fraction of the total surface energy budget of a desert, so dew probably contributes negligibly to the overall energy balance.

Convective Heat Transfer

The rate of convective heat transfer from the desert surface to the atmosphere is directly proportional to the temperature difference between the surface and the air. The resistance to heat transfer is determined by wind speed and surface roughness. For a constant temperature difference, increasing wind speed will decrease the resistance and increase the rate of heat transfer. Increasing surface roughness will also decrease resistance and increase heat transfer. (Details of transport models and processes can be found in many references; see Monteith, 1973; Thom, 1975; Campbell, 1977.)

There are no simple, direct methods for modeling convective heat transfer. Indirectly the convective term can be taken as the residual after other terms in the energy budget have been estimated. Peak instantaneous rates equal net radiation minus soil heat storage for dry surfaces. For wet surfaces, where nearly all of the net radiation goes into evaporation of water, convective heat transfer is near zero.

To estimate the magnitude of the mean annual convective heat loss from deserts, previous estimates of long-wave and evaporative heat loss can be used. If long-wave loss accounts for around 40 percent of the absorbed short-wave radiation and latent heat loss for 10 percent, then the average convection rate must be half or more of the absorbed short wave, or around 100 W/m².

Canopy and Soil Heat Transfer and Storage

Heat is stored in the atmosphere, the canopy, and the soil (figure 5-1). (Storage in the atmosphere will not be discussed here.) Munn (1966) tells how to estimate canopy heat storage. He gives peak instantaneous storage rates of 35 W/m² for a dense forest, which is around 5 percent of the maximum instantaneous net radiation. Since forest biomass is much greater than that of deserts, canopy heat storage in deserts is negligible. Average heat storage over a diurnal or annual cycle is, of course, zero.

An analysis of soil heat storage is given by Monteith (1973) and in more detail by van Wijk (1963). The maximum rate of heat storage in the soil can be estimated using some of Monteith's equations. If the maximum surface temperature is assumed to be 25°C above the mean, the thermal conductivity of the soil is 0.5 W m⁻¹ C⁻¹ and the diurnal damping depth (depth at which the diurnal temperature variation is 0.37 of its surface value) is 10 cm, then the rate of heat storage in the soil would be 180 W/m², or perhaps 20 percent of the net radia-

TABLE 5-3. *Summary of the Important Components of the Desert Energy Budget, Expressed as Percentages of Absorbed Short-Wave Radiation*

Component	Mean annual	Peak daytime wet soil	Peak daytime dry soil
Net long wave	30–50	10	20
Soil heat storage	0	10	20
Latent Heat	5–10	70	0
Convection	40–60	10	60

Note: Mean annual values as well as peak daytime rates are shown.

tion for a dry soil surface. The soil heat storage averaged over a day would be near zero. The actual value can be estimated using the annual damping depth in place of the diurnal damping depth in Monteith's equation. For an annual damping depth of 2 meters, with other parameters as before, the peak annual storage rate would be about 9 W/m². This would occur in late spring and late fall. The average annual storage rate is, of course, zero.

Heat is transported by conduction, convection, and evaporation condensation within the soil (figure 5-1). In terms of the energy budget, conduction is of primary importance. Convection refers to heat transported by moving soil water. The amount of heat transported by this mechanism would always be negligible because water fluxes in soil are small. Latent heat transfer in soil is also very small, except possibly in freezing soil (Fuchs et al., 1978). (More detail on rates of latent heat transfer in soil is provided in chapter 6.)

Energy Budget Summary

The major contributions to the energy budget for an annual cycle and for peak times during a clear day with wet and dry surfaces in terms of percentage of net short-wave radiation are summarized in table 5-3. For the annual cycle, the absorbed solar radiation is dissipated mainly by convection and net long-wave radiation. This is also the case for the instantaneous energy budget of dry soil, except that a significant quantity of heat goes to storage in the soil during the day. When the soil surface is wet, the incoming energy is dissipated primarily by evaporation, but the amount of time that surfaces are wet is not large in the desert.

THE WATER BUDGET

The water budget for a desert surface is shown in figure 5-2. Input of water to the system is from precipitation and dew. Losses are by evapotranspiration and deep percolation. Storage of water in the system is mainly in the soil, although some water is stored in the canopy and, after precipitation or dew, on the surface of leaves and soil. The soil storage reservoir is arbitrarily divided

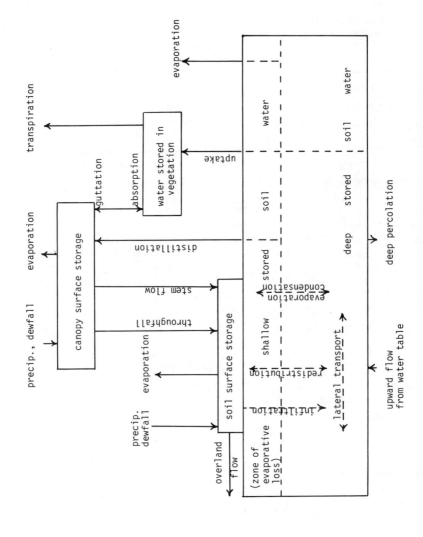

FIGURE 5-2. *Water storage and exchange in a soil-plant-atmosphere system.*

into a shallow and a deep compartment. Water in the shallow compartment is subject to loss by evaporation and uptake by shallow roots of desert plants (chapter 3). Water stored deep in the soil is not subject to rapid loss by evaporation and can be used by deep-rooted perennials. The dividing line between the layers is not well specified, and its depth is a function of a number of factors, which will be discussed later.

Precipitation and Dew

The primary input of water in deserts is precipitation. (Characteristics of desert precipitation are treated in chapter 10.) Some aspects of precipitation on a microscale are indicated by figure 5-2. Interception of precipitation by the canopy will reduce precipitation below the canopy relative to that in open spaces. In addition, some vegetation tends to concentrate intercepted water and channel it down stems to soil directly beneath the plant (Satterlund, 1972; chapter 7). Drifting of snow around plants can also concentrate precipitation in the vicinity of the plant (Hinds, 1971). These effects are interesting and are undoubtedly important to the desert water balance, but the complexities are such that general modeling efforts have so far been unable to cope with them. It is difficult to assign magnitudes to microscale precipitation fluctuations though experience suggests that fluctuations of at least 100 percent in amount of water delivered to a particular location are common. These differences are partially compensated by the fact that plant roots draw water from those locations where it is most available, so differences are evened out with time. The possible importance of the channeling effect of vegetation can be illustrated by considering the disposition of water that might be received in a 5 mm summer storm. This amount of water, if applied uniformly, would wet the soil to a depth of 3 or 4 cm and would soon be lost by evaporation. However, if the same water were applied to one-fourth that area, it might wet the soil to approximately 15 cm, thus providing a plant with some water. In addition, the collected water would be stored beneath the plant crown where the soil might be shaded, and local evaporation might be reduced compared to adjacent locations.

A large and ambiguous literature exists on the importance and quantity of dew in deserts. Reviews can be found in Monteith (1963) and Wallin (1967). An examination of dew as part of the water budget of crops is given by Rutter (1975). From the standpoint of modeling a desert system, Monteith's approach is most helpful. He computes the maximum quantity of dew deposition possible on the basis of the energy budget of the surface. Maximum rates of dew deposition occur when the air is saturated. The rate of dew deposition from a saturated atmosphere is a function only of the air temperature and the net isothermal radiation (table 5-2). The temperature function is weak, so for most purposes the latent heat transfer to the surface will be around half the net isothermal radiation, or about 40 W/m². This is equivalent to 0.06 mm/hr of dew deposition. Actual rates of dew deposition are less than this amount because of reduced net isothermal radiation due to overcast sky, air with relative humidity lower than unity, and some fraction of the energy for net isothermal radiation being supplied by stored soil heat. Maximum nightly dew deposition rates on artificial surfaces are shown by Monteith to range from 0.17 to 0.45 mm. He considers these numbers to be consistent with the energy budget calculations. If dew were condensed at the maximum measured rate every night of the year, the annual total would be 164 mm, a substantial contribution to the water budget of the desert. However, the actual dew deposition is probably one-fourth to one-half this value.

The source of dew is important if we wish to model the water budget of the desert. Some of the dew is evaporated from the soil and condensed on the canopy, thus resulting in no net gain of water by the system. This component of dew is termed *distillation*. Water from the atmosphere that is deposited on the surface, termed *dewfall,* actually adds water to the system. Monteith's calculations show that one-fourth to one-half of the dew is from the atmosphere, so the annual input of water to the desert by dewfall is probably 10 to 40 mm. This input is generally worth considering in any desert water budget and is of considerable importance when water is particularly scarce.

Assessment of the importance of dew to plants is difficult. Dew on the surfaces of leaves and on the soil is quickly evaporated in the morning. For the dew to be useful to the plant, it must be absorbed. Foliar absorption is indicated as one of the fluxes in figure 5-2. The magnitude of foliar absorption depends on several factors, including the moisture deficit of the plant and resistances in the liquid and vapor flow paths from the external leaf surfaces to the mesophyll cells (Montieth, 1963; Wallin, 1967). Total absorption apparently does not occur, since leaves do not remain dry during dewfall. However, some plants, particularly lichens, absorb enough dew to assure a favorable water balance during dry periods and allow continued photosynthesis, at least for a few hours in the morning (Lange et al., 1975; chapter 3).

Another complication to modeling dewfall in the desert is the ability of plants to concentrate dew. Although the total rate of dew deposition for a large area cannot exceed the value given by the energy budget calculation, the amount of dew intercepted by a single plant part may be much greater than the projected area of the plant part. Thus, plants may concentrate dew and derive more benefit from it in terms of a more favorable water budget than can be predicted on the basis of the average water budget of an area.

Transpiration and Evaporation

Water from the desert is lost primarily by evaporation and transpiration. Which of these is the dominant process is determined by the evaporative demand when precipitation occurs and the amount of water delivered to the surface in each precipitation event (Campbell and Harris, 1977).

Transpired water comes from storage in the soil or plant. Hillel (1972) likens this storage reservoir to a bank that is robbed and embezzled daily. In the desert, the robber and embezzler is evaporation, which takes its share from surface storage as water infiltrates the soil and then continues with time to draw water from several centimeters at the surface of the soil. When soil or plant surfaces are wet, the rate of evaporation is determined by atmospheric demand and is near the potential rate (chapter 8). As surfaces dry, the resistance to vapor transport increases and evaporation rates decrease.

The total amount of water lost from plants following a precipitation event is equal to the surface stored water on the plants. Rutter (1975) reviews information on surface storage capacities for several different vegetation types and gives values ranging from around 0.1 to 0.4 mm of water stored per square centimeter of leaf surface area. Leaf area index in deserts is low so total surface storage in deserts is considerably less than that reported by Rutter, but the total quantities of water being considered are lower also. Typical losses from vegetation surface storage for deserts would probably be a few tenths of a millimeter per storm. Since this amount of water is taken out of every storm, the storm efficiency (water stored per unit of water applied) increases with the total precipitation in the storm.

In addition to the water evaporated from plant and soil surface storage, stored soil water moves to the surface by unsaturated flow and evaporation (chapter 6). The amount of water so evaporated depends on the atmospheric demand, the hydraulic properties of the soil and the amount of surface cover. For gravels, pebble pavement, and similar surfaces, the unsaturated hydraulic conductivity is near zero, and the surface dries as soon as the surface-stored water evaporates. For soils with high unsaturated conductivities, the soil may dry to quite low potentials before the surface dries.

Evaporation of water from soil is generally considered to be a two-stage process. The first stage of drying is considered complete when the soil surface dries. A dry soil surface is an indication that the loss of water is no longer controlled by atmospheric demand and is now under the control of soil factors. Modeling of this control is shown in chapter 11. The second stage of drying is characterized by a falling evaporation rate as a dry layer in the soil forms. The thicker the dry layer, the greater the vapor diffusion resistance of the layer and the slower the loss. Finally, unsaturated flow of water up to the wetting front just balances the rate of evaporation and diffusion of water through the dry layer. The rate of water loss at this stage is typically quite constant and low, perhaps a fraction of a millimeter per day.

For widely spaced storms and a given soil type, the amount of water lost to evaporation per storm is, like surface evaporation, fairly constant. Increasing the storm frequency or the size of the storm or decreasing the rate of evaporation between storms increases the quantity of water available for storage and later transpiration. Winter storms store more soil water than summer storms because the shallow storage is not depleted by evaporation between storms. Obviously many factors are interacting in this part of the system, and definitive estimates of quantities of water involved can only be found by direct measurement or through an adequate model of the system (Campbell and Harris, 1977; chapter 11).

Surface and Vegetation Storage

A characteristic of desert vegetation is that it is not uniformly distributed over the soil surface (chapter 3). Moreover water distribution on a microscale is also not uniform. Individual plants or clumps of plants may concentrate dew and precipitation by interception. As Walter (1973) points out, infiltration, overland flow, and surface storage characteristics of the desert are such that precipitation is also concentrated (see also chapter 7). The importance of this concentration effect to water conservation for plant use is obvious when the magnitude of evaporation losses is considered along with the fact that they represent a relatively constant loss from the system, more or less independent of amount of precipitation. Concentration of water by overland flow and surface storage allows more of the water from a small rain to reach deep soil storage than would be the case with uniformly distributed water.

Soil surface storage is in the form of depressions or surface irregularities that trap the water in pools of various sizes, as well as droplets that cling to soil and stones. Desert storms are often of high intensity and short duration (chapter 10), and desert soils may have low infiltration rates, some even being hydrophobic. Surface storage holds the water in one place for periods of time long enough that infiltration can occur.

Water storage within the plant can be estimated by knowing the water content of the tissue and the amount of tissue present per unit area of ground surface. If we assume that there is around 1 kg of plant material per square meter of ground surface, half of which is water, then the total water stored in the vegetation is around half a millimeter. Typical water content fluctuations are around 10 percent of the fresh weight, so changes in storage would be around 0.05 mm, a number that is small even in comparison with the amount of water stored during a nightly dewfall. Apparently canopy storage is not a significant component of the water budget, although it may be important to the water budget of an individual plant under water stress conditions.

Transport and Storage of Water in the Soil

Water enters deep soil storage by infiltration from soil surface storage, upward flow from a water table, and lateral transport (figure 5-2). Water is lost from storage by evaporation, deep percolation, transpiration, and possibly lateral transport. Water is transferred from one place to another in storage by redistribution and evaporation-condensation. It is convenient to consider these processes separately and to reserve special names for the various processes, but in terms of modeling the behavior of the soil moisture system, all aspects of transport into, within, and out of the soil are governed by the Darcy-Buckingham equation for water flow in soil, modified to include the possibility for thermally induced flow of water or water vapor (chapter 6). No distinctions need to be made in the water flow models between infiltration and redistribution (see chapter 11). The flux is simply determined by the direction of the potential gradient and the hydraulic conductivity of the soil.

In deserts, deep percolation and upward flow from water tables are generally negligible, although in specific cases, such as playa areas, this may not be the case. Lateral transport in the unsaturated zone of the soil is negligible except on a microscale. Water transport by evaporation-condensation is negligible in terms of the total water balance but may be significant for some processes (chapter 6).

The moisture stored in the soil provides plants with a more or less continual supply of water in spite of infrequent and unpredictable inputs from precipitation. It is important to be able to predict the amount of water available from storage for plant use. This prediction is difficult, however, because of the transient nature of the soil moisture system. The amount of water available to plants from shallow storage is particularly difficult to predict because it is a function of depth and evaporation rate as well as other soil factors.

The terms *field capacity* and *permanent wilting point* (Daubenmire, 1959) have long been used to describe the upper and lower limits of soil moisture in the soil water reservoir. *Field capacity* is used to denote the water content of soil when the rate of change of water content in the profile becomes slow following a rain or irrigation. *Permanent wilting point* is the water content of the soil below which water cannot be extracted by plants. The difference between field capacity and permanent wilt water contents multiplied by the depth of the rooting zone is the water holding capacity of the soil reservoir. Technically, water loss to evaporation should be subtracted, but, except for shallow-rooted plants, this would be a small fraction of the total stored water.

The permanent wilt point for a soil is not difficult to define unambiguously. Plants that adapt to drought and reduce transpiration rates to values near zero can withdraw water from the soil at water potentials near the lowest daytime water potentials of the leaves. Permanent wilting point is often taken as the water content of the soil at −1,500 Joules per kilogram (J/kg) water potential. Desert plants characteristically reach water potentials much lower than this (chapter 7). Thus the permanent wilting point for desert vegetation may be lower than for most mesic plants. The difference in total stored water, however, is usually not great because of the low water capacity of most soils at low water potential. This is not to say that the added available water is not important to plant growth; it probably is because demands are usually low when the soil is this dry, but in terms of the total water budget, the increment is not great.

Field capacity is much more difficult to define. In the past, correlations have indicated that the water content at either −10 or −30 J/kg water potential could be used as estimates of field capacity. However, since field capacity is a function of the hydraulic conductivity of the profile rather than the water potential of the soil, it is unlikely that any set potential can be used to estimate field capacity. Field capacity is also a function of the arbitrary choice of a negligible drainage rate. For agricultural purposes, where water is replenished every few days, this may be one or two orders of magnitude higher than it would be for a desert soil, which may go months between periods of recharge. A reasonable negligible rate might be 10 percent or so of the actual evapotranspiration rate.

Estimates of field capacity can be made if the hydraulic conductivity function of the soil profile is known. Gardner (1970) showed that the rate of change of water content in an initially wet soil profile is equal to the hydraulic conductivity of the profile. Given an arbitrary definition of field capacity that designates a negligible drainage rate of 0.1 mm/day, the profile water content at which the hydraulic conductivity is 0.1 mm/day would be the field capacity water content. Table 5-4 compares calculated field capacity water contents and potentials for a uniform profile of Gilat fine sandy loam soil for three profile drainage rates. Calculations were made using the moisture retention and hy-

TABLE 5-4. *Field Capacity Water Potential and Water Content for a Uniform Profile of Gilat Fine Sandy Loam Soil as a Function of Rate of Change of Profile Water Content*

Rate of change of profile water content (mm/day)	Field capacity water potential (J/kg)	Field capacity water content (m³/m³)
1	− 19	0.26
0.1	− 48	0.21
0.01	−120	0.17

draulic characteristics given by Gardner et al. (1970). For such a profile, a field capacity water content between −10 and −30 J/kg would appear reasonable for an irrigated soil that would be recharged every few days and is supplying water for evapotranspiration at a rate of around 7 or 8 mm per day. For a desert soil, where negligible loss rates are much lower, the field capacity water potential would be around −100 J/kg.

To continue using Gilat fine sandy loam as an example, the permanent wilting point (water content at −5,000 J/kg) would be around 0.07 m³/m³, so the storage capacity would be around 0.2 m³/m³, or 200 mm per meter rooting depth. Sandier soils would, of course, have lower water holding capacities, but the presence of layering in the soil profile decreases the profile hydraulic conductivity and increases the field capacity water content. Storage capacities of around 100 to 200 mm per meter may therefore be considered reasonable for desert soil.

To illustrate the increase in available water that may result from low water potentials of some desert plants, the water content of the Gilat soil at −1,500 J/kg is 0.1 m³/m³. Thus an additional 15 percent, or 30 mm of water per meter of rooting depth, is made available between −1,500 and −5,000 J/kg.

Summary of the Water Budget

Precipitation is the primary source of water for most deserts; it probably accounts for 90 percent or more of the water input. Dew generally accounts for less than 10 percent of the moisture input but may be more important in some deserts. Essentially all of the moisture received by dew and precipitation is evaporated or transpired. Deep percolation losses and stream flow, though sometimes present, are local effects and generally account for little of the water loss from the desert. Water is stored primarily by the soil over long periods and by soil surface storage for short periods, long enough to allow infiltration to occur. The storage capacity of desert soils is usually sufficient to hold soil moisture within 1 to 2 meters of the soil surface, where it is available for absorption by plants.

INTERACTIONS BETWEEN SYSTEM COMPONENTS

There are several obvious interactions between the processes shown in figure 5-1 and those in figure 5-2. These are processes in which both latent heat and water vapor are transported. Such interactions are important to recognize in constructing a model because, if they are strong, solution of one model would be impossible without a simultaneous solution of the other. This may add considerably to the complexity of the model. The importance of latent heat flow in soil to the total soil heat flux is still open to question (Kimball et al., 1976). The influence of temperature gradients on soil water flow is important only in specific situations (chapter 6). Evaporation and transpiration are such important components of the energy budget that they must always be included. Fortunately, there are methods of accounting for interactions in the models of these components (see chapter 11). If it is assumed that evapotranspiration is at the potential rate, then aspects of the water budget have little effect on the calculation. If the soil is sufficiently dry that the rate of water loss is relatively predictable and constant, again the two budgets can be solved separately. Only in the intermediate area, where evapotranspiration rates are adjusting to the heat load and the heat load is being influenced by the transpiration rate, does modeling become difficult.

LIMITS TO MODELING

Transport models such as those to be presented in later chapters of this book are generally one-dimensional and are intended to describe the average behavior of a system. The models use point measurements of transport coefficients and driving forces to describe the fluxes of mass and energy in the system. On a microscale, the system is not one-dimensional. On a macroscale the one-dimensional equations are probably reasonably correct, but the local transport coefficients and driving forces may not apply. The transport coefficients must take into account the microscale three-dimensionality of the system to be valid. The atmospheric transport models satisfy this requirement, at least to some extent. The atmosphere is reasonably well mixed, and the transport coefficients represent semiempirical relationships between fluxes and driving forces. Models for transport in soil and water uptake by plants, however, generally do not account for the microscale three-dimensionality of the system. Given the uneven distribution of applied heat and moisture in the desert, this could be a severe limitation on desert soil heat and water flow models.

SUMMARY

The collection of equations that describes all fluxes and storages of energy and mass within the desert system can be regarded as a model of the soil-plant-atmosphere system of the desert. The primary source of energy is solar radiation. For the annual cycle, the absorbed solar radiation is dissipated mainly by convection and net long-wave radiation. This is also the case for the instantaneous energy budget of dry soil, except that a significant quantity of heat goes to storage in the soil during the day. When the soil surface is wet, the incoming energy is dissipated primarily by evaporation, but the amount of time that surfaces are wet is not large in the desert.

Precipitation is the primary source of water for most deserts and probably accounts for 90 percent or more of the water input. Dew generally accounts for less than 10 percent of the moisture input but may be more important in some deserts. Essentially all of the moisture received by dew and precipitation is evaporated or transpired. Deep percolation losses and steam flow, though sometimes present, are local effects and generally account for little of the water loss from the desert. Water is stored primarily by the soil over long periods and by soil surface storage for short periods, long enough to allow infiltration to occur. The storage capacity of desert soils is usually sufficient to hold soil moisture within 1 to 2 meters of the soil surface, where it is available for absorption by plants.

REFERENCES

Biscoe, P. V., R. K. Scott, and J. L. Monteith. 1975. Barley and its environment III. Carbon budget of the stand. *J. Appl. Ecol.* **12**:269–293.
Campbell, G. S. 1977. *An Introduction to Environmental Biophysics*. Springer-Verlag, New York, 159 pp.
Campbell, G. S., and G. A. Harris. 1977. Water relations and water use patterns for *Artemisia tridentata* in wet and dry years. *Ecology* **58**:652–659.
Daubenmire, R. 1959. *Plants and Environment*. John Wiley, New York. 422 pp.
Fuchs, M. 1972. The control of the radiation climate of plant communities. In D. Hillel, ed., *Optimizing the Soil Physical Environment Toward Greater Crop Yields*. Academic Press, New York.
Fuchs, M., G. S. Campbell, and R. I. Papendick. 1978. An analysis of sensible and latent heat flow in a partially frozen unsaturated soil. *Soil Sci. Soc. Am. J.* **42**:379–385.
Gardner, W. R. 1970. Field measurement of soil water diffusivity. *Soil Sci. Soc. Am. Proc.* **34**:832–833.
Gardner, W. R., D. Hillel, and Y. Benyamini. 1970. Post irrigation movement of soil water: I Redistribution. *Water Resour. Res.* **6**:851–861.
Hillel, D. (ed.). 1972. *Optimizing the Soil Physical Environment Toward Greater Crop Yields*. Academic Press, New York, 240 pp.
Hinds, W. T. 1971. On the ecological importance of drifting snow in the Desert Biome. Report on the US/IBP Desert Biome Abiotic Specialists' Meeting, Tucson, Arizona, Mar. 6–7, 1970.
Kimball, B. A., R. D. Jackson, R. J. Reginato, F. S. Nakayama, and S. B. Idso. 1976. Comparison of field measured and calculated soil-heat fluxes. *Soil Sci. Soc. Am. J.* **40**:18–25.
Lange, O. L., E. D. Schulze, L. Kappeu, V. Basehbom, and M. Evenari. 1975. Adaptations of desert lichens to drought and extreme temperature, pp.

20–37. In N. F. Hadley (ed.), *Environmental Physiology of Desert Ecosystems,* Dowden, Hutchinson and Ross, Stroudsburg, Pa.

Monteith, J. L. 1963. Dew: facts and fallacies, pp. 37–56. In A. J. Rutter and F. H. Whitehead, eds., *The Water Relations of Plants,* Blackwell Scientific Publications, Oxford.

Monteith, J. L. 1973. *Principles of Environmental Physics.* American Elsevier, New York, 241 pp.

Munn, R. E. 1966. *Descriptive Micrometeorology.* Academic Press, New York, 245 pp.

Ross, J. 1975. Radiative transfer in plant communities, pp. 13–56. In J. L. Monteith, ed., *Vegetation and the Atmosphere,* Academic Press, New York.

Rutter, A. J. 1975. The hydrological cycle in vegetation, pp. 111–154. In J. L. Monteith, ed., *Vegetation and the Atmosphere,* Academic Press, New York.

Satterlund, D. R. 1972. *Wildland Watershed Management.* Ronald Press, New York, 370 pp.

Sellers, W. D. 1965. *Physical Climatology.* University of Chicago Press, Chicago, 272 p.

Thom, A. S. 1975. Momentum, mass and heat exchange of plant communities, pp. 57–110. In J. L. Monteith, ed., *Vegetation and the Atmosphere,* Academic Press, New York.

van Wijk, W. R. 1963. *Physics of Plant Environment.* North Holland Publishing Co., Amsterdam, 382 pp.

Wallin, J. R. 1967. Agrometeorological aspects of dew. *Agric. Meteor.* **4:**85–102.

Walter, H. 1973. *Vegetation of the Earth.* Springer-Verlag, New York, 237 p.

6

Flow of Water and Energy under Desert Conditions

William A. Jury, John Letey, Jr., and *Lewis H. Stolzy*

Much of the effort of soil physicists over the last thirty years has been directed toward establishing quantitative descriptions of water flow through porous materials. Unfortunately most of this work has been performed on uniform samples in controlled laboratory environments, and only quite recently (Nielsen et al., 1973; Biggar and Nielsen, 1976) have researchers become concerned with the limitations of applying laboratory-based methods to field experiments.

Description of soil water and energy transport processes is even less developed for extreme environments, such as those found in deserts. This deficiency is the result of inadequate experimental work and because the physical conditions (large temperature gradients, high temperatures, and dry soils) are outside the assumptions used in most theoretical investigations.

Several climatological and soil physical characteristics are common to most deserts. Rainfall tends to be seasonal and intense, occasionally causing surface runoff. There are long periods of hot, dry weather between rainy seasons, resulting in thorough soil drying. The soils tend to be coarse textured and have little water-holding capacity. Plant cover is incomplete, so that evaporation is a large part of the total water loss. Many plant species have developed a drought tolerance and need little moisture for survival.

The principal mechanisms of water transfer also vary with the season. Liquid movement is most important when water is redistributing following precipitation, and water vapor movement, which is influenced by temperature gradients, is dominant in hot, dry soil.

The purpose of this chapter is to review and discuss research relevant to describing water and energy movement through desert soils. First we will present general heat and water flow equations and then apply them to specific desert environments. Experimental work measuring the physical parameters used to describe water movement in desert soils and studies testing the theoretical models will be discussed, with special emphasis on the work done under the IBP Desert Biome.

FUNDAMENTAL REPRESENTATION OF WATER AND HEAT FLOW

Components of the Soil-Water Potential

The conventional definition for the total water potential H_t in head units is the amount of useful work per unit weight of pure water that must be done by means of externally applied forces to transfer reversibly and isothermally an infinitesimal amount of water from the standard state to the soil liquid phase at the point under consideration. The energy state of the water may be altered by pressure effects p, by the presence of the soil matrix h, by the presence of solutes within the soil solution s, or by the weight of the nonrigid soil matrix in a swelling soil o. In addition, the energy state of soil water depends on elevation z.

Pressure Potential p

The pressure potential p is the component of the total potential that is affected by a change in the external pressure on the soil water. This could be caused either by a hydrostatic pressure within the liquid phase or by a soil gas pressure in excess of atmospheric pressure.

Matric Potential h

The soil matric potential h is that portion of the soil-water potential that is due to adsorptive forces of the solid matrix on the soil solution. These adsorptive forces create a concave curvature of the air-water interface within the porous medium, which lowers the energy state of the water with respect to free water. The sum $h + z$ of the matric and gravitational potentials is called the hydraulic head and is given the symbol H.

Osmotic Potential s

The osmotic or solute potential s is that portion of the total potential due to the presence of dissolved solutes in the soil water. Because the water molecules possess a dipole moment, there results an electrostatic attraction to the solute ions, and the water is held in a bound state of energy lower than that of the reference state. When a semipermeable membrane that passes water and restricts solutes (such as a plant root) is placed at the interface between a solution and pure, free water, the pure water will cross the membrane into the solution until the pressure potential of the solution is equal and opposite to the solute potential. Because a membrane is needed to exhibit the effect of the solute potential in liquid flow, it is mainly of interest in plants. However, solutes in water do affect vapor density and vapor pressure, so that solute potential should be taken into account when considering water movement in the vapor phase.

Overburden Potential o

When the soil matrix is not rigid but is free to move, water in the soil experiences a pressure due to the weight of the solid material above it. This pressure is called the overburden potential and is of importance in swelling soils.

These components are general enough to specify completely the state of water in isothermal systems. Because of the rather specialized nature of the desert environment, we will be concerned primarily with the matric and gravitational components when discussing liquid water movement and with the matric and solute potential components when discussing vapor movement.

Gravitational Potential z

Water in the soil feels a force from the gravitational field of the earth. The gravitational potential energy z is defined as the energy carried by a unit weight of water due to its elevation with respect to reference height.

Flux Laws

Isothermal Liquid Flow

In a series of experiments on saturated sand columns, Darcy (1856) found that the flux of water percolating through the porous medium in the vertical direction directly proportional to the water potential gradient, or

$$J_1 = -K \, d(p+z)/dz, \tag{6.1}$$

where the proportionality constant K is known as the hydraulic conductivity. For a saturated soil, K is generally considered a constant, although it may change with time due to particle rearrangement within the solid matrix or due to microbial activity. In structured field soils, the conductivity may have a directional dependence and also be dependent upon the chemical composition of the water.

Years later, Darcy's law was extended to unsaturated soils by making the hydraulic conductivity a strongly varying function of the matric potential or water content of the porous medium (Buckingham, 1907), or

$$J_1 = -K(h) \, d \, (h+z)/dz. \tag{6.2}$$

This relationship has received thorough testing under laboratory conditions (Gardner and Fireman, 1958; Jackson et al., 1963; Neilsen et al., 1962). Measurements for a variety of porous materials have shown that the hydraulic conductivity will vary over many orders of magnitude between saturation and the lower limit for liquid water flow.

It is also possible to write Darcy's law in a form utilizing the volumetric water content Θ as the independent variable:

$$J_1 = -K(h) \left[(\partial h / \partial \Theta) d\Theta / dz + 1 \right] = -D_{W1} (\Theta) d\Theta / dz - K(\Theta), \qquad (6.3)$$

where $D_{W1} (\Theta)$ is used to symbolize $K(h)\, \partial h / \partial \Theta$ and is referred to as the liquid soil water diffusivity.

Water Vapor Flow

If the assumption is made that the total gas pressure P is constant throughout the porous medium, the flux of vapor may be described by a form of Fick's law for binary diffusion, modified to take into account the effects of the porous medium (Philip and deVries, 1957):

$$J_V = -f(a)\, D_a \left[\rho / (\rho - \rho_V) \right] d\rho_V / dz, \qquad (6.4)$$

where D_a is the binary diffusion coefficient for water vapor in air, ρ is the total gas density, ρ_V is the water vapor density, a is the volumetric air content, and $f(a)$ is a geometric factor modifying the path of gas flow within a porous medium. The factor $[\rho/(\rho - \rho_V)]$ is a small correction for the effects of air diffusion.

Heat Flow

There is some difficulty in writing an expression for the heat flow in a medium where fluid flow is also occurring because several mechanisms that are not superimposable will contribute to the flow of heat. These terms may be grouped in this way:

1. The Fourier or sensible heat flux, which is the contribution of pure heat conduction from atom to atom across the moist porous medium.
2. Convective heat flux, which represents sensible heat carried along by the moving vapor and liquid.
3. Latent heat flux carried along by the moving vapor.

Following deVries (1958) we can write these terms as

$$J_h = -\lambda^* (h,T) dT / dz + C_V (T - T_o) J_V + C_1 (T - T_o) J_1 + L J_V, \qquad (6.5)$$

where the first term represents the contribution from heat conduction; λ^* would be the thermal conductivity of a porous medium if we did not allow either liquid or vapor to move. The second and third terms represent the transfer of sensible heat by fluid convection in vapor and liquid phases, respectively. C_1 is the liquid-specific heat, and C_V is the vapor-specific heat. The fourth term represents the transfer of latent heat by vapor movement, where L is the latent heat of vaporization at reference temperature T_o. The formulation neglects heat transfer by air convection and by radiation, since these effects are usually small in soil (deVries, 1952).

Coupled Heat and Water Flow

In their present form, equations 6.2 and 6.4 do not take into account the interaction between water, energy, and solutes within the porous medium. By expanding these equations we can separate the influences of salt concentration gradients, temperature gradients, and water content gradients.

By applying the chain rule,

$$d(h+z)/dz = (\partial h/\partial\Theta)_{T,S} d\Theta/dz + (\partial h/\partial T)_{\Theta,S} dT/dz +$$

$$(\partial h/\partial s)_{T,\Theta} \frac{ds}{dz} + 1, \tag{6.6}$$

we may rewrite the liquid water flux equations 6.2 and 6.3 as

$$J_1 = -D_{W1} d\Theta/dz - D_{T1} dT/dz - D_{S1} ds/dz - K, \tag{6.7}$$

where we have defined

$$D_{T1} = K(h) (\partial h/\partial T)_{\Theta,S} \tag{6.8}$$

as the thermal liquid soil water diffusivity and

$$D_{S1} = K(h) (\partial h/\partial s)_{T,\Theta} \tag{6.9}$$

as the osmotic liquid soil water diffusivity.

Similarly, the water vapor flux (equation 6.4) may be expanded into thermal, solute, and water content gradient terms by applying the chain rule to the vapor density, or

$$J_V = -f(a)D_a [\rho/(\rho - \rho_V)] \{(\partial\rho_V/\partial\Theta)_{T,S} d\Theta/dz +$$

$$(\partial\rho_V/\partial T)_{\Theta,S} dt/dz + (\partial\rho_V/\partial s)_{T,\Theta} ds/dz\}, \tag{6.10}$$

which may be rewritten as

$$J_V = -D_{WV} d\Theta/dz - D_{TV} dT/dz - D_{SV} ds/dz, \tag{6.11}$$

where D_{WV}, D_{TV}, and D_{SV} are the vapor soil water diffusivity, the thermal vapor soil water diffusivity, and the osmotic vapor soil water diffusivity, respectively.

In discussing water vapor movement in a nonisothermal porous medium, Philip and deVries (1957) postulated two enhancement mechanisms that would cause vapor movement in excess of that predicted by equation 6.4 or 6.10. First, they argued that water vapor could traverse liquid islands in a subsaturated porous medium by condensation and subsequent evaporation, and that up to the point of liquid continuity, the volume occupied by the liquid should be considered as space available for vapor diffusion so that $f(a)$ in equation 6.10 is replaced by $f(a + \Theta)$. Second, they argued that the temperature gradients across vapor-filled pores might be in excess of the temperature gradients across the whole porous medium and that an enhancement factor should be added to the temperature gradient in the second term of equations 6.10 and 6.11.

Combining equations 6.7 and 6.11 gives the total moisture flux (liquid plus vapor), or

$$J_W = -D_W d\Theta/dz - D_T dT/dz - D_s ds/dz - K. \qquad (6.12)$$

Equation 6.5 for heat transport already contains the coupling effects of associated water movement. The second and third terms in it describing the convection of sensible heat within the liquid and vapor phases are negligible for water flow rates normally encountered within a porous medium. The remaining terms may be put in a form compatible with equations 6.7, 6.10, and 6.11 by substituting 6.10 for the vapor flux and recollecting terms:

$$J_h = -LD_{WV} d\Theta/dz - (\lambda^* + LD_{TV}) dT/dz - LD_{TS} ds/dz =$$
$$-LD_{WV} d\Theta/dz - \lambda dT/dz - LD_{SV} ds/dz, \qquad (6.13)$$

where λ is the effective thermal conductivity including the contribution of thermally driven latent heat flux of vapor.

Irreversible Thermodynamics Formulation

Much of the early work done in this field in the area of coupled heat and water flow was cast in the formalism of irreversible thermodynamics (Cary and Taylor, 1962a, b). Although the flux equation derivations are quite complex, the final results are similar to equations 6.7, 6.10, and 6.11, except that the driving forces are soil water potential and temperature gradients. Jury (1973) derived the following expressions for total moisture flux J_W and heat flux J_h:

$$J_W = -L_{MM} dH/dz - \frac{L_{WT}}{T} dT/dz \qquad (6.14)$$

and:

$$J_h = -L_{TW} dH/dz - \frac{L_{TT}}{T} \frac{dT}{dz} \qquad (6.15)$$

where $L_{TW} = L_{WT}$ follows from the principles of irreversible thermodynamics. It may be shown (Jury, 1973) that the physical approach of equations 6.7, 6.10, and 6.13 and that of irreversible thermodynamics are compatible if the Clausius-Clapyron equation is used to derive one from the other.

Conservation Equations

Water

Application of the equation of continuity for the liquid and vapor phases within a porous medium results in

$$\partial\Theta_v/\partial t + \partial J_v/\partial z = E, \tag{6.16}$$

$$\partial\Theta_1/\partial t + \partial J_1/\partial z = -E, \tag{6.17}$$

and

$$\partial\Theta/\partial t + \partial J_w/\partial z = 0, \tag{6.18}$$

where Θ_v is the volumetric vapor content (expressed as equivalent liquid volume), Θ_1 is the liquid water content, and Θ is the total moisture content, and E is the evaporation (>0) or condensation (<0) rate per unit volume within the porous medium. In almost all circumstances, the time rate of change of volumetric vapor content in equation 6.16 is negligible relative to the other two terms. Similarly the distinction between total and liquid moisture content need not be made, except at extreme dryness.

For isothermal systems, or when using the irreversible thermodynamics approach, it may be advantageous to cast the transient water flow equations in terms of temperature and water potential. In the isothermal case, the time rate of change of water content may be expressed in terms of the time rate of change of soil matric potential by using

$$\partial\Theta/\partial t = (\partial\Theta/\partial h)_{T,S} \, \partial h/\partial t = C_w(h,s)\partial h/\partial t \tag{6.19}$$

where C_w is the water capacity.

Combining the conservation equation 6.18 with the flux equation 6.12 gives the differential equation for water transport, or

$$\partial\Theta/\partial t = \partial/\partial z \, [D_w\partial\Theta/\partial z + D_T\partial T/\partial z + D_s\partial s/\partial z + K]. \tag{6.20}$$

Equation 6.20 requires much experimental information and the use of high-speed computers to calculate water flow patterns. As a result, only a few simulations have been performed (Jury, 1973).

Heat

To write the transient heat flow equation we must first form an expression for the heat content per unit volume Q of the porous medium

$$Q = C_d(T-T_o) + C_V \Theta_V (T-T_o) + C_1 \Theta_1 (T-T_o) +$$

$$\rho_1 \Theta_V L - \rho_1 \int_0^{\Theta_1} W d\Theta_1,$$

(6.21)

where C_d is the heat content per unit volume of the dry porous medium, ρ_1 is liquid water density, and W is the differential heat of wetting of the porous medium. If we ignore other sources of heat within the medium, we can write an equation for the conservation of heat energy:

$$\partial Q/\partial t + \partial J_h/\partial z = 0.$$

(6.22)

Combining equations 6.13, 6.21, and 6.22 results in an extremely complex expression, which after simplification (Jury, 1973) yields

$$\partial/\partial z \, (\lambda \partial T/\partial z) + \partial/\partial z \, (\rho_1 L D_{WV} \partial \Theta_1/\partial z) = C \partial T/\partial t,$$

(6.23)

where

$$C = C_d + C_V \Theta_V + C_1 \Theta_1$$

(6.24)

is the volumetric heat capacity of the moist porous medium.

As in the case of equation 20, few calculations have been performed with equation 6.23 (Jury, 1973).

Application to Arid Zones

These formal theoretical equations are used to solve water flow in specific situations using appropriate boundary conditions. The analysis and measurement of water flow through soil has largely been restricted to isothermal conditions when water flow is primarily in the liquid state as compared to vapor flow. Under desert conditions, soils are often quite dry so that analyses of water movement under dry conditions must be considered. Furthermore, environmental conditions are such that temperature gradients may significantly affect heat and water movement through desert soils. In this section, we will review both liquid and vapor flow under isothermal conditions, followed by consideration of heat and water flow under thermal gradients.

ISOTHERMAL WATER FLOW

Until the soil dries to a potential of approximately $-15,000$ cm (-15 bars), the air-filled pores are very nearly saturated with water vapor. As soils dry beyond this point, the water vapor density in the pores decreases more rapidly. Under wetter conditions ($h > -1,000$ cm), isothermal water flow is entirely in the liquid state, with essentially no vapor flux. Under drier conditions, isothermal water flow may be both in the liquid and vapor phases.

The flux of liquid water can be adequately described with Darcy's law (equation 6.2). To apply 6.2 to the movement of water through soil, one must measure the soil water transport coefficient (K) and matric potential (h). Although the basic theory and earliest measurements were put forth by Buckingham (1907), it was many years later before sufficiently sophisticated equipment was available to measure K and h over a large range of water contents. With the development of the tensiometer (Richards, 1928) and the use of the pressure plate (Richards, 1949) to measure hydraulic conductivity (Gardner, 1956), quantitative tests of the transport equations became possible. Subsequently a number of steady state and transient experiments have verified equations 6.2 and 6.18 (Gardner and Fireman, 1958; Jackson et al., 1963; Nielsen et al., 1962; Rawlins and Gardner, 1963) for isothermal monotonic processes.

Several methods of obtaining hydraulic conductivity and diffusivity of unsaturated soils have been reviewed by Klute (1972). Gardner (1956), using data from pressure plate outflow, was one of the first to determine hydraulic conductivity at moisture contents lower than the tensiometer range (approximately -800 cm). Gardner's method was limited to approximately $-15,000$ cm matric potential because of the limitations of the pressure plate. Studies conducted in our laboratory as part of the Desert Biome successfully extended the measurement of hydraulic conductivity to potentials of approximately $-50,000$ cm by using soil psychrometers for measuring water potential (Mehuys et al., 1975). Extending the measurement of hydraulic conductivity to dry ranges is important for describing water flow under desert conditions when soil water contents can become very low. Data presented in figure 6-1 illustrate typical relationships between hydraulic conductivity and soil water potential. These data are from soils obtained from the Sonoran Desert in Arizona and the Mojave Desert in Nevada during the Desert Biome study. Hydraulic conductivity varied over several orders of magnitude as the water potential decreased. There was a significant difference in hydraulic conductivity between the two soils under the more moist conditions but the difference decreased at very dry conditions.

Almost all measurements of hydraulic conductivity have been made on sieved soils in the laboratory. Gravel and stones are removed from the samples prior to measuring hydraulic conductivity. However gravel and/or stones are present in quantity in many desert soils and should not be ignored. The effect of stones on the hydraulic conductivity of soils was investigated by Mehuys and others (1975). This investigation was carried out under the Desert Biome objectives, and measurements were made on three desert soils from validation sites of the Desert Biome. Experiments were conducted in the laboratory on soil columns with and without stones, and the hydraulic conductivity was measured over the potential range of -50 to $-50,000$ cm. It was concluded that if the hydraulic conductivity was stated as a function of matric potential, the conductivity values were very similar for samples with and without stones. This result occurred because the water potential as measured by tensiometers or psychrometers is not affected by stones because these instruments respond to moisture changes in the soil portion only. When the conductivity was expressed as a function of water content, the apparent conductivities were higher

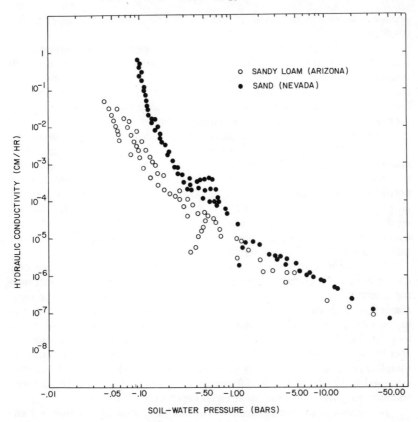

FIGURE 6-1. *Hydraulic conductivity as a function of soil-water pressure during desorption of a sandy loam (Sonoran Desert, Arizona) and a sand (Mojave Desert, Nevada).*

for a given water content when stones were present than when stones were removed. A simple correction of water contents of stone-free samples based on the stone volume of each soil adequately accounted for differences observed when water contents were computed on a total volume basis (Mehuys et al., 1975).

The equations presented earlier assume a unique relationship between hydraulic conductivity and potential or soil-water content. When both wetting and drying of the porous medium takes place, the relationship between hydraulic conductivity and potential depends upon whether it is observed on the wetting or drying cycle (Poulovassilis, 1962; Topp and Miller, 1966). The observed hysteresis in the hydraulic conductivity-potential relationship causes the description of flow processes to become much more complicated. Some recent computer simulations (Watson, 1974; Reeves and Miller, 1975) have attempted to study the influence of hysteresis on water movement, but at the present time little is known about the importance of hysteresis under natural conditions.

Soil temperature has an effect on water flow even under isothermal conditions. The hydraulic conductivity varies with temperature and is generally taken to be inversely proportional to the temperature dependence of the coefficient of viscosity of water (Cary, 1965). This means that the value for the conductivity at a given water content may be different at different times of the year, and a modification should, in principle, be made.

Leaching of soil profiles is usually not extensive under desert conditions. Because of this, appreciable solutes can accumulate within the profile. Nonuniform distribution of salts through the profile may lead to solute concentration gradients, which create osmotic potential gradients. In principle, osmotic potential gradients can contribute to liquid water flow (equation 6.7). Letey et al. (1969), however, found that the coefficient D_{s1} (equation 6.9) was very small under moderately wet conditions. For practical purposes, the effect of osmotic potential gradients can be neglected as a factor in liquid water movement under moderately wet conditions.

Most experimental studies on water flow through soils have been conducted in the laboratory. Studies in the field have been hampered by measurement errors and spatial variability in the transport coefficients. For these reasons, the measured values contain a great deal of variability. Although increased accuracy could be obtained by analyzing field samples in the laboratory, studies have shown that disturbed sample measurements of transport coefficients give different values from in situ measurements. The effect of sampling errors due to variability has been shown by Nielsen et al. (1973). They observed order of magnitude differences in saturated hydraulic conductivity values among adjacent samples at equal depth in a 50 ha field.

Although certain computer model calculations based on equations 6.2 and 6.18 using measured coefficients (Nimah and Hanks, 1973; Feddes et al., 1974) have been shown to be in fair agreement with observed soil-water changes, there is increasing concern about measuring errors in field soil-water movement (Fluhler et al., 1976). Evans et al. (1975) found a variety of values for infiltration rates into bare soil and around vegetation under desert conditions.

ISOTHERMAL VAPOR FLOW

Water may move through the soil in response to vapor density gradients (equation 6.4). The vapor density at any point in the porous medium in thermodynamic equilibrium with the associated liquid phase is affected by temperature, osmotic potential, and matric potential of the liquid water:

$$\rho_v(h,s,T) = \rho_v^* (T) \ exp \ (-g(h+s)/RT), \tag{6.25}$$

where ρ_v^* is saturated vapor pressure and g is the acceleration of gravity.

For practical purposes, the matric and osmotic terms must be lower than about $-15,000$ cm before any noticeable lowering of the vapor density occurs $(\rho_v/\rho_v^* = 0.989$ at $h + s = -15,000$ cm). Thus, isothermal flow of water vapor

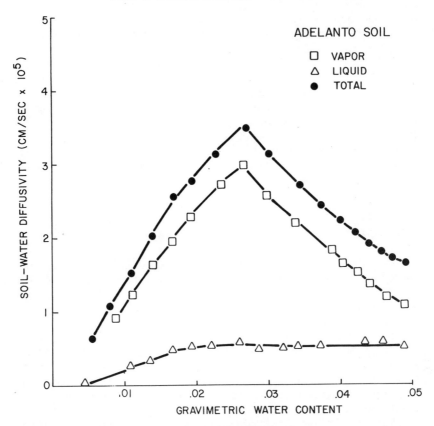

FIGURE 6-2. *Total, vapor, and liquid diffusivity coefficients for Adelanto loam at an ambient pressure of 730 mm Hg and 25°C (from Jackson, 1965).*

will occur only under extreme conditions of dryness or salinity in the soil. Water vapor flux under isothermal conditions is a diffusion process. Equation 6.4 may be considered to be simply Fick's first law of diffusion where the diffusion coefficient for water vapor is multiplied times the vapor density gradient. The term $f(a)$ is included in equation 6.4 to account for the geometric effects of the soil and water matrix.

Rose (1963) measured isothermal soil-water diffusivities in the dry range where vapor movement is dominant and found them to be much larger than diffusivities calculated from gaseous hydrogen diffusion measurements in the same medium. This confirmed the existance of a vapor-liquid interaction, which enhanced vapor flow over that of an inert gas, as suggested by Philip and DeVries (1957).

In practice, liquid and vapor water movement in response to matric potential gradients are not separated; rather the total water flux J_W is measured. Jackson (1964a, b, c, 1965) conducted laboratory experiments where liquid and vapor water flow components were separated (figure 6-2). At very small water contents, the liquid diffusivity is very low and continues to decrease with decreasing soil-water content, eventually approaching zero. At these very low water contents, the vapor diffusivity is larger than the liquid diffusivity. The isothermal vapor diffusivity increases as the soil-water content decreases, reaching a maximum, after which this coefficient decreases with further soil drying.

When salt is present in appreciable quantities, such as near precipitated salt granules or when the soil surface is salt crusted, a vapor density gradient may develop sufficient to cause appreciable vapor movement. In this event, the third term of equation 6.11 is not negligible and should be used to evaluate water flux properly. A series of experiments looking at water movement near crystalline salt (Scotter and Raats, 1970; Scotter, 1974a, b) showed substantial movement in response to osmotic gradients.

THERMAL GRADIENT EFFECTS ON WATER FLOW

Desert environments commonly are subjected to widely fluctuating atmospheric temperatures. High daytime temperatures and low nighttime temperatures are common. These temperature fluctuations lead to thermal gradients within the soil, which can cause water transfer and thus may be an important mechanism for water movement in desert soils.

The second factor in equation 6.12 accounts for the total water flux in response to thermal gradients. Letey (1968) reviewed published research results from which the coefficient D_T could be calculated. One significant finding of that review was that the value of D_T was relatively constant over a wide range of soil-water contents. Furthermore, the value did not vary greatly between different investigators and different soils.

It is generally considered that water flow in response to thermal gradients is mostly vapor transfer as compared to liquid flow. Cary (1965) presented the following equation for the flow of water vapor through soil as effected by the temperature gradient:

$$J_V = \frac{\beta p D_A L}{R^2 T^3} \frac{dt}{dz} , \qquad (6.26)$$

where p is vapor pressure, D_A is the diffusion coefficient of water vapor, L is the latent heat of vaporization, β is a unitless factor, and R is the gas constant. All of the terms in equation 6.26 can be either measured or calculated except for β, which is a geometric and enhancement factor that accounts for the presence of the soil-water system. Theoretically the value of β equals 1 for vapor movement across an air gap.

The terms preceeding the temperature gradient in equation 6.26 are equivalent to D_{TV} of equation 6.11. Several of these terms are temperature dependent. Letey (1968) determined that the combination of these terms would increase as the temperature increased. Thus, the value of D_{TV} would be expected to increase as the average temperature increased.

Philip and DeVries (1957) described a model to predict water vapor flux in response to thermal gradients. They considered the effects of tortuosity, liquid-vapor interactions, microscopic thermal gradients, and air phase corrections in developing their model. A summary of the results of calculating β from Philip and DeVries's model for various soil materials with different porosities and water contents is given in table 6-1. Note that except for high percentages of saturation, the value of β remains fairly constant over a fairly wide range of water contents. Furthermore, the value of β does not change very greatly as the total porosity of the system changes. These general results from Philip and DeVries's model are in agreement with observed behavior that the transmission coefficient is relatively constant over a range of water contents and soil packings. Wheeler (1972) applied the Philip and DeVries (1957) model to calculate water flux in response to temperature gradients for studies conducted under the Desert Biome. He found that the calculated water vapor flux was essentially constant in the range of matric potential from $-1,000$ to $-40,000$ cm. Again, this observation is consistent with the data reviewed by Letey in which the observed water vapor flux was quite independent of soil water potential.

The value of β calculated from Philip and DeVries theory is less than or equal to 1. The value of β measured in the experiments reviewed by Letey varies from about 1 to 3, with most values being in the range of 1 to 2. One possible explanation for the higher measured value of β is that the Philip and DeVries model assumes that all thermally driven water is in the vapor phase. Most of the experimental data reviewed did not differentiate water that moved

TABLE 6-1.   *Values of the Vapor Phase Temperature Gradient Enhancement Factor η and the Total Enhancement Factor β*

Percent saturation	$\varphi = 0.3$		$\varphi = 0.4$		$\varphi = 0.5$	
	η	β	η	β	η	β
Quartz Sand Solid Fraction						
100	2.92	0.0	2.52	0.0	2.21	0.0
80	2.81	0.4	2.40	0.4	2.10	0.5
60	2.74	0.7	2.33	0.8	2.03	0.8
40	2.70	0.8	2.27	0.9	1.96	1.0
20	2.67	0.9	2.21	0.9	0.89	0.9
0	3.23	1.0	2.45	1.0	1.97	1.0
Clay Mineral Solid Fraction						
100	2.11	0.0	1.96	0.0	1.7	0.0
80	2.06	0.3	1.90	0.4	1.6	0.5
60	2.04	0.5	1.86	0.6	1.6	0.8
40	2.05	0.6	1.85	0.7	1.5	0.9
20	2.09	0.6	1.85	0.7	1.5	0.9
0	3.03	0.9	2.35	0.9	1.6	1.0

Note: The theory of Philip and DeVries (1957) is used for various porosities φ.

in the vapor and liquid phases. Any movement of water in the liquid phase in response to thermal gradient in the experiments would result in a higher calculated value for β.

It is fortuitous that the value of D_{TV} is relatively constant over a wide range of soil-water conditions. Indeed reasonable estimates of water flow in response to thermal gradients can be calculated by merely measuring temperature gradients within the soil. The value of D_{TV} can vary over a range of approximately 1×10^{-3} to 4×10^{-3} cm² deg⁻¹ hr⁻¹. Values between 1 and 2×10^{-3} appear to be most commonly observed at temperatures of approximately 20°C. The value of the coefficient should be modified for the average temperature as described by Letey (1968).

As part of the Desert Biome study, Jury and Bellantuoni (1976a, b) conducted a field experiment to investigate the effect of large surface rocks covering soil on water and heat flow patterns. They found that the rocks significantly altered the energy balance at the surface, producing generally lower temperatures under the rocks. By placing thermal conductivity probes under the rocks and adjacent soil, they observed that water at 10 cm depth remained under the rock while being lost from adjacent soil ostensibly by evaporation with a possible contribution from thermally induced movement (figure 6-3). In a separate laboratory experiment on rock-covered soil sealed against evaporation, they observed water movement toward the soil under the rock that was caused by

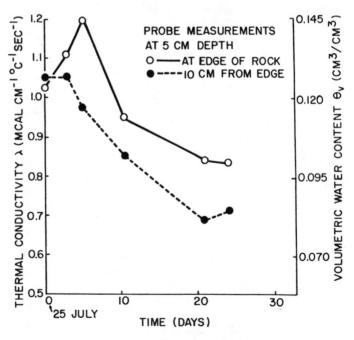

FIGURE 6-3. *Thermal conductivity readings at the 5 cm depth as a function of time during July 25 to August 15 experiment (25 cm diameter rock) (after Jury and Bellantuoni, 1976b).*

thermal gradients (figure 6-4). They concluded that any surface cover that altered the surface energy balance such as a litter layer under a desert bush or stones could cause moisture to be collected and stored from surrounding soil areas. Water flow in response to thermal gradients may thus result in concentrating water from a relatively dry environment into localized zones, which may be significantly important to the desert organisms.

In a series of experiments at Death Valley, California, in the Desert Biome, Stark (1970) and Stark and Love (1969) measured the water balance of desert plants by gravimetric sampling and estimated that a large fraction of the plants' water needs were being satisfied by upward movement of water vapor at night, presumably because of thermal gradients.

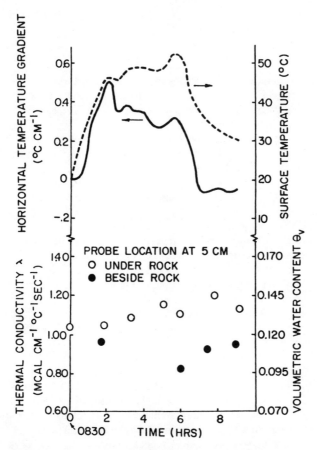

FIGURE 6-4. *Thermal conductivity readings as a function of time at the 5 cm depth under the rock (○) and at 10 cm adjacent to the rock edge (△) along with horizontal temperature gradient at the 2.5 cm depth and surface temperature (after Jury and Bellantuoni, 1976b).*

MODIFIED HEAT FLOW

The terms of most importance in describing heat flow in soils are conduction of heat through the medium and convection of latent heat by moving water vapor. Because the water vapor movement may be predominantly described by a term proportional to temperature gradients, the general heat flow equation 6.13 can be simplified by neglecting the terms proportional to water content gradients and salt content gradients. This approximation is valid except at extremely low water contents where water content gradients may have a substantial influence on heat flux (Kimball et al., 1976) and in cases where crystalline salt is present. With this approximation, equation 6.13 becomes

$$J_h = -\lambda \ \frac{dT}{dZ} \ . \tag{6.27}$$

Inserting the modified flux relations into the conservation equations 6.18 and 6.22 yields the representation of transient heat and water flow. The modified equations are much easier to work with and should give results that are adequate for most field applications.

Early laboratory studies of heat movement in soil were summarized by DeVries (1952) who formulated a theory of the thermal conductivity of granular materials (DeVries, 1952, 1963). Although a calibration factor is needed to apply the theory at low water contents, calculations based on this model have often been found to be in good agreement with laboratory measurements (DeVries, 1963; Jury and Miller, 1974).

The relative importance of water vapor transport on heat flow increases at high temperatures such as near the soil surface where neglecting latent heat transport could cause up to 50 percent error in estimating heat flow (Westcot and Wierenga, 1974). DeVries's model accounts for both the water vapor movement and its temperature dependence (DeVries, 1963).

Measured values of the thermal conductivity λ and thermal diffusivity λ/C have frequently been found to depend on the method of measurement used. Hadas (1968) argued that the anomalies in his data could have been caused by mass flow of water vapor due to soil air movement. He also has cited thermal contact resistance between the soil and the probe (Hadas, 1974) as a possible cause of variations in measurements with methods.

Application and testing of the above theory of heat and water vapor movement in field systems have been hampered by extreme difficulties in measuring all of the appropriate transport coefficients. Observations have shown, however, that vapor movement driven by temperature gradients can result in substantial water content changes near the surface (figure 6-5).

Rose (1968) conducted a field experiment on a bare surface loamy sand initially watered to 30 cm. He obtained the liquid diffusivity and hydraulic conductivity relations from laboratory measurements, estimated storage change from gravimetric samples, measured water content and temperature gradients in the soil, assumed the vapor moisture diffusivity was negligible,

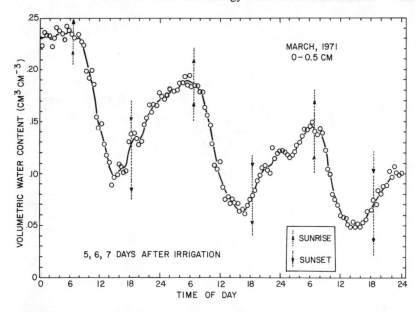

FIGURE 6-5. *Volumetric water content in the 0–0.5 cm depth versus time for three days in March 1971 (after Jackson, 1973).*

calculated D_{T1} from a model by Philip and DeVries (1957), and calculated water vapor flux by difference. Figure 6-6 shows the contribution of various terms to the water balance at two depths for different times after irrigation. It shows that water vapor flux was initially large and ultimately the dominant form of water transport cycling in phase with the soil heat flow. Neither gravity nor thermally induced liquid flow was important for the system. Rose also calculated the vapor flow coefficient (D_{TV}) except for enhancement due to liquid water and compared it with the measured values. He found enhancement factors up to 10 although the error estimates were large.

Jackson et al. (1974) conducted a two-week bare soil experiment on Adelanto loam on which water content samples were taken at half-hour intervals. Using laboratory coefficients and field-measured gradients, he estimated the water fluxes of vapor and liquid and compared them with the model of Philip and DeVries (1957). He found that in fairly wet and very dry soil, the theory was unsuccessful and that the best fit to experimental observations was found by assuming that water flow was not influenced by temperature gradient. At intermediate water contents, they found that the complete theory, including the effect of temperature gradients, did the best job of describing the data.

Related experiments in heat flow by the same group (Kimball et al., 1976) tested DeVries's (1963) theory against the field measurements. Agreement was achieved only when latent heat transfer due to water vapor movement was left out of the calculation.

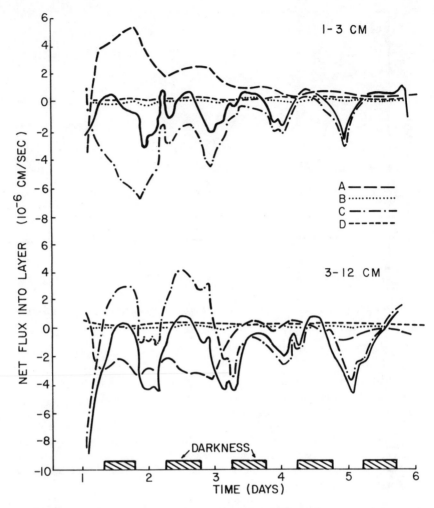

FIGURE 6-6. *Time history for depth intervals of the net flux terms* A *(caused by water content gradients),* B *and* C *(thermal liquid and vapor flux),* D *(gravitational), and* E *(water storage changes) (after Rose, 1968).*

SUMMARY AND CONCLUSIONS

The varied experimental results reviewed here illustrate the difficulties encountered in studying heat and water flow. Each of the transfer coefficients must be known as a function of water content and temperature before the flux relations can be used. In the field tests, this has often been accomplished by making measurements on disturbed cores in the laboratory, a procedure certain to introduce error into the field water and heat balances.

Under most circumstances water movement in the liquid phase is dominant in the soil. The discussion, however, has served to emphasize the unique aspects of the desert environment. During prolonged periods without rainfall or artificial irrigation, the soil profile in the desert environment becomes sufficiently dry that the majority of water movement is made in the vapor phase. This vapor phase movement is strongly influenced by temperature gradients. Under these circumstances, complex models describing the coupled interaction of heat and moisture flow are needed to make a mathematical, physical formulation of the transfer process. The best efforts in modeling this process are still under investigation.

In the interim, it will suffice to treat liquid water flow in the simplified manner (equation 6.2), which is independent of temperature and salt concentrations, and to use equation 6.26 to describe vapor flow. Heat flow will be adequately represented in most circumstances by using equation 6.27.

REFERENCES

Biggar, J. W., and D. R. Nielsen. 1976. Spatial variability of the leaching characteristics of a field soil. *Water Resour. Res.* **12**:78–84.

Buckingham, E. 1907. *Studies on the Movement of Soil Moisture.* U.S. Dept. Agric. Bur. Soils Bull. 38.

Cary, J. W. 1965. Water flux in moist soil: Thermal vs. suction gradients. *Soil Sci.* **100**:168–175.

Cary, J. W., and S. A. Taylor. 1962a. The interaction of the simultaneous diffusions of heat and water vapor. *Soil Sci. Soc. Am. Proc.* **26**:413–416.

Cary, J. W., and S. A. Taylor. 1962b. Thermally driven liquid and vapor phase transfer of water and energy in soil. *Soil Sci. Soc. Am. Proc.* **26**:417–420.

Darcy, H. 1856. *Les fountaines publiques de la ville de Dijon.* Dalmont, Paris.

DeVries, D. A. 1952. *Het warmtegeleidingsvermogen van grond Med.* Landbouwhogeschool, Wageningen 52, 73 pp.

DeVries, D. A. 1958. Simultaneous transfer of heat and moisture in porous media. *Trans. Am. Geophys. Un.* **39**:909–916.

DeVries, D. A. 1963. Thermal properties of soil, pp. 210–235. In van Wijk (ed.), *Physics of Plant Environment.* North Holland Publishing Co., Amsterdam.

Evans, D. D., S. Nnaji, T. W. Sammis, and G. Hansen. 1975. Water infiltration under desert conditions. US/IBP Desert Biome Res. Memorandum 75–39.

Feddes, R. A., E. Bresler, and S. P. Neuman. 1974. Field test of a modified numerical model for water uptake by root systems. *Water Resour. Res.* **10**:1199–1206.

Fluhler, H., M. S. Arkadani, and L. H. Stolzy. 1976. Error propagation in determining hydraulic conductivities from successive water content and pressure head profiles. *Soil Sci. Soc. Am. J.* **40**:830–836.

Gardner, W. R. 1956. Calculation of capillary conductivity from pressure plate outflow data. *Soil. Sci. Soc. Am. Proc.* **20**:317–320.

Gardner, W. R., and M. Fireman. 1958. Laboratory studies of evaporation from soil columns in the presence of a water table. *Soil Sci. Soc. Am. Proc.* **85**:244–249.

Hadas, A. 1968. A comparison between two methods of determining the thermal conductivity of a moist soil. *Soil Sci. Soc. Am. Proc.* **32**:20–30.

Hadas, A. 1974. Probability involved in measuring the soil thermal conductivity and diffusivity in a moist soil. *Agric. Meet.* **13**:105–113.

Jackson, R. D. 1964a. Water vapor movement in relatively dry soil. I. Theoretical considerations and sorption experiments. *Soil Sci. Soc. Am. Proc.* **28**:172–176.

Jackson, R. D. 1964b. Water vapor movement in relatively dry soil. II. Desorption experiments. *Soil Sci. Soc. Am. Proc.* **28**:464–466.

Jackson, R. D. 1964c. Water vapor movement in relatively dry soil. III. Steady-state experiments. *Soil Sci. Soc. Am. Proc.* **28**:467–470.

Jackson, R. D. 1965. Water vapor movement in relatively dry soil. IV. Temperature and pressure effects on sorption diffusivities. *Soil Sci. Soc. Am. Proc.* **29**:144–148.

Jackson, R. D., D. R. Nielsen, and F. S. Nakayama. 1963. On diffusion laws applied to porous materials. *USDA-ARS Bull.* pp. 41–86.

Jackson, R. D., R. J. Reginato, B. A. Kimball, and F. S. Nakayama. 1974. Diurnal soil water evaporation: Comparison of measured and calculated soil water fluxes. *Soil Sci. Soc. Am. Proc.* **38**:861–866.

Jury, W. A. 1973. *Simultaneous Transport of Heat and Moisture through a Medium Sand.* Ph.D. dissertation, Univ. of Wisconsin.

Jury, W. A., and E. E. Miller. 1974. Measurement of the transport coefficients for coupled flow of heat and moisture in a medium sand. *Soil Sci. Soc. Am. Proc.* **38**:551–558.

Jury, W. A., and B. Bellantuoni. 1976a. Heat and water movement under surface rocks in a field soil. I. Thermal effects. *Soil Sci. Soc. Am. J.* **40**:505–509.

Jury, W. A., and B. Bellantuoni. 1976b. Heat and water movement under surface rocks in a field soil. II. Moisture effects. *Soil Sci. Soc. Am. J.* **40**:509–513.

Kimball, B. A., R. D. Jackson, R. J. Reginato, F. S. Nakayama, and S. B. Idso. 1976. Comparison of field-measured and calculated soil-heat fluxes. *Soil Sci. Soc. Am. J.* **40**:18–25.

Klute, A. 1972. The determination of the hydraulic conductivity and diffusivity of unsaturated soils. *Soil Sci.* **113**:264–276.

Letey, J. 1968. Movement of water through soil as influenced by osmotic pressure and temperature gradients. *Hilgardia* **39**:405–418.

Letey, J., W. D. Kemper, and L. Noonan. 1969. The effect of osmotic pressure gradients on water movement in unsaturated soil. *Soil Sci. Soc. Am. Proc.* **33**:15–18.

Mehuys, G. R., L. H. Stolzy, J. Letey, and L. V. Weeks. 1975. The effect of stones on the hydraulic conductivity of relatively dry desert soils. *Soil Sci. Soc. Am. Proc.* **39**:37–42.

Nielsen, D. R., J. W. Biggar, and J. M. Davidson. 1962. Experimental consideration of diffusion analysis in unsaturated flow problems. *Soil Sci. Soc. Am. Proc.* **26**:107–111.

Nielsen, D. R., J. W. Biggar, and K. T. Erh. 1973. Spatial variability of field-measured soil-water properties. *Hilgardia* **42:**215–260.

Nimah, M. N., and R. J. Hanks. 1973. Model for estimating soil water, plant, and atmospheric interrelations. *Soil Sci. Soc. Am. Proc.* **37:**522–527.

Philip, J. R., and D. A. DeVries. 1957. Moisture movement in porous materials under temperature gradients. *Trans. Am. Geophys. Union* **38:**222–232.

Poulovassilis, A. 1962. Hysteresis of pore water: An application of the concept of independent domains. *Soil Sci.* **93:**405–412.

Rawlins, S. L., and W. H. Gardner. 1963. A test of the validity of the diffusion equation for unsaturated flow of soil water. *Soil Sci. Soc. Am. Proc.* **27:**507–511.

Reeves, Mark, and E. E. Miller. 1975. Estimating infiltration for erratic rainfall. *Water Resourc. Res.* **11:**102–110.

Richards, L. A. 1928. The usefulness of capillary potential to soil moisture and plant investigators. *J. Agric. Res.* **37:**719–742.

Richards, L. A. 1949. Methods of measuring soil moisture tension. *Soil Sci.* **68:**95–112.

Rose, C. W. 1968. Water transport in soil with a daily temperature wave. *Aust. J. Soil Res.* **6:**31–57.

Rose, D. A. 1963. Water movement in porous materials. *Brit. J. Appl. Phys.* **14:**256–262, 491–496.

Scotter, D. R. 1974a. Salt and water movement in relatively dry soil. *Aust. J. Soil Res.* **12:**27–35.

Scotter, D. R. 1974b. Factors influencing salt and water movement near crystalline salts in relatively dry soil. *Aust. J. Soil Res.* **12:**77–86.

Scotter, D. R., and P. A. C. Raats. 1970. Movement of salt and water near crystalline salt in relatively dry soil. *Soil Sci.* **109:**170–178.

Stark, N. 1970. Water balance of some warm desert plants in a wet year. *J. Hydrol.* **10:**113–126.

Stark, N., and L. D. Love. 1969. Water relations of three warm desert species. *Isr. J. Bot.* **18:**175–190.

Topp, G. C., and E. E. Miller. 1966. Hysteretic moisture characteristics and hydraulic conductivities for glass bead media. *Soil Sci. Soc. Am. Proc.* **31:**312–314.

Watson, K. K. 1974. Some applications of unsaturated flow theory. *Agronomy* **17:**359–400.

Westcot, D. W., and P. J. Wierenga. 1974. Transfer of heat by conduction and vapor movement in a closed soil system. *Soil Sci. Soc. Am. Proc.* **38:**9–14.

Wheeler, M. L. 1972. *Application of Thermocouple Psychrometers to Field Measurements of Soil Moisture Potential.* Ph.D. dissertation, Univ. of Ariz.

7

Water as a Factor in the Biology of North American Desert Plants

James A. MacMahon and *David J. Schimpf*

This chapter deals with the theory of soil-plant-atmosphere water relations, provides a survey of the adaptations of desert plants to limited and unpredictable water supplies, and shows the effect of such water relations on ecosystem structure. We have elected to attempt a comprehensive treatment of North American deserts rather than survey other desert regions with which we have much less experience.

On the basis of the biologically mediated flow of water in nature, many authors refer to a soil-plant-atmosphere continuum (SPAC) (Kozlowski, 1972; Oertli, 1976). The plant, by transpiration of water absorbed through its roots, is an intimate link between the soil and the atmosphere. The passage of water along this pathway links the plant to its environment via physiological processes such as photosynthesis and growth. Thus, production of the energy that will be the very basis for the existence of biological communities is intimately tied to transpiration. A number of researchers have been able to correlate productivity to transpiration. Rosenzweig (1968), for example, presents tight regressions of net above-ground production on actual evapotranspiration (see also Lieth, 1976).

We assume throughout this discussion that desert plants obtain their water from the soil. While aerial uptake is possible through shoot radiative cooling below the dew point, high leaf resistance (Babu and Went, 1978) and predominant meteorological conditions militate against sizable uptake in most cases (Stark and Love, 1969; Went, 1975). Condensation from fog does seem to be significant in parts of Baja California (Rundel, 1978; Nash et al., 1979). Rapid leaf growth of ocotillo (*Fouquieria splendens*) results from the presence of liquid water on the buds (Lloyd, 1905).

In arid areas, where soil water quantities are low and unpredictable (Trewartha, 1968. pp. 161–163), plants must possess sophisticated physiological and morphological adaptations to facilitate the use of this elusive resource.

It is important to clarify our conceptual approach to this and other ecological topics. We believe that if an organism (in this case a plant) can get to a place and survive under the conditions existing there, then the plant will be part of the community or ecosystem occurring in that place at that time. This philosophical position is that of individualistic or continuum bias of community studies (Gleason, 1939; McIntosh, 1967; MacMahon, 1979). Getting there is a matter of dispersal dynamics. To a significant extent, these dynamics involve stochastic processes and the proximity of migrules to an area open to occupation. In general we will not address problems of dispersal, even though it is possible that transport by surface water flow might be a factor in migrule dispersal.

Given that dispersal occurs, once a migrule reaches an area, it must in turn survive, perhaps germinate, grow, survive, and compete (or otherwise interact) with other species in the area if it is to occur there. Finally, long-term persistence of a species in an ecosystem usually implies that reproduction must occur.

Water, obviously, can play a role in all of these processes. A complication is that water as an environmental factor seldom acts alone; temperature and salts, for example, interact with it to determine evaporative stresses on plants. We specifically ignore the complications of the presence of higher soil salt content. (For a review of halophytes and halophytic conditions, see Reimold and Queen, 1974; Ungar 1979; and Waisel, 1972.) Despite these complications, our approach will be to consider water somewhat independently of other factors. To include all environmental interactions is clearly beyond the scope of this chapter.

Our mode of presentation is summarized in figure 7-1, which shows that the individual plant is part of the soil-plant-atmosphere continuum, and the interactions affect a series of plant life-cycle processes, which themselves cause the plant to be part of the vegetation component of an ecosystem. It should be obvious that each of these levels of response contains components that may feed back on each other; for example, landscape pattern can affect plant life-cycles characteristics, which in turn affect the soil-plant-atmosphere continuum (SPAC).

PLANTS AS PART OF THE SOIL-PLANT-ATMOSPHERE CONTINUUM

Theory

The flow of water in the soil-plant-atmosphere continuum depends on the presence of a gradient of decreasing water potential energy from the soil through the plant and finally to the atmosphere.

Whether in the plant or in the soil, water potential (Ψ) is, for constant temperature and gravity (Ψ_g), represented by

$$\Psi = \Psi_s + \Psi_p + \Psi_m, \tag{7.1}$$

where Ψ_s is the osmotic potential (due to dissolved solutes), Ψ_p is a pressure potential component (usually zero in an open system like soil, negative in xylem, and positive for turgid cells), and Ψ_m is the matric potential (the sum of capillary and colloidal forces interacting with water). Free pure water is taken,

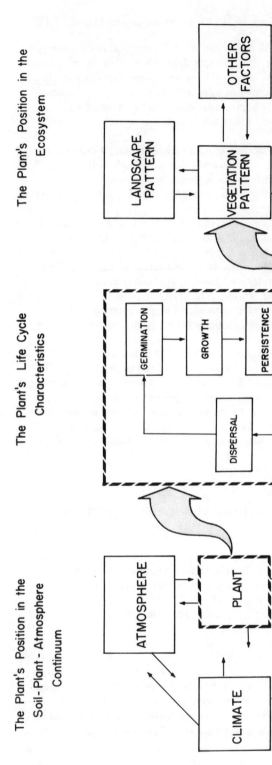

The Plant's Position in the
Soil-Plant-Atmosphere
Continuum

The Plant's Life Cycle
Characteristics

The Plant's Position in the
Ecosystem

FIGURE 7-1. *Aspects of desert plant biology potentially affected by water. The series on the left places an individual plant within the context of the abiotic factors that affect its water dynamics (SPAC). The central portion enlarges the plant to show the processes in the life cycle of a plant, which can be affected by water. Note that not all possible reciprocal effects are shown. The right-hand series of interactions shows the plants interacting with other components to form an ecosystem. Some plant interactions (for example, competition) are not depicted on this figure but are important to desert plant biology.*

for reference, to have $\Psi = 0$. This thermodynamic approach to water derives from Slatyer and Taylor (1960), Slatyer (1967), Kramer (1969), and Oertli (1971, 1976).

Another integrating formula expresses Ψ as a function of continuum demands (Richter, 1976):

$$\Psi = \Psi^{soil}_{stat} + \Psi_g + \Psi_f \tag{7.2}$$

where Ψ^{soil}_{stat} is the static soil-water potential, Ψ_g is gravitational potential depending on density of water and on the geographically variable water constant (but usually equal to 0.1 bars m^{-1}), and Ψ_f is the frictional potential (the work necessary to overcome friction of water in the pathway). Methods of measuring the components of these two formulas have been reviewed by Brown and van Haveren (1972) and Slavik (1974) and are not reviewed in detail here.

One measure common in field studies should be mentioned briefly, however. Total water potential (Ψ^{plant}) is measured either by psychrometers or with a pressure chamber. When a pressure chamber is used, only xylem pressure potential is actually measured. This (Ψ^{xylem}) is an adequate approximation of Ψ because few dissolved substances occur ($\Psi_s \cong 0$) and matric potentials are low ($\Psi_m \cong 0$) (Ritchie and Hinckley, 1975).

A major characteristic of the soil-plant-atmosphere continuum is the presence of resistance to water flow throughout the system. Flow in any section of the system is represented, then, by

$$J = \frac{-\triangle\Psi}{R} \;\;, \tag{7.3}$$

where J is the flux in volume/area/time, $-\triangle\Psi$ is potential drop, and R is resistance. Rewriting the equation, resistance is simply $-\triangle\Psi/J$. These resistances in the plant may appear as complex, branched, parallel pathways (Oertli, 1976).

To relate leaf water potential (Ψ^{leaf}) to soil (Ψ^{soil}), including the resistances, we can use the summary formula,

$$\Psi^{leaf} = \Psi^{soil} + \triangle\Psi. \tag{7.4}$$

Consult Slatyer (1967), Weatherly (1970), and Oertli (1971) for a more detailed discussion.

Plants in an initially wet but subsequently unwatered soil create a flow of water into their leaves, which decreases Ψ^{soil}. This is often a diurnal cycle of plant Ψ such that at dawn $\Psi^{soil} = \Psi^{root} = \Psi^{leaf}$, and during the day a gradient occurs where $\Psi^{soil} > \Psi^{root} > \Psi^{leaf}$. These relationships are shown in figure 7-2.

With this general background we can address specific attributes of North American desert plants as they affect the soil-plant-atmosphere continuum.

Result: Water Potential

The result of the plant's generally responding in nature according to the theory presented above is the development of a tissue water potential that

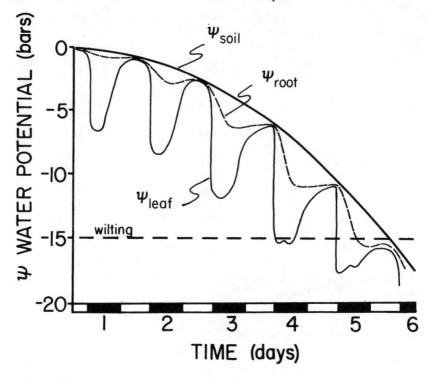

FIGURE 7-2. *Hypothetical changes in water potential of root, soil, and leaves of a plant in an initially wet ($\Psi^{root} \cong 0$) soil. The same evaporative conditions are assumed for each day (redrawn, by permission, after Slatyre, 1967).*

tracks soil-water potential if the plant is poikilohydric or differs by some value depending on the plant's specific strategy. While differences in total Ψ control water flux in the SPAC, components of Ψ^{plant} may be the important variables for specific plant responses. In general, Ψ_p is important for cell expansion and stomatal aperture, while Ψ_s affects biochemical reactions (Wiebe, 1972; Hsiao, 1973).

The total water potential of living plants varies from a high of about 0 bars, since even with $\Psi^{xylem} > 0$ (guttation may occur) total potential is probably not positive (O'Leary, 1970), to a low of less than -100 bars. Some desert plants have the ability to carry on photosynthesis even at these very low water potentials. Table 7-1 summarizes some extreme values. Not all of these values represent plants actively photosynthesizing. The only Ψ^{plant} reported for an annual is, to our knowledge, -10 bars (Ehleringer et al., 1979). It should be mentioned that the lower values in this table may be beyond the reliable range of standard psychrometric or pressure bomb equipment (Wiebe, pers. comm.).

TABLE 7-1. *Some Minimum Tissue Water Potentials (Ψ^{plant}) for Apparently Healthy North American Desert Plants.*

Species	Minimum water potential (−bars)	Notes	Source of data
Sonoran Desert			
Acacia greggii	48		Solbrig et al. (1977)
	44*	Minimum value tested	Szarek & Woodhouse (1978a, b)
Ambrosia (Franseria) deltoidea	85*	Also see Szarek & Woodhouse (1977)	Halvorson & Patten (1974)
Cercidium microphyllum	36	36.3 (leafless) Solbrig et al. (1977), 27.6 leafed	Halvorson & Patten (1974)
	31*	minimum value tested	Szarek & Woodhouse (1978a, b)
Chilopsis linearis	20		Odening et al (1974)
Encelia farinosa	37*		Solbrig et al. (1977) Odening et al. (1974)
Eriogonum fasciculatum	76		Halvorson & Patten (1974)
Ferocactus acanthodes	6	After 7 mo. drought	Nobel, 1977b
Krameria grayi	74		Halvorson & Patten (1974)
Larrea tridentata	40–65	Predawn values in Feb. and Sept., respectively	Oechel et al. (1972b)
Notholaena parryi	15*	Note this is a poikilohydrous fern & endures much lower tissue water potentials	Nobel (1978)

119

TABLE 7-1. *continued*

Species	Minimum water potential (−bars)	Notes	Source of data
Olneya tesota	35*		Szarek & Woodhouse (1976)
Opuntia basilaris	18*	Acidification rate ≅ 0	Szarek (1974), Szarek & Ting (1975)
Prosopis juliflora	45*		Strain (1970)
Simmondsia chinensis	62	Photosynthesis stops ≅ −40 (Al-Ani et al., 1972)	Halvorson & Patten (1974) Odening et al. (1974)
Viguiera tomentosa	46	Baja California	Solbrig et al. (1977)
Great Basin Desert			
Artemisia tridentata	64 60–70		Branson et al. (1976) Campbell and Harris (1977)
Atriplex confertifolia	114*		Moore et al. (1972)
Atriplex corrugata	107		Branson et al. (1976)
Atriplex nuttallii	103		Branson et al. (1976)
Atriplex (Grayia) spinosa	79		Branson et al. (1976)
Ceratoides (Eurotia) lanata	120*		Moore et al. (1972)
Chrysothamnus greenei	84		Branson et al. (1976)
Chrysothamnus nauseosus	41		Branson et al. (1976)
Distichlis spicata	46*		Detling & Klikoff (1973)

Species	Value	Note	Reference
Sarcobatus vermiculatus	63		Branson et al. (1976)
	44*		Detling & Klikoff (1973)
Suaeda depressa	78		Detling & Klikoff (1973)
Suaeda fruticosa	53*		Detling & Klikoff (1973)
Tetradymia spinosa	50		Branson et al. (1976)
Chihuahuan Desert			
Larrea tridentata	52–22	Aug.–Oct. in areas without caliche	Cunningham & Burk (1973)
Larrea tridentata	70–23	Areas with caliche	Cunningham & Burk (1973)
Mojave Desert			
Ambrosia dumosa	50	Loses leaves about here	Bamberg et al. (1975)
Atriplex hymenelytra	42*		Pearcy et al. (1974)
Krameria parvifolia	48–72*	Small positive CO_2 uptake	Bamberg et al. (1975)
Larrea tridentata	51–65*	Small positive CO_2 uptake	Bamberg et al. (1975)
Lycium andersonii	41–52	Loses leaves ≅ 50	Bamberg et al. (1975)
Lycium pallidum	44–51	Loses leaves ≅ 50	Bamberg et al. (1975)
Tidestromia oblongifolia	25*		Björkman et al. (1972)

Note: Asterisked values indicate photosynthesizing plants. See Scholander et al. (1965) for additional data and technique, and Syvertsen et al. (1975) for a caveat on the use of predawn xylem potentials.

Strategies of Plants to Deal with Water Availability in Deserts

Generally plants can be classified along a continuum of available environmental water supplies where species adapted to total or partial submergence in water are termed *hydrophytes*; those adapted to moderate water supplies are termed *mesophytes*, and those adapted to arid areas are termed *xerophytes* (Levitt, 1972).

Walter and Stadelmann (1974) point out confusion in the use of the term *xerophyte*. They note that workers have incorrectly used the term to include all plants growing in arid regions. Clearly some species occupy moist microsites in an otherwise dry background and are not xerophytes. Similarly, according to a restricted concept of xerophytes (Seddon, 1974), succulents, halophytes, and annuals (ephemerals) are not included.

Thus true xerophytes are "those nonsucculent and nonhalophytic plants of arid regions which maintain living above-ground organs throughout the year, including drought periods, and obtain their water supply from local precipitation or atmospheric moisture only" (Walter and Stadelmann, 1974). In turn true xerophytes can be subdivided into poikilohydrous, malacophyllous, sclerophyllous (or aphyllous), and stenohydrous xerophytes. Although such a classification is useful, a scheme based on a general theory of response of plants to stress, proposed by Levitt (1972), seems conceptually of broader application and is adopted here (figure 7-3).

Drought Escaping

Ephemerals, or as they are often called, annuals, cannot withstand drought except in the form of seeds. Historically these species have been thought to differ little from mesophytes (Levitt, 1972).

Annuals in North America fall into two rather discrete groups: those that germinate and complete their development in the winter and spring (winter annuals) and those that develop in the summer or early fall (summer annuals).

The distribution of these two types of annuals correlates with the seasonal rainfall distribution so characteristic of North American deserts. Simplistically, the Mojave Desert has winter annuals and winter rainfall, the Sonoran Desert has winter and summer annuals and biseasonal (winter and summer) rainfall, and the Chihuahuan Desert has summer annuals and rainfall. The Great Basin Desert, although receiving more than half of its precipitation in the winter, has few native annual species. For spatial variation within these general trends, see MacMahon (1979).

Recently, Johnson (1976) and Mulroy and Rundel (1977) suggested a suite of characteristics of annuals that can be considered as adaptive to a desert existence. They point out that summer annuals are relatively tall in stature, weedy (occur on disturbed ground), include many grasses, have foliage not very xerophytic (lack hairs), have simple and entire leaves or leaflets, and seldom have basal leaf rosettes. Winter annuals show generally the converse of all of these characteristics.

One area of particularly interesting contrast between the two annuals'

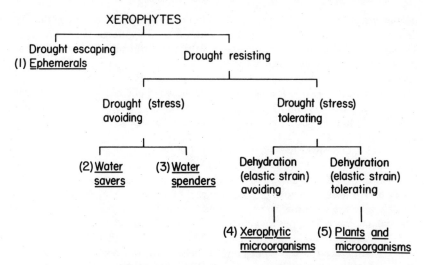

FIGURE 7-3.   *A system of classification of true xerophytes (from Levitt, 1972 by permission; copyright © 1972 by Academic Press, Inc.).*

characteristics is associated with their photosynthetic pathways. Two strategies have been elucidated for plants generally (Johnson, 1975), which are termed C_3 and C_4 metabolism. Briefly, C_4 (so named because CO_2 reacts to form a four-carbon compound) plants have optimum carbon fixation at high temperatures and light intensities and have high net production rates and relative water use efficiencies (Black, 1973).

Most C_4 annuals are summer annuals. This correlates to high summer temperatures and light intensity. The C_3 annuals are winter annuals. They germinate during a cool period, suited to the lower-temperature photosynthesis optimum as compared to C_4 species. Additionally, C_3 species may initiate their early growth in a rosette form, which, being close to the ground surface, would heat more during cold, suboptimum temperature periods of winter. As seasonal temperatures increase, the plant may change life form and grow up and out of the soil surface microenvironment. Additionally, Mulroy and Rundel (1977) interpret the leaf dissection among C_3 species as an adaptation to permit a decreased boundary layer effect and concomitant greater exchange of air (CO_2) at the leaf surface. Some entire-leaved C_3 species (such as *Camissonia*) may have high CO_2 uptake rates (Mooney et al., 1976; Ehleringer et al., 1979). Finally, winter annuals are highly plastic in their ability to track the environment and produce large numbers of flowers and seeds during favorable years.

Drought Avoiding, Water Savers

Water-conserving species generally rely on morphological adaptations such as impervious cuticle and surface area reduction to reduce water loss. Succulent species can expand their stems to store considerable water when it becomes available (MacDougal and Spalding, 1910). They also behaviorally limit the amount of time their stomates are open when the air is hot and dry. Thus gas exchange frequently occurs at night; night transpiration exceeds that during daylight (Ehrler, 1969). The CO_2 taken up at night is assimilated by species with what is known as crassulacean acid metabolism (CAM) and stored in the form of malate (malic acid) until daylight when photosynthesis can occur without the plant's opening its stomata (Kluge and Ting, 1979). This strategy is clearly adaptive in arid situations (Johnson, 1975; Kluge, 1976; Ting et al., 1972).

CAM metabolism has been reported for 18 families and 109 genera of angiosperms (Szarek and Ting, 1977). Of this number the two families Agavaceae (leaf succulents) and Cactaceae (stem succulents) are groups that typify North American deserts. The geographic distribution of the two families is such that the Sonoran has a plethora of cacti of varying life forms, the Chihuahuan has both types of succulents, and the Mojave has cacti in the west and Agavaceae in the form of *Yucca* in the east and at higher elevations. The Great Basin Desert is essentially devoid of succulents from these groups, at least as dominant components (Johnson, 1976; MacMahon, 1979).

In the two conspicuous groups of CAM plants (leaf succulents and stem succulents), a controversy has arisen as to their ability to shift from CAM metabolism to C_3 metabolism under favorable conditions (Hartsock and Nobel, 1976). Currently the data suggest that stem succulents (such as *Opuntia basilaris*) do not shift from CAM to C_3 metabolism. Rather rainfall or irrigation enhances CAM, depending on the age of the plant (Hanscom and Ting, 1977). Leaf succulents may switch photosynthetic pathways (cf. Eickmeier and Bender, 1976). Recent data on response of succulents (not all of them desert species) to water stress suggest several modes of effect: C_3 species that change to CAM, C_3 that change to internal CO_2 cycling, and CAM plants that do not change (Hanscom and Ting, 1978).

Water Spenders

Species that lose water at a high rate, as long as it is available, are termed *water spenders*. This counterintuitive strategy is based on observation of many species, particularly those along ravines and arroyos (phreatophytes). Walter (1962) explained this apparent paradox when he noted that because of the great plant-plant distance in deserts, each individual has a large soil volume from which to extract water. Root distribution data may not support this supposed relationship.

Adaptations for water spending include a high ratio of conducting to nonconducting tissue; high root to shoot ratio; high water-absorbing potential; the possibility of absorbing dew or otherwise being somewhat hygroscopic; and the ability to become a water saver under extreme stress (Levitt, 1972). Such phreatophytic plants as mesquite *Prosopis juliflora*, tamarisk *Tamarix* sp., and apache plume *Fallugia paradoxa* are included in this group.

Drought Tolerating, Dehydration Avoiding

Some species of plants have good tolerance to drought but avoid dehydration to a large extent. In fact this group probably blends into the next group, tolerant nonavoiders, because under extreme circumstances even the best nonavoider (such as *Larrea*) may lose its leaves, an avoidance mechanism.

Species such as palo verde (*Cercidium microphyllum*) retain water by having small, ephemeral leaves. In fact for some species, stem photosynthesis rivals leaf photosynthesis. While some species (for example, *Fouquieria*) show little stem photosynthesis during the leafless period (Mooney and Strain, 1964); under favorable circumstances this changes, and for some species, the leafless period may show appreciable stem photosynthesis. The latter case is exemplified by *Cercidium floridum*, which has high concentrations of stem chlorophyll (Adams and Strain, 1968), in fact more than in leaves on a per unit area analysis (Adams et al., 1967; Adams and Strain, 1969). The green stems produce 40 percent of the yearly total photosynthate. Net photosynthesis in a leafless tree was 86 percent as great as that in the leaves of a foliated tree. Photosynthesis rate per unit area of surface is similar for leaves and stems (Adams and Strain, 1969). Perhaps one of the most interesting species in this group is ocotillo (*Fouquieria splendens*) and, by inference, its relatives *F. macdougalli*, *F. diguetii* and *F. (Idria) columnaris*. Other desert species not in this adaptive category also carry on stem photosynthesis to advantage (for example, *Gutierrezia sarothrae*) (De Puit and Caldwell, 1975b) and *Atriplex confertifolia* (Wiebe et al., 1974).

All of the dehydration avoiders close their stomata when water stress is very slight. This decreases water loss, thus maintaining higher ψ^{plant}. With no gas exchange occurring, the plants begin to starve; they are not known to have CAM to avoid the problem as do succulents. Their leaves turn yellow, purportedly as nutrients are translocated to stem tissue, and then drop (Daubenmire and Charter, 1942). Similar patterns occur in *Jatropha cardiophylla* and *Euphorbia heterophylla* (Walter and Stadelmann, 1974). Species respond to the presence of moisture following drought by rapid leafing out (Mooney and Strain, 1964).

Many microorganisms also fall into this group.

Drought Tolerating, Dehydration Tolerant

This grouping of species suggests by its name that ψ^{plant} of the included species simply tracks ψ^{soil} with no detrimental effects at almost any water potential value. Indeed for extreme species such as resurrection plants (Gaff and Hallam, 1974; Gaff, 1977; Eickmeier, 1979b), mosses (Alpert, 1979), and lichens, this is the case. For a discussion of these physiological phenomena, see Bewley (1979).

For other forms, there is some sort of avoidance. Parenthetically we note that the two drought-tolerating categories (dehydration avoiders and tolerators) are not as distinctly separated as the other adaptation categories. These are the forms termed *malacophyllous xerophytes* by Walter and Stadelmann (1974). Many of these species respond by producing seasonally dimorphic leaves (such as *Encelia farinosa*) (Shreve, 1923, 1924; Walter, 1962), and finally when very dry conditions persist, they either lose their leaves (as *Ambrosia dumosa* and *A. deltoidea* do) or, except under harshest conditions, remain evergreen (*Larrea tridentata*).

The dimorphic leaves may differ in size, pubescence, thickness, and internal to external leaf area ratios (A^{mes}/A) (Cunningham and Strain, 1969; Ehleringer et al., 1976; Nobel, 1977a; Smith and Nobel, 1977; Strain, 1969). Nobel (1978) experimentally determined, at least for *Encelia farinosa,* that "irradiation appeared to have its major influence on leaf thickness, A^{mes}/A and adsorptance, with secondary effect on leaf length; ψ^{soil} affected primarily leaf length, growth rate and water status and secondarily A^{mes}/A."

In addition to seasonal dimorphism, differences exist in the morphology and function of leaves from different parts of the plant: sun leaf/shade leaf contrasts (such as *Hyptis emoryi*) (Nobel, 1976a).

It is not possible in a short chapter to review all of the adaptations of plants—such as anatomical (Carlquist, 1975, p. 207) or morphological (Dittmer, 1969; Hevly, 1963; Smith, 1978)—to varying moisture regimes. Many papers in recent years have looked at such areas as water-use efficiency changes under different moisture regimes, effects of tissue water potential on photosynthesis, seasonal and diurnal patterns of water potential, and photosynthesis. For some references to North American desert species, we list the following: *Acacia greggii* (Strain, 1969; Szarek and Woodhouse, 1978a and b); *Agave deserti* (Nobel, 1976b); *Agave lecheguilla* (Eickmeier and Adams, 1978); *Agropyron spicatum* (De Puit and Caldwell, 1975b); *Ambrosia deltoidea* (Szarek and Woodhouse, 1976, 1977); *Artemisia tridentata* (De Puit and Caldwell, 1973, 1975a, 1975b; Campbell and Harris, 1977); *Atriplex canescens* (Dwyer and De Garmo, 1970); *Atriplex confertifolia* (Caldwell et al., 1977; Love and West, 1972; Moore et al., 1972); *Atriplex hymenelytra* (Pearcy et al., 1974; Sánchez-Diaz and Mooney, 1979); *Atriplex lentiformis* (Pearcy and Harrison, 1974); *Atriplex nuttallii* (Branson et al., 1976); *Atriplex (Grayia) spinosa* (Branson et al., 1976); *Ceratoides (Eurotia) lanata* (Caldwell et al., 1977; Love and West, 1972; Moore et al., 1972); *Cercidium floridum* (Adams et al., 1967; Adams and Strain, 1969); *Cercidium microphyllum* (Shreve, 1914; Szarek and Woodhouse, 1978a and b); *Chilopsis linearis* (Odening et al., 1974); *Chrysothamnus nauseosus* (Branson et al., 1976); *Encelia farinosa* (Nobel et al., 1978; Odening et al., 1974; Smith and Nobel, 1977; Strain, 1969); *Ferocactus acanthodes* (Nobel, 1977b); *Fouquieria splendens* (Mooney and Strain, 1964); *Gutierrezia sarothrae* (De Puit and Caldwell, 1975a, b; Dwyer and De Garmo, 1970); *Hilaria mutica* (Dwyer and De Garmo, 1970); *Hymenoclea salsola* (Strain, 1969); *Hyptis emoryi* (Smith and Nobel, 1977); *Larrea tridentata* (Dwyer and De Garmo, 1970; Mallery, 1935; Mooney et al., 1976–1977; Odening et al., 1974; Oechel et al., 1972a, b; Strain, 1969, 1970; Syvertsen et al., 1975); *Mirabilis tenuiloba* (Smith and Nobel, 1977); *Muhlenbergia porteri* (Dwyer and De Garmo, 1970); *Notholaena parryi* (Nobel, 1978; Nobel et al., 1978); *Olneya tesota* (Szarek and Woodhouse, 1976, 1977); *Opuntia basilaris* (Hanscom and Ting, 1977; Szarek and Ting, 1974, 1975; Szarek et al., 1973); *Prosopis juliflora*

(Dwyer and De Garmo, 1970; Strain, 1970); *Prosopis glandulosa* (Wendt et al., 1968); *Salsola kali* (Dwyer and Wolde-Yohannis, 1972); *Sarcobatus ver-miculatus* (Branson et al., 1976); *Simmondsia chinensis* (Adams et al., 1977, 1978; Al-Ani et al., 1972; Tal et al., 1979); *Sporobolus flexuosus* (Dwyer and De Garmo, 1970); *Tetradymia spinosa* (Branson et al., 1976); *Tidestromia oblong-ifolia* (Sánchez-Diaz and Mooney, 1979). See also the reviews by Ehrler (1975), Johnson (1975), and Ting and Szarek (1975). Recently a model of *Larrea* carbon allocation, incorporating water status, was published by Cunningham and Reynolds (1978).

Consequences of water-use efficiency from different photosynthesis methods (C_3, C_4, CAM) may determine the composition of regional floras (Teeri and Stowe, 1976; Stowe and Teeri, 1978; Teeri et al., 1978; Doliner and Jolliffe, 1979), or local species assemblages along an altitudinal transect (Eick-meier, 1978, 1979a).

WATER AND DESERT PLANT LIFE CYCLE CHARACTERISTICS

It is clear that many parts of a plant's life cycle are affected by water (figure 7-1). If all parts of the life cycle are not completed, the individual plant will cease to exist, and its species may cease to exist in a particular locality. We now discuss some strategies of desert plant life cycles that appear tuned to the water stress of arid lands.

Germination

Information on germination in deserts comes from both observations in the field and controlled experiments. Among North American desert species, information has been published for more annual than perennial species. Theory of water relations of germination developed for plants in general probably applies equally well to desert taxa and will be considered first; a general treatment of germination water relations is that by Hillel (1972). Our emphasis on water should not be taken to mean that soil chemistry (such as effects of gypsum on *Gaillardia,* Secor and Farhadnejad, 1978), temperature (see for example, Capon and Van Asdall, 1967; Freeman et al., 1977; McCleary and Wagner, 1973), or other factors (for example, Alcorn and Kurtz, 1959) are unimportant. Throughout this section we will use *germination* in the broad sense, including emergence.

Theory

The probability that a nondormant seed will develop into a photosynthesizing seedling depends on the amount of water it can acquire from the soil and the amount of soil it must penetrate to reach the soil surface. If the soil is drying through time, the rate at which the seed acquires water also affects this probability.

Soil-water potential affects four important characteristics of the environment of the germinating seed: the magnitude of the water potential gradient from seed to soil, resistance to water movement along that gradient, exchange area between soil water and seed, and mechanical strength of the solid matrix that the seedling must penetrate. Solute potential and matric potential have equivalent effects only on the magnitude of the gradient. Resistance, exchange area, and mechanical strength change strongly with soil-water content but not soil-solute content (Collis-George and Williams, 1968). Decreased soil matric potential reduces the magnitude of the water potential gradient but results more importantly in an increase in resistance to flow. In addition, the exchange area between soil water and seed is reduced, diminishing flux potential. The more complex responses of the soil system to decreased water content mean that seeds usually germinate more readily in solutions than in soil at an equivalent water potential (for example, Wood et al., 1976).

Sensitivity to water stress is not uniform throughout the germination process. The initiation of germination has a $\psi^{\text{substrate}}$ minimum several bars higher than that permitting radicle emergence/elongation (McDonough, 1975; Hegarty and Ross, 1978). Barbour (1968) noted greater sensitivity to water stress for germination of *Larrea* than for root elongation. Initiation of germination is probably the life-cycle stage requiring the highest ψ^{plant}.

Soil-water potential above a species-specific critical value affects the rate of germination but not the total germination percentage (Hadas and Russo, 1974). Below this critical value, total percentage declines (Williams and Shaykewich, 1971). These studies have in common a negligible rate of soil drying. In deserts, soils often begin to dry soon after precipitation events, more rapidly so when soil and air temperatures are high, as in summer. This may increase the critical water potential for successful germination, since the rate of germination becomes crucial for the establishment of a photosynthesizing seedling before surface soil dries out.

Drying also affects the mechanical strength of the soil. In a sandy clay, impedance to penetrating seedlings was maximal on the fourth day of drying ($\Theta_m = 0.06$), being two to three times that at field capacity (Arndt, 1965). Frelich et al. (1973) concluded that lower soil-water potential slowed emergence sufficiently that concomitant increased hardness in the surface crust could reduce the number of grass seedlings emerging before available water becomes exhausted.

Germination in North American Deserts

Field studies have generally consisted of observations following precipitation events or manipulations of the amount of water falling on an area (for examples, Horton et al., 1960). Seeds from desert populations have also been germinated under laboratory conditions.

Selected aspects of laboratory experiments on water relations of desert plant germination are summarized in table 7-2. In many cases, the water potentials tested were so widely spaced that the critical values reported are not highly accurate. As expected, these results showed reduced rate of germination with lower $\Psi^{substrate}$, regardless of whether final germination percentage was lower. Had soil been the germination substrate, the critical values of Ψ would probably have been higher (for example, Wood et al., 1976). Studies of germination in soil with Ψ controlled by a method such as Kaufmann's (1969) would be more indicative of field behavior.

In another study, barley, corn, buckwheat, and bush beans germinated at lower soil-water potentials than did *Salsola kali, Ambrosia (Franseria) dumosa, Atriplex canescens,* and *Atriplex (Grayia) spinosa* from the Mojave (Wallace and Romney, 1972). In general, there is nothing to suggest that desert species can germinate at appreciably lower water potentials than can mesophytic species.

Many desert species of *Atriplex* have seeds enclosed by persistent utricles or bracts. Moisture enters the picture here in a different way, being required to leach substances from these (Cornelius and Hylton, 1969) or to promote fungal growth and hence mechanical softening (Vest and Cottam, 1953) before germination occurs.

In the field, Steenbergh and Lowe (1969) observed seedling emergence of saguaro (*Cereus giganteus*) after 20 mm or more of rain in the previous four to six days. Most field studies have dealt with annual species in the Mojave. In general, the minimum precipitation in an event sufficient to bring on germination and emergence is 15 to 25 mm (Beatley, 1974b; Juhren et al., 1956; Tevis, 1958a), though as little as 6 mm may suffice for some species (Juhren et al., 1956).

Hidden within this generality are many problems that must be considered concurrently with precipitation total. The effect of the precipitation event depends not only on the total rainfall but also on the duration; a slow rain brings on more germination than a cloudburst yielding the same precipitation total (Juhren et al., 1956; Soriano, 1953). For some species, germination percentage declines beyond a certain optimal rainfall (Juhren et al., 1956). The physiological controls of these behaviors remain to be determined clearly, as does any adaptive significance. Precipitation too light to induce germination may affect seed response to subsequent greater precipitation. For a general physiological review of this topic, see Hegarty (1978).

Artificial sprinkling of desert soil-annual seed systems has been studied in both field and laboratory. Tevis (1958b) sprinkled sandy soils with well water in the field at different times of the year. An application totaling 100 mm resulted in two to three times as many emerged seedlings per unit area as a 40 mm event and three to five times as many as a 13 mm event. Interestingly, a real rain of 23 mm in January resulted in a higher density of emerged seedlings than artificial rain did in that month. The reason may be differences in pH of rain versus well water, a factor that could affect the leaching of germination-inhibiting chemicals. *Salsola kali* emerged with as little as 3 mm water added, and full emergence required only 13 mm (Dwyer and Wolde-Yohannis, 1972).

Temperature interacts strongly with precipitation in effects on germination. For annuals in the Mojave, the amount of the first rain of the winter and the temperatures immediately following it were the most important determinants of germination (Juhren et al., 1956). Tevis (1958b) induced germination of *Abronia villosa* in all months by sprinkling. More water was needed for germi-

TABLE 7-2. *Germination Response of Some North American Desert Plant Species to Water Potentials Controlled in the Laboratory*

Species	Highest Ψ tested at which percentage was reduced (−bars)	Highest Ψ tested at which percentage was zero (−bars)	Osmoticum	Source of data
Agave parryi var. parryi	5	*	Carbowax 4000	Freeman (1975)
Agave lecheguilla	10	*	Carbowax 4000	Freeman (1973b)
Atriplex canescens	7	15	Mannitol	Springfield (1966)
Atriplex polycarpa	4.2	16.8	NaCl	Chatterton & McKell (1969)
Atriplex polycarpa	3.6	*	NaCl	Sankary & Barbour (1972)
Atriplex (Grayia) spinosa	6	*	Polyethylene glycol MW 1540	Wood et al. (1976)
Atriplex (Grayia) spinosa	8	17	NaCl	Wood et al. (1976)
Bouteloua eriopoda	11	*	Mannitol	Knipe & Herbel (1960)
Descurainia pinnata	Not reported	8	Not reported	Klikoff et al. (1975)
Eragrostis chloromelas	3	20	Mannitol	Knipe & Herbel (1960)
Eragrostis lehmanniana	7	20	Mannitol	Knipe & Herbel (1960)
Fouquieria splendens	5	*	Carbowax 4000	Freeman (1973a)
Halogeton glomeratus	1	9	Vapor exchange	Cronin (1965)
Halogeton glomeratus	Not reported	9	Not reported	Klikoff et al. (1975)
Hilaria jamesii	10	*	Mannitol	Knipe (1968)

Species				
Hilaria mutica	11	*	Mannitol	Knipe & Herbel (1960)
Larrea tridentata	1.5	*	Mannitol	Knipe & Herbel (1966)
Larrea tridentata	2	10	Sucrose	Barbour (1968)
Lapidium perfoliatum	Not reported	8	Not reported	Klikoff et al. (1975)
Muhlenbergia porteri	11	*	Mannitol	Knipe & Herbel (1960)
Nicotiana trigonophylla	7	12	Mannitol	Wells (1959)
Sporobolus flexuosus	7	11	Mannitol	Knipe & Herbel (1960)
Sporobolus airoides	1	*	Mannitol	Knipe (1968)
Sporobolus airoides	8	*	Mannitol	Knipe (1971)
Sporobolus airoides	8	*	Carbowax 200	Knipe (1971)
Sporobolus airoides	3	*	Carbowax 4000	Knipe (1971)
Taeniatherum asperum	8	*	Polyethylene glycol MW 1540	Young et al. (1968)

Note: An asterisk indicates that the lowest $\Psi_{substrate}$ tested was too high to prevent germination completely.

131

nation in the July–September period than in the winter, which is the best season for growth for this cool-adapted species. Perennials in the western Mojave germinate in the fall, with the exception of *Eriogonum* (Went, 1948) and *Atriplex hymenelytra* (Went and Westergaard, 1949). Went (1948) suggested that this permits extensive root development during the winter, when precipitation is highest and most dependable and evaporative potential is lowest. A different germination timing might be expected in the Chihuahuan, where precipitation is characteristic of the summer but not the winter.

Juhren et al. (1956) reported summer annuals germinating with no more precipitation than that required for winter annuals, perhaps because higher summer temperatures permit faster seedling development (Tevis, 1958b). Their comparisons deal with C_4 summer annuals as opposed to C_3 winter annuals; it would be interesting to compare the precipitation minima for C_3 and C_4 summer annuals in the southeastern Sonoran (Mulroy and Rundel, 1977).

It has been suggested that desert annuals germinate more rapidly than other plant groups do. Baker (1972) noted that desert annuals form an exception to the trend of greater seed weight with drier environments in California in that desert annuals' seeds are smaller than one would predict from their dry environment. Presumably the populations are physiologically adapted for rapidity of germination and early growth so that they can draw water from deeper horizons without germinating from greater depths (which would require larger seeds). Data on their germination rates as compared to other plant groups are largely wanting. However, Went (1949) observed that seeds from the driest site in Joshua Tree National Monument germinated faster than seeds of the same species from moister sites.

Growth

The growth of desert plants is directly related to the availability of moisture. The timing of the availability of moisture is extremely important because many desert (as well as nondesert) species have refractory periods where they can make little use of water; winter annuals, for example, respond most to fall rains (Beatley, 1974b). We do not treat ecosystem-wide productivity, a topic covered in two future IBP synthesis volumes. For a general review of productivity in arid zones, see Fischer and Turner (1978).

It is not our purpose to be exhaustive here, but species shown to respond directly to available soil moisture, in terms of growth, include: *Encelia farinosa*, which has longer leaves and higher growth rates with higher Ψ^{soil} (Smith and Nobel, 1978); *Hyptis emoryi* and *Mirabilis tenuiloba* (Smith and Nobel, 1977); *Parthenium argentatum* (Veihmeyer and Hendrickson, 1961); *Plantago insularis* (Klikoff, 1966); *Yucca elata* (Smith and Ludwig, 1976, 1978); *Yucca baccata* (Wallen and Ludwig, 1978); *Chilopsis linearis* (De Pree and Ludwig, 1978); *Cercidium, Ambrosia, Prosopis* and *Larrea* (Klikoff, 1967); *Larrea* being taller but less dense (no./ha) (Beatley, 1974a); a number of Mojave species (Bamberg et al., 1976; Beatley, 1974b) and Chihuahuan species (Dwyer and De Garmo, 1970); Sonoran annuals (Inouye, et al., unpublished); *Ambrosia dumosa, Ceratoides (Eurotia) lanata* and *Lycium andersonii* (Romney et al., 1978); *Atriplex confertifolia* (Fernandez and Caldwell, 1975;

Hodgkinson et al., 1978); the fern *Notholaena parryi* (Nobel, 1978); whole suites of species receiving extra water from road runoff (Johnson et al., 1975); intraspecific variation in growth characteristics (McMillen and Peacock, 1964; Peacock and McMillan, 1965). On the other hand, too much water can cause growth to cease (*Ephedra funera* and *Larrea*) or be unaffected (*Yucca*) (Romney et al., 1978). For general reviews of biology, including water relations of two conspicuous desert genera, see the volumes on *Prosopis* (Simpson, 1977b) and *Larrea* (Mabry et al., 1977).

Absolute rates of growth vary widely. Some species are notoriously slow growers. Saguaro, for example, grows about 0.15 m in ten years (Hastings and Alcorn, 1961).

Water, in part, mediates a number of growth relationships of desert plants. In *Ferocactus acanthodes* the amount of water diverted to flowers equals 6 percent of the stem weight (Nobel, 1977b). At least one agave puts so much dry matter into flower production (1.25 kg per year) that this equals the whole yearly normal photosynthetic output. Water is transferred from leaves to the inflorescence; the approximately sixty-eight leaves of a plant decreased 24.9 kg in wet weight, of which only 7.1 kg was attributable to transpiration (Nobel, 1977c).

The season of water use for growth may vary topographically. For example, Turner (1963), in a study of four Sonoran subtrees, found that the upland pair (*Olneya tesota* and *Cercidium microphyllum*) depend mainly on summer rain for radial growth, while the lowland species (*Cercidium floridum* and *Prosopis juliflora*) may "have genetically determined tolerances enabling them to make use of both winter and summer precipitation for growth."

One aspect of desert plant growth of special interest is the ratio of below-ground to above-ground biomass. Previously it was assumed that in response to desert conditions, plants invested relatively heavily in below-ground production (see, for example, Glendening, 1941), thus competing for scarce supplies of water. Barbour (1973) has doubted this and presents data from Garcia-Moya and McKell (1970) to substantiate his point.

Recent studies (Wallace et al., 1974) suggest a mean root-to-shoot ratio for ten Mojave desert species of 0.77 (0.37 *Atriplex*—1.40 *Lycium*). Similar values were obtained for the Sonoran desert (Thames, 1975). Only in Great Basin desert species do high values seem to occur; 4.09 *Atriplex confertifolia* and 6.77 *Ceratoides lanata* (Caldwell et al., 1977) are examples. The low value in the Mojave (0.37) is for *Atriplex confertifolia*, the same species with a ratio of 4.09 in the Great Basin. This vast difference, if real, is unexplained to date.

Although some species, such as *Prosopis*, may have roots extending to over 50 m (Simpson, 1977b), the vertical distribution of roots is generally confined to the upper meter even in areas with subtrees (figure 7-4). Note that there is essentially a rootless area in the upper 5 to 10 cm. This may permit the presence of annuals or shallow-rooted cacti when the soils are wetted and simply be too dry or hot for roots at other times. This gap does not seem as prominent in the Great Basin (MacMahon, unpublished data). Few native annuals occur in the Great Basin. Perhaps these abundant roots of perennials preempt them. Several nonnative species are present on disturbed sites (Young et al., 1972).

The root standing crop data cited above generally do not differentiate live

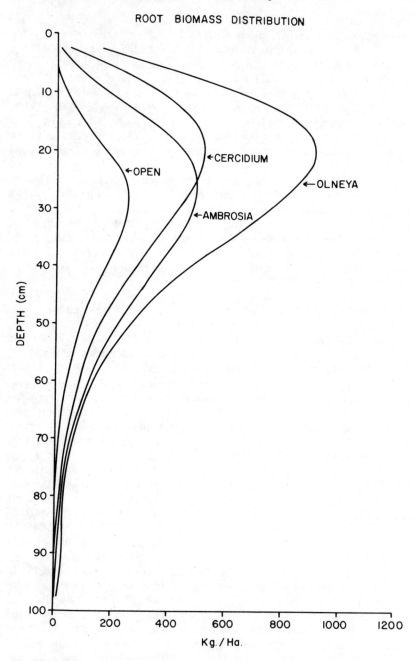

FIGURE 7-4. *Distribution of root biomass under four conditions (areas dominated by* Ambrosia, *areas dominated by* Olneya, *and plant interspaces) on the Silver Bell bajada, near Tucson, Arizona (from Barbour et al., 1977 by permission).*

and dead roots. Different ratios derive when productivity data (g C m^{-2} yr^{-1}) are used. For *Ceratoides* the ratio is 3.09 (108/35) and for *Atriplex confertifolia* 3.53 (152/43), based on data from Caldwell et al. (1977), updated from Caldwell and Camp (1974) for the Great Basin.

Obviously root distribution patterns affect the soil moisture extraction pattern of the soil column (Cable, 1977a, b; Sturges, 1977; Tiedemann and Klemmedson, 1977).

Persistence

The low Ψ^{plant} tolerated by many desert species (table 7-1; Clark et al., 1974) is most significant for allowing an individual to persist until favorable conditions return; the quantity of additional soil water taken up by developing such low internal potentials is small. Soil water is required for plants to live, though many forms, such as cacti, can persist for several years without measurable soil-water uptake. There are changes in the species composition of desert plant communities over time (Hastings and Turner, 1965). Such compositional changes are due to failure of species to reproduce and/or the failure of adults to persist. Climatic changes, including water quantity and seasonal distribution, can be a driving variable in such vegetation responses. Small increases or decreases in mean rainfall might cause conditions leading to local extinction of a species, perhaps via changed competitive relationships. Creosote bush (*Larrea*), for example, seems to be limited at the upper extreme by 183 mm of rainfall per year (Beatley, 1975; Wallace and Romney, 1972). Obviously differences in the seasonal distribution of the rainfall and rainfall effectiveness cause variations in the plant use of any given rainfall quantity. Nonetheless, too much water is detrimental to many desert plants (see, for example, Brum, 1973).

In favorable sites many desert species have long life expectancies. Fairy ring clones of *Larrea* may live 1,049 to 3,077 years (Vesek et al., 1975a; Sternberg, 1976); saguaro more than 175 years (Shreve, 1910); and *Fouquieria* (*Idria*) *columnaris* 700 to 800 years (Humphrey, 1974). One implication of this longevity is that many species can endure unfavorable conditions for long time spans (decades), never reproducing, and yet populations can persist because the adults last long enough that the probability of at least one good episode of reproduction and establishment during their lifetime is high.

Interestingly, some short-lived species may flower and die after shorter lifetimes when water stress is high or after longer lifetimes when stress is low for a sufficiently long interval. Species such as *Astragalus lentiginosus, Erioneuron (Tridens) pulchellum* and perhaps *Sphaeralcea* sp., *Mirabilis purdica* and *Eriogonum inflatum* can be considered facultative in this respect (Beatley, 1970).

Another aspect of water's affecting persistence of desert species can be assumed from some linked facts about nitrogen dynamics. A number of authors have shown that in wet years, or under artificial watering conditions, soil nitrogen is limiting to desert plants (Romney et al., 1978; Wallace and Romney, 1972), perhaps affecting plant survival. Soil crust algae are known to produce nitrogen forms usable by plants (Snyder and Wullstein, 1973). Sagebrush (*Artemisia*) actually picked up labeled ^{15}N from algae (Mayland and McIntosh,

1966). Since rainfall increases the activity of the soil crust algae, it may aid the plants at times when nitrogen would otherwise be limiting (see West and Skujins, 1978). Litter decomposition rates increased with the increased soil-water potential beneath artificially watered *Atriplex confertifolia* under field conditions, which might alter the supply of materials required for growth (MacMahon et al., 1975).

Clearly, through direct and indirect ways, water in deserts can vary the life span of individual plants. For desert-adapted species, too much water may lead to susceptibility to pathogens or enhance establishment of competitors (for example, grassland species) such that desert species can no longer persist. This, in part, might be the cause of historical changes in desert vegetation, though recent, perhaps man-related, changes are generally in the opposite direction (Hastings and Turner, 1965).

Reproduction

Little has been written on the relationships between water status and reproductive development in desert plants. This situation reflects the lower level of scientific interest in the water relations of flowering as compared to the controlling functions of photoperiod and temperature. Yet plant water status may control flowering in desert plants to a greater degree than it does in plants from environments where moisture is more abundant or reliable. Even less information is available on water relations of desert plant asexual reproduction; we do not treat this topic. Although this section emphasizes flowering as a response to plant water status, flowering may also affect water status. Nobel (1977c) showed that monocarpic flowering in the century plant *Agave deserti* required tremendous quantities of water, which could only be supplied by intraplant transfer from the succulent leaves.

Plant water status may affect reproductive potential in a number of ways. The quantity of biochemical resources within the plant that can be mobilized for reproduction will usually be greater when the plant has been physiologically active because of favorable water status. Water stress may render leaves ineffective in promoting flowering under normally inductive photoperiods (Aspinall and Husain, 1970), depress the number of floral primordia and their rate of initiation (Slatyer, 1969), or prevent normal female gametophyte development (Moss and Downey, 1971).

Information on desert plant reproductive behavior comes largely from observational data correlated with precipitation events or site differences in moisture availability. In the Mojave, vigorous reproduction by perennials followed heavy rain between January and mid-March; the amount of soil moisture at the outset of the spring growth period determined the initial flowering response (Ackerman and Bamberg, 1974). *Ephedra nevadensis,* however, produced another heavy cone crop in a year when precipitation was scant, and other species flowered sparsely. *Larrea tridentata, Ceratoides (Eurotia) lanata,* and *Ambrosia dumosa* flowered more lightly in response to the more unpredictable rains of late spring, summer, and fall. Successful fruiting did not always ensue, depending upon the quantity of rain and the species involved.

Some species, such as *Atriplex (Grayia) spinosa,* went dormant in the summer and had no reproductive responses elicited by summer rains. In the Chihuahuan, C_3 and CAM species flowering occurs mostly in spring, while C_4 species flower more in summer (Syvertsen et al., 1976). In the Sonoran, flowering of *Fouquieria splendens* seems timed to periods of pollinator availability rather than to rainfall (Waser, 1979), in contrast to leaf production.

In cool deserts, drier than average years truncated phenological development of *Atriplex confertifolia* and *Ceratoides (Eurotia) lanata,* with noncompletion of reproduction or low seed set (West and Gasto, 1978). Rains after June were generally ineffective in promoting reproduction, except for some flowering during one warm, wet August–September period. When perennials in artificial contour furrows were compared to those on unfurrowed sites, differences in reproductive development occurred (Wein and West, 1971). The furrows presumably collected more water for percolation into the soil. For some species, such as *Atriplex confertifolia,* individuals in the furrows flowered and fruited in years when nearby controls did not. Flowering occurred earlier in furrows for *A. corrugata,* but later and longer in the warm season grass *Hilaria jamesii.* All *Atriplex* species (including *A. nuttallii*) produced a greater biomass of seeds/plant when located in a furrow.

In the saguaro (*Cereus [Carnegiea] giganteus*) the occurrence of flowering in the population is lower on marginal sites; flowering there occurs largely in washes or on protected slopes, where moisture is presumably more available (Brum, 1973). The percentage of fruit set is also lower on the marginal sites. Differences in fruit production are correlated with Chihuahuan precipitation patterns in *Chilopsis linearis* (De Pree and Ludwig, 1978), *Yucca baccata* (Wallen and Ludwig, 1978), and *Yucca elata* (Campbell and Keller, 1932; Smith and Ludwig, 1976, 1978).

Fruit (and seed) production of perennials in the Mojave was 1.4 to 11 times as great as that of controls when irrigated with 50 cm water beyond the 8.5 cm precipitation the site received (Hunter et al., 1976). *Larrea tridentata* and *Lepidium fremontii* showed the lowest responses and *Sphaeralcea ambigua* the highest increase. Fruit production by winter annuals on the same Mojave site has been followed for a number of years (Turner and McBrayer, 1974; Turner, 1975, 1976). Mean production and mean precipitation for the preceding October–May are presented in table 7-3. A doubling or trebling of precipitation

TABLE 7-3.   *Fruit Production and Growing Season*
Precipitation for Winter Annuals at
Rock Valley, Nevada

Spring	Oct.–May precipitation (cm)	Winter annuals, fruits (kg/ha)
1973	23	200.5
1974	7	3.3
1975	11	5.2

Note: Data courtesy of F. Turner.

was associated with forty- to sixty-fold increases in fruit yield. Inouye et al. (unpublished) present regressions of *Erodium cicutarium* fecundity on density for watered and unwatered plots in the Sonoran.

Although absolute levels of flowering may be low in dry years, the proportion of above-ground growth committed to reproduction may be high. In *Larrea tridentata*, up to 43 percent of the above-ground production is allocated to reproductive structures in dry years, compared to 0.5 percent for well-watered individuals (Barbour et al., 1977). Taxa that are competitive equals in moist situations may have marked seed production differences under dry conditions (Friedman and Elberse, 1976).

Because seeds are such vital resources for many desert animals, more studies are needed to establish predictions of seed output from meteorological data. See, for example, the recent attempt for *Larrea* by Cunningham and Reynolds (1978). Assumptions that seed production is linearly related to precipitation (see, for example, Davidson, 1977) may not be sound with respect to year-to-year variations at one site, in light of the data in table 7-3.

In summary, desert perennials require higher water availability for germination and establishment than for persistence and growth of adults. Water requirements for reproduction are not as well understood. Establishment of a new adult in an opening in the ecosystem requires a relatively lengthy period of favorable moisture leading to infrequent episodes of recruitment into the population. This contrasts with patterns of establishment in openings in less extreme biomes.

COMMUNITY RESULTS OF SPAC INTERACTIONS

Water is the resource most often limiting plant growth in desert ecosystems; soil nitrogen may become limiting in years of extremely high precipitation (Romney et al., 1978). Plants interact with one another in ways that modify the availability of water for them. Water availability may be increased or decreased by interactions that may be intraspecific or between species.

In this section we deal both with the processes (interactions) and products (spatial patterns). Through time, these interactions contribute to the formation of spatial patterns in the vegetation. These patterns are also affected by the physical structure of the site, by plant-plant interactions with respect to other factors, and perhaps by plant interactions with animals, facts long recognized (see Livingston, 1910). Generally the role of water as mediator in interactions has been inferred without rigorous testing of its primacy. Interactions may be such that one plant directly influences the water status of the environment of another plant, or there may be indirect effects (such as allelopathy) on the capacity of the other plant to obtain or retain water.

Interactions centered around water might occur in any stage of the plant life cycle. Times of active growth are expected to show the strongest interactions. Even during germination, a seed may affect water status in soil 1 cm away from the seed surface (Dasberg, 1971). However, passive processes, such as shedding of plant parts, shading by inactive shoots, or trapping of wind-blown debris by canopies, may also be important. We will take up the process

and product of interaction for annuals and perennials including shrubs, subtrees, and stem succulents.

Annuals

From observations of competing desert annuals, Went (1973) concluded
that mortality is significant only early in the life cycle; thereafter the effect of
neighbors is one of uniform stunting and reduced seed production. In contrast,
Klikoff (1966), found mortality occurring throughout the life cycle of *Plantago
insularis* var. *fastigata*. The mortality rate was higher when moisture stress
was greater.

Juhren et al. (1956) suggested that dense canopies of annuals prevent
subsequent germination by some allelopathic interference. The fact that germination occurred in soil removed from beneath the canopy might be taken as
evidence that germination inhibition under the canopy may be caused by the
reduced red-to-far-red radiation ratio (see, for example, Taylorson and Borthwick, 1969). Tevis (1958b) was unable to show germination inhibition by a more
open annuals' canopy.

The horizontal distribution of annuals in relation to the position of shrubs
or subtrees has received much attention. In general, the biomass or density of
annuals has been shown to be greater beneath the shrub canopy than in the
intershrub spaces (Went, 1942; Muller, 1953; Muller and Muller, 1956; Mott
and McComb, 1974; Halvorson and Patten, 1975; Patten, 1978). This was not
true, though, for winter annuals at a site in the Sonoran (Thames, 1974).

Within this general pattern, individual species of perennials and annuals
exhibit differing degrees of spatial association. Some annuals do not seem to
depend on shrubs, while others, such as *Rafinesquia neomexicana*, occur essentially nowhere except under perennial canopies (Went, 1942; Muller, 1953).
Certain perennial species seem to harbor more of the shrub-dependent annuals
than do other shrubs (Went, 1942; Muller, 1953; Muller and Muller, 1956).

The mechanism for such association has usually been inferred to include
enhanced water availability under the species associated with dependent annuals. Muller (1953) and Muller and Muller (1956) argued that such shrubs have
canopies effective at trapping wind-blown debris beneath them over long average lifetimes, leading to an increased soil organic content and fine particulate
inorganic content, with consequent greater water-holding capacity. Mott and
McComb (1974) suggested that the greater depth to hardpan and higher nitrogen content (Garcia-Moya and McKell, 1970) within under-shrub mounds favored productivity of the annuals. At a Sonoran site, Patten (1978) found more
efficient use of solar radiant energy by winter annuals beneath perennial
canopies, as compared to annuals in the open.

Negative associations between shrubs and annuals have also been reported (Adams et al., 1970; Thames, 1975; Friedman et al., 1977). A Sonoran
site had greatest biomass density of summer annuals in spaces between perennials. *Larrea* canopies, for example, covered 17 percent of the site but super-
posed only 8 percent of the annuals' biomass (Thames, 1975). This was largely
due to the distribution of *Bouteloua aristidoides*, the dominant summer annual

species. Not all of the other summer annuals showed the same pattern. Likewise, different species of winter annuals exhibited nonrandom dispersion with respect to the shrubs at this same site, even though the aggregate of species did not (Thames, 1974).

Friedman et al. (1977) found biomass density of annuals to be less on north-facing slopes of the Negev Desert than on the presumably drier south-facing slopes. They attributed the reduction in annuals to allelopathic interference from *Artemisia herba-alba,* which dominates the north-facing slopes. Density of annuals was even smaller directly beneath the canopy. South-facing slopes are dominated by *Zygophyllum dumosum,* which showed no allelopathic interference with annuals.

Adams et al. (1970) found annuals negatively associated with mounds under perennials in California. The distribution of annuals was strongly correlated with water repellency of the soil in the mounds. The effect on annuals and the repellency varied among perennial species and was intensified by burning of the perennials.

Not all of the spatial variance in annual plant parameters is ascribable to differences in water availability. Differential seed predation with respect to species as well as under-canopy versus open sites also appears to be important (Beatley, 1976; Inouye et al., unpublished; Nelson and Chew, 1977).

Perennials

Interactions among perennials have largely been inferred from spatial patterns. Among the few process studies is that of Sheps (1973). She found that *Larrea tridentata* seedlings died quickly beneath adult *Larrea.* Survival and size of seedlings increased with greater distance from adults. Because supplemental watering of seedlings did not avert their death beneath adults, Sheps concluded that allelopathic interference was operating within this species (cf. Knipe and Herbel, 1966). Cable (1977b) showed that soil under *Larrea* and *Ambrosia deltoidea* dried more rapidly than it did between shrubs, but it did not become ultimately drier.

General Dispersion

Since most authors infer competition from dispersion data, we will discuss competition here. In fact, the pattern is the result of all biotic interactions among species and their responses to the physical milieu.

Spacing and pattern in plant communities have been topics of interest in ecology for several decades. Hill (1973) gives three different purposes for which analysis of pattern may be used: "(i) relating differences in local environment to differences in the vegetation; (ii) determining the approximate scale of an autogenic mosaic . . ." (iii) suggesting or checking theories about the competition and establishment of plants in the community."

Desert plant groups appear to have each of the three general dispersion patterns: clumped, random, and regular.

Random dispersion is expected in a homogeneous environment where seeds are widely dispersed by the plant and no intense competition occurs. Clumped or aggregated pattern may occur either in a heterogeneous environment or where plants reproduce vegetatively or have seeds of limited dispersal ability. Kershaw (1973) states that regular dispersion most likely results from "a high density of individuals within a uniform area, with active competition limiting both the total density over the area and at the same time the spatial distribution of an individual relative to its neighbors." Obviously in an environment where a critical commodity like water is scarce, the dispersion patterns of plants may reflect the dispersion pattern of available water.

For North American deserts, the most work done on the pattern of any species has concerned creosote bush *Larrea tridentata*. At a series of desert sites in California, Woodell et al. (1969) claimed that *Larrea* exhibited regular dispersion in low rainfall areas and clumped dispersion in higher rainfall areas, suggesting that regular spacing may have been a result of competition for water. This thesis stirred some controversy. First was an attack by Anderson (1971), who argued that regular or not, root competition for water was not likely as the cause and effect reason for the patterns. King and Woodell (1973) followed with a refutation. Barbour (1969) found a tendency toward regularity in *Larrea* in drier sites in the Mojave and Sonoran deserts as opposed to random or clumped dispersion in the more mesic Chihuahuan. Later, Barbour (1973) questioned the theory of competition for water-producing regular dispersion patterns. Recently MacMahon (Barbour et al., 1977) analyzed spatial patterns of a number of pairs of North American desert perennials and showed either regular or clumped dispersion depending on the dispersion metric employed in data analysis.

Yeaton and his coworkers (Yeaton and Cody, 1976; Yeaton et al., 1977) have looked at the dispersion pattern of perennials in a northern Mojave site and an upland Sonoran site. On the Mojave site, considering all the possible pairwise relationships of two cacti (*Opuntia acanthocarpa* and *O. ramosissima*) and a yucca (*Yucca schidigera*), the greatest neighbor distances suggest the presence of competition. Additionally, there is no difference in the degree of competition between any of the pairs. Another observation is that individuals of different species occur significantly closer together than do individuals of the same species. On another Mojave site, Wallace and Romney (1972) showed clumped dispersions among many perennial species. An analysis of all pairwise combinations of 28 species of perennials showed that 229 pairs were positively associated, 24 pairs were negatively associated, and 321 pairs were mutually exclusive.

Yeaton's studies of the Sonoran site (Yeaton et al., 1977) considered *Larrea tridentata, Ambrosia deltoidea, Opuntia fulgida, Cereus giganteus,* and *Fouquieria splendens,* which together comprise 95 percent of the individuals and 94 percent of the cover on his plots. All intraspecific nearest-neighbor data suggest competition. The interspecific data suggest that *Larrea* competes with all species except *Cereus, Ambrosia* only competes with *Larrea,* and *Cereus* competes with no other species.

From studies along a climatic gradient across the Sonoran and Mojave, Phillips (1978) concluded that for *Larrea*-dominated sites, no correlation existed between several dispersion metrics and rainfall (whether expressed as total as coefficient of variation or as seasonality). Phillips did find increasing regularity of dispersion with greater shrub size (and presumably age), suggesting competitive interactions.

Fonteyn and Mahall (1978), in an elegant field experiment with *Larrea* and *Ambrosia dumosa*, measured Ψ^{plant} in response to mechanical removal of either or both species. Plant water potential was highest when all other shrubs were cut out and lowest in nonmanipulated plots and plots where only conspecifics were cut. Removal of the other species produced Ψ^{plant} higher than that in control plots, clearly indicating that the two species were competing with each other for water. The meaning of these results for any mechanism producing the dispersion patterns Fonteyn and Mahall report is not clear, but this may be a problem arising from the metric chosen for dispersion.

Such complex interactions are not unexpected. The factors allowing overlap of competing species include, among other things, differences in the vertical distribution of roots (see figure 7-4; Solbrig et al., 1977; and Yeaton et al., 1977).

Several relationships other than exploitation competition contribute to dispersion patterns of desert plants. On a local scale, allelopathy might be important, although Barbour (1973) questions the veracity of previous claims (see, for example, Went, 1955).

Competition can be the biotic interaction accounting for pattern. Several other factors appear to be important, at least for North American deserts. These include the nurse-plant phenomenon, changes in vegetation associated with local scale microtopography (and, by inference, water relations), and the relationship of plants to broader topographic patterns such as bajadas, with their concomitant variation in water availability and perhaps safe sites (sensu Harper, 1977, p. 112) for seed germination.

Nurse Plants

Many desert perennials, and most notably cacti, begin their lives under the canopies of other species (see, for example, Brum, 1973; Humphrey, 1974; McDonough, 1963; Steenberg and Lowe, 1976, 1977; Turner et al., 1966). This phenomenon, referred to as nurse plants, appears to be instrumental in a cyclical species replacement between *Larrea* and *Opuntia leptocaulis* in the northern Chihuahuan (Yeaton, 1978). Some plants may establish under conspecifics (see, for example, Sherbrooke, 1977). Not all perennials gain advantage through nurse plant relationships. For example, *Prosopis juliflora* and *Cercidium microphyllum* seedlings are not favored through association with shrubs (Paulsen, 1950; Shreve, 1911). Nurse plant effects (figure 7-5) may be caused by the additional organic matter under the crowns of nurse plants, their shade, or perhaps other characteristics (Barth and Klemmedson, 1978; Tiedemann and Klemmedson, 1973a, b; West and Skujins, 1978). Most such correlations are best interpreted as the cause and effect change, in a positive direction, of the water balance of the nursed species. An exception would be the apparent stimulating effect of desert litter (and included fungi) on desert plant growth

FIGURE 7-5.   *The nurse-plant phenomenon. Several young saguaros* (Cereus giganteus) *on the left and one organpipe cactus* (Cereus thurberi) *growing in the shade of a paloverde* (Cercidium microphyllum) *at Organ Pipe Cactus National Monument, Arizona.*

despite moisture content (Sheps, 1973). Recently, Steenberg and Lowe (1976, 1977) demonstrated that the saguaros under the cover of paloverde (*Cercidium*) survived freezing periods more often than individuals in the open did, suggesting a strong amelioration of the thermal environment of the young plants beneath the nurse's canopy.

A result of the occurrence of small plants under larger ones is that aerial photographic sampling of desert vegetation that contains subtrees seriously underestimates shrub cover. Table 7-4 compares data from an enumerated hectare of Sonoran Desert near Maricopa, Arizona, to estimates derived from aerial photography. Notice there is no error for the subtree *Cercidium* or large cacti *Cereus*, forms not occurring under other species on this plot.

Effects of Microtopography

Local variations in topographic relief, less than a few centimeters in difference, may, in a water-insufficient environment, drive the dispersion pattern of plants. Aerial photographs show that plants frequently cluster along microrelief channels (figure 7-6). In fact the species-species dispersion relationships may

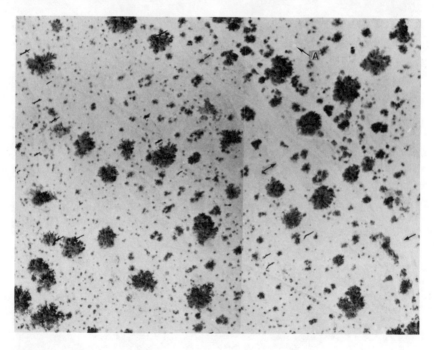

FIGURE 7-6. *Aerial photograph of a one hectare, upper bajada, Sonoran Desert site near Maricopa, Arizona. Enumeration of plants can be found in Barbour et al. (1977) and table 7-4. Details of the bajada are presented in Phillips and MacMahon (1978). The three arrows in the right half of the photo point out microrelief washes. The arrow in the upper right marked A points to a 1 x 1 meter square for size calibration.*

TABLE 7-4. *Comparison of Aerial Photography Estimates to the Actual Values of Density and Dominance of an Enumerated Hectare of Sonoran Desert Vegetation near Maricopa, Arizona*

Species	Density (ind/ha)			Dominance (m²/ha)		
	Actual	Photo	% Error	Actual	Photo	% Error
Larrea tridentata	429.63	292.59	−31.9	713.14	569.22	−20.18
Encelia farinosa	370.38	120.36	−67.5	231.13	84.54	−63.43
Ambrosia dumosa	444.43	335.19	−24.58	237.12	138.01	−41.8
Cercidium microphyllum	27.77	27.77	—	632.43	859.89	+35.96
Hymenoclea monogyra	185.18	114.80	−38.0	134.14	88.3	−34.17
Lycium andersonii	105.56	64.81	−38.6	142.33	136.60	− 4.03
Ambrosia deltoidea	111.12	74.08	−33.3	27.33	21.98	−19.58
Opuntia acanthocarpa	33.33	27.77	−16.68	61.78	31.03	−49.78
Sphaeralcea sp.	3.71	3.71	—	2.26	2.69	+19.10
Trixis californica	1.85	1.85	—	2.65	0.52	−80.25
Cereus giganteus	7.41	7.41	—	0.65	0.41	−37.39

significantly change over the surface of a square hectare in ways that suggest plant response to microtopographic relief and its concomitant effect on soil water availability (figures 7-7 and 7-8), as well as local competitive interactions, are complex and may significantly alter interpretation of the very nature of intraspecies or interspecies interactions. Gulmon and Mooney (1977) and Sánchez-Diaz and Mooney (1979), in studies of *Atriplex hymenelytra* and *Tidestromia oblongifolia,* found many characteristics that segregated these species in the extremely arid sites studied in Death Valley. At least some segregation was due to microsite differences, which may be more important than interspecific competition for this species pair.

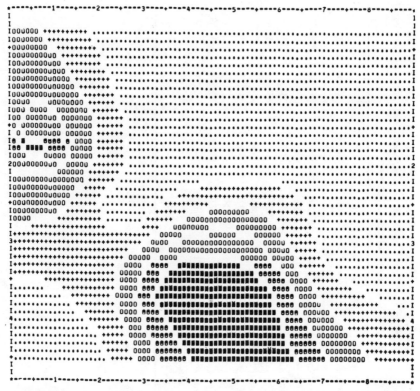

FIGURE 7-7. *A computer-generated, interpolation smoothed representation of nearest-neighbor distances of* Larrea *to* Larrea *on the enumerated site shown in figure 7-6. The darker the overprinting, the closer the neighbors. Measurements of the distance from every* Larrea *to the closer* Larrea *in each of four quadrants were obtained, averaged, and plotted as a data point. These points are then the basis used to draw isophenes of mean nearest-neighbor distances, the maximum and minimum neighbor distances are used as end points, and all values between these are divided into five equal interval categories. In this case, and in figure 7-8, the darkest overprint areas, when analyzed alone, show significant contagion; the lightest overprint area shows random dispersion (measures are described in Barbour et al., 1977).*

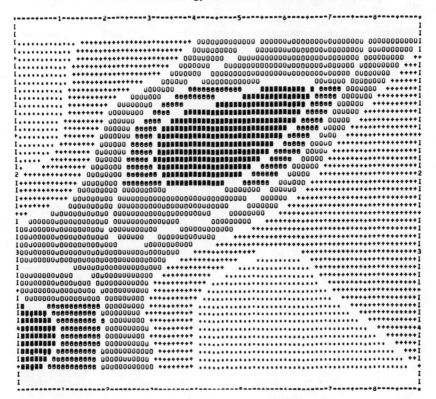

FIGURE 7-8. *Same as figure 7-7 but for* Larrea-Cercidium *nearest-neighbor distances.*

Not all local variation in soil moisture properties can be inferred from microtopography. Wagenet and Jurinak (1978) discovered great horizontal heterogeneity in soluble salt content (and thus Ψ_s) within a topographically uniform desert shale substrate. Man-made structures such as roads and power lines may enhance local moisture availability (Johnson et al., 1975; Vasek et al., 1975b).

Working with somewhat larger topographic variation, Freeman et al. (1976) found a greater staminate/pistillate population ratio for the dioecious *Atriplex confertifolia* on drier sites as compared to moister sites a few meters away. These workers presented several hypotheses that could account for such distributions.

Distribution along Bajadas

A feature of much of the basin and range physiographic province of North America (the site of North American deserts) (MacMahon, 1979) is the presence of sloping, coalesced alluvial fans emanating from the adjacent mountain ranges (bajadas). These features are characterized by particle sorting such that the upper bajada soils are coarse textured and the lower bajadas and plains are fine textured. Trends of vegetation change along these soil coarseness gradients (and presumably water availability gradients) are documented (Barbour and Diaz, 1973; Livingston, 1910; Mutz, 1979; Niering et al., 1963; Phillips and MacMahon, 1978; Stein and Ludwig, 1979; Whittaker et al., 1968; and Yang and Lowe, 1956) (figures 7-9 and 7-10).

An example of such species changes is presented in figure 7-11. Phillips and MacMahon (1978) present data on soil particle size changes and salinity changes along the same bajada. There is strong inferential reason to believe that water availability is the driving variable in this sequence of species changes along the topographic gradient. MacMahon (1979) further summarizes bajada trends for North American deserts. Solbrig and Orians (1977) and Solbrig et al. (1977) develop general theories about desert plant communities that relate to responses to conditions on bajadas.

The general pattern along the bajada, from top (coarse soil) to the bottom, is one of decreasing perennials species density and life form diversity (see figure 7-11). Creosote bush (*Larrea*) increases in cover from very low values (tops) to over 60 percent in nonsaline flats (Barbour et al., 1977). Solbrig et al. (1977) give values of 118 shrubs per hectare, composed of two species on the flats; the upper bajada had over 1,000 shrubs and 20 species per hectare. Phillips and MacMahon (1978) found similar trends; however, the lower parts of their bajada were somewhat saline. Klikoff (1967) attributes such changes to differences in water stress patterns. The fine soils of lower bajadas retain water in their upper layers but do not permit percolation to any great depth. Coarse soils permit greater percolation due to less water retention in upper layers. Thus annuals, with their shallow rooting strategies, are more abundant in the flats or where they occur under the moderate shade of shrubs with open canopies (for example, *Cercidium* and *Larrea*) (Halvorson and Patten, 1975; Solbrig et al., 1977). Careful scrutiny of root profile diagrams (figure 7-4) suggests that perennials' roots do not occupy the upper 5 to 10 cm of soil. Thus annuals, or shallow-rooted perennials (cacti) when present and removing water, probably do not interfere with perennials. The ephemeral nature of annuals permits use of a transient water source since these same fine-textured soils lose water due to evaporation at a rate higher than coarse soils (Alizai and Hulbert, 1970). Recently general theory has been proposed that accounts for the increased moisture retention of soils underlaid by coarse-textured layers, the condition existing on middle to upper bajadas (Clothier et al., 1977).

Miscellaneous

Stark and Love (1969) suggest that surface stones may act as condensation loci for water vapor moving from lower soil horizons under appropriate temperature regimes. They cite the concentration of roots of Mojave perennials (such as *Atriplex hymenelytra* and *Peucephyllum schottii*) under such stones as evidence for the biological effects of this phenomenon. Our observations in the Sonoran of blue-green algae beneath translucent stones (such as quartz) indi-

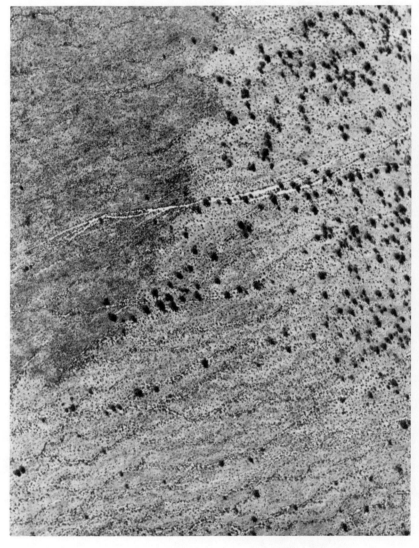

FIGURE 7-9. *Aerial view of an upper bajada near Maricopa, Arizona, where subtrees (Cercidium and Olneya) drop out. The site is that sampled by Phillips and MacMahon (1978). The bajada drops from the top of the photo to the bottom.*

FIGURE 7-10. *Aerial view of the lower part of a bajada near Maricopa, Arizona (see figure 7-9). Mid-bajada is in the upper right; the flat flood plain, dominated by mesquite (Prosopis), is on the lower left. Note that on the bajada, plants are clearly clumped along channels of various sizes; subtrees follow the larger channels.*

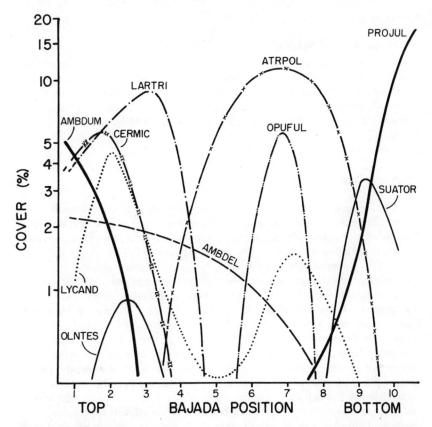

FIGURE 7-11. *Change in plant community species composition (measured as % cover) along a 5 km bajada near Maricopa, Arizona. Values are means derived from two parallel transects. Species with neither transect cover value over 1 percent are omitted. Curves are smoothed for illustrative purposes. Actual values and values of soil particle size and soil salinity can be found in Phillips and MacMahon (1978). AMBDEL:* Ambrosia deltiodea; *AMBDUM:* Ambrosia dumosa; *ATRPOL:* Atriplex polycarpa; *CERMIC:* Cercidium microphyllum; *LARTRI:* Larrea tridentata; *LYCAND:* Lycium andersonii; *OLNTES:* Olneya tesota; *OPUFUL:* Opuntia fulgida; *PROJUL:* Prosopis juliflora; *SUATOR:* Suaeda torreyana.*

cate that the possible nitrogen fixation by such algae, as well as temperature differences, may also figure in such rooting patterns.

A conspicuous feature of many desert soils is the presence of a petrocalcic layer termed *caliche,* which affects individual plant water relations complexly (Cunningham and Burk, 1973). Such interactions may have ecosystem-wide consequences (see, for example, Burk and Dick-Peddie, 1973). For a more detailed treatment, see MacMahon (1979) and MacMahon and Wagner (in press).

Effects of Washes

Plants requiring more than the generally available amounts of moisture in desert areas frequently aggregate along washes (for example, *Fallugia paradoxa* and *Prosopis juliflora*) (figure 7-10). This is simply the exaggerated effects of the same processes discussed previously concerning microsite differences. Shrub height and width generally increased with higher Ψ^{soil} along a Chihuahuan wash, while plant density decreased (Balding and Cunningham, 1974).

Temporal Changes

To this point we have dealt with changes in desert ecosystems through space. Changes through time also occur and may be in part water mediated. Conspicuous changes have occurred over geological time; for general reviews see Axelrod (1950) and Van Devender and Spaulding (1979). Wells and Hunziker (1976) examined the origins of the *Larrea*-dominated areas.

Shorter-term changes may be mediated by climate or other factors, such as human activities (see, for example, Hastings and Turner, 1965; Shreve and Hinckley, 1937; Niering et al., 1963). One particular process of vegetation change over relatively short intervals is the successional recovery of plant cover following disturbance. Because of the extreme nature of desert environments, classical succession may not occur; that is, an orderly progression of species composition resulting in a climax may not ensue. Rather, the climax species, being adapted to those extremes, colonizes the openings without prior occupation by "subclimax" species. See MacMahon (1979) and MacMahon and Wagner (in press) for reviews of North American desert succession. Site-to-site variation in water availability may affect the rate or obviousness of such vegetation change. See, for example, Vasek et al. (1975a).

Plant Interactions with Other Community Components

We have discussed at some length plant-plant interactions at the community level. A perusal of the right side of figure 7-1 suggests that there are many other community interactions that could be addressed. Some of these have been reviewed recently (MacMahon, 1979), but we will point out a few here. Throughout this chapter we have ignored the reciprocal interactions of plants with soil. Presence of petrocalcic horizons, gypsum (see, for example, Powell and Turner, 1977), and other indurated horizons obviously have significant effects on plant communities. Conversely plants modify the soil properties. Many references to these interactions can be found in MacMahon (1979) and MacMahon and Wagner (in press).

Plant species density (number of species per area) or diversity (H') depends in part on moisture in deserts (Barbour et al., 1977; Billings, 1949; Branson et al., 1967; Johnson, 1976; Muller, 1939, 1947; Mulroy and Rundel, 1977; Nash et al., 1977; Noy-Meir, 1973; Shreve and Wiggins, 1964; Solbrig and

Orians, 1977; Solbrig et al., 1977; Wittaker and Niering, 1964, 1965; Yang and Lowe, 1956). Life forms may also vary along gradients of water availability. Whole strategy suites of plants may differ in correlation to the annual dispersion pattern of rainfall (Simpson, 1977a). All of these plant community characteristics can directly affect the diversity and behavior of the animal component of the community, including lizards (Pianka, 1977), birds (Tomoff, 1974), mammals (Brown, 1975), and insects (Davidson, 1977; Moldenke, 1976; Otte, 1976; Spellenberg and Delson, 1977).

Because all of these taxa do not respond to water availability in the same ways, their competitive relationships may shift along climatic gradients. Such shifts may be manifested for strong competitors exhibiting geographical complementarity (for ants and rodents, see Brown and Davidson, 1977; for other vertebrates, see Schall and Pianka, 1978).

None of this even alludes to the trophic interactions of plants and animals, relationships that are well studied (see, for example, Beatley, 1976) and the basis of a recent general theory (Fretwell, 1977). White (1976, 1978) proposes that plant water status, through effects on the proportions of different nitrogenous compounds, markedly modifies the quality of the plant as food for herbivores. Hypothesized lower palatability of C_4 versus C_3 species (Caswell et al., 1973) has not been definitely validated (Boutton et al., 1978). Both free and metabolic water obtained from plants may be an important resource for desert animals (see, for example, Edney, 1974; Ghobrial and Nour, 1975; Schmidt-Nielsen, 1964).

Very little has been published on plant pathogens in desert ecosystems. Based on experience elsewhere, the water status of the host plant, soil, or atmosphere would be expected to play an important role in plant interactions with parasitic microbes (Kozlowski, 1978). Boyle (1949) concluded that a saguaro disease incited by a bacterium, *Erwinia carnegieana*, was not related to precipitation amount. Diseases occluding the xylem, such as the *Fusarium* infections of senita, *Cereus (Lophocereus) schottii*, reported by McLaughlin (1934), could adversely change plant water relations. Turning to vascular parasites, it is our subjective impression that dodder (*Cuscuta denticulata*) is more abundant in wetter than average years in the Mojave. In the foggy deserts of Baja California, *Cuscuta veatchii* often covers plants of *Bursera* spp. and *Pachycormus* spp., especially during very rainy periods (Humphrey, 1974, p. 161; Shreve and Wiggins, 1964).

The epiphyte *Tillandsia recurvata* (heno pequeño) occurs commonly on *Fouquieria diguetii, F. (Idria) columnaris, Cereus (Pachycereus) pringlei, Pachycormus discolor,* and *Yucca valida* in the Vizcaino region of Baja (Humphrey, 1974). This epiphytism, usually associated with high rainfall areas, is undoubtedly due to the frequent fog of this area.

Water is the driving variable of importance for almost all contemporary desert community interactions and probably the basis of desert community evolution in the past (Wells and Hunziker, 1976; see MacMahon, 1979, for a review). The unpredictable changes in water abundance are so important that general models treating desert systems as pulse-reserve systems have been developed (Noy-Meir, 1973, 1974). This paradigm suggests that the whole system turns on with water, stores material for the dry interval, and then shuts down until the next water event. The strong link between erratic precipitation and vegetation phenology makes it more difficult to optimize timing of human use of deserts, including livestock grazing (West and Gasto, 1978).

Directional changes through time in desert ecosystems are probably often linked to some alteration of water regimes (Hastings and Turner, 1965). Even in contemporary systems, water is the main ecosystem influent, with the possible exception of man's chemicals (Wood and Nash, 1976) and physical impacts (Vollmer et al., 1976).

One hopes that in the future we will be able to use water as an input variable to an ecosystem model that will predict the vagaries of desert dynamics. We seem far from this lofty goal, though useful generalizations can be made (Noy-Meir, 1973, 1974; Solbrig and Orians, 1977). At the organismal level, several interesting modeling attempts have recently appeared (Cunningham and Reynolds, 1978; Orians and Solbrig, 1977).

Acknowledgments

We thank Martyn Caldwell, Kathryn Mutz, and Herman Wiebe for their comments on an earlier version of the manuscript. Constance V. Braun, Donald L. Phillips, Fred Turner, and John Thames provided and/or helped to collect some data used herein. Bette Peitersen was an exceptional help. Linda Finchum typed all drafts of the manuscript. This work was made possible, in part, by the US/IBP Desert Biome (NSF Grant GB-32139).

REFERENCES

Ackerman, T. L., and S. A. Bamberg. 1974. Phenological studies in the Mojave Desert at Rock Valley (Nevada Test Site), pp. 215–226. In H. Lieth (ed.), *Phenology and Seasonality Modelling.* Springer-Verlag, New York.

Adams, J. A., F. T. Bingham, M. R. Kaufmann, G. J. Hoffman, and D. M. Yermanos. 1978. Responses of stomata and water, osmotic, and turgor potentials of jojoba to water and salt stress. *Agron. J.* **70:**381–387.

Adams, J. A., H. B. Johnson, F. T. Bingham, and D. M. Yermanos. 1977. Gaseous exchange of *Simmondsia chinensis* (jojoba) measured with a double isotope porometer and related to water stress, salt stress and nitrogen deficiency. *Crop Sci.* **17:**11–15.

Adams, M. S., and B. R. Strain. 1968. Photosynthesis in stems and leaves of *Cercidium floridum:* spring and summer diurnal field response and relation to temperature. *Oecol. Plant.* **3:**285–297.

Adams, M. S., and B. R. Strain. 1969. Seasonal photosynthetic rates in stems of *Cercidium floridum* Benth. *Photosynthetica* **3:**55–62.

Adams, M. S., B. R. Strain, and I. P. Ting. 1967. Photosynthesis in chlorophyllous stem tissue and leaves of *Cercidium floridum:* accumulation and distribution of ^{14}C from $^{14}CO_2$. *Plant Physiol.* **42:**1797–1799.

Adams, S., B. R. Strain, and M. S. Adams. 1970. Water-repellent soils, fire, and annual plant cover in a desert scrub community of southeastern California. *Ecology* **51:**696–700.

Al-Ani, H. A., B. R. Strain, and H. A. Mooney. 1972. The physiological ecology of diverse populations of the desert shrub *Simmondsia chinensis*. *J. Ecol.* **60**:41–57.

Alcorn, S. M., and E. B. Kurtz. 1959. Some factors affecting the germination of seed of the saguaro cactus (*Carnegia gigantea*). *Amer. J. Bot.* **46**:526–529.

Alizai, H. U., and L. C. Hulbert. 1970. Effects of soil texture on evaporative loss and available water in semi-arid climates. *Soil Sci.* **110**:328–332.

Alpert, P. 1979. Desiccation of desert mosses following a summer rainstorm. *Bryologist* **82**:65–71.

Anderson, D. J. 1971. Pattern in desert perennials. *J. Ecol.* **59**:555–560.

Arndt, W. 1965. The impedance of soil seals and the forces of emerging seedlings. *Aust. J. Soil Res.* **3**:55–68.

Aspinall, D., and I. Husain. 1970. The inhibition of flowering by water stress. *Aust. J. Biol. Sci.* **23**:925–936.

Axelrod, D. I. 1950. Evolution of desert vegetation in western North America. *Carnegie Inst. Wash. Publ.* **590**:215–306.

Babu, V. R., and F. W. Went. 1978. The effect of dew on plant water balance in desert shrubs. *Ann. Arid Zone* **17**:1–11.

Baker, H. G. 1972. Seed weight in relation to environmental conditions in California. *Ecology* **53**:997–1010.

Balding, F. R., and G. L. Cunningham. 1974. The influence of soil water potential on the perennial vegetation of a desert arroyo. Southwest. *Natur.* **19**:241–248.

Bamberg, S. A., G. E. Kleinkopf, A. Wallace, and A. Vollmer. 1975. Comparative photosynthetic production of Mojave Desert shrubs. *Ecology* **56**:732–736.

Bamberg, S. A., A. T. Vollmer, G. E. Kleinkopf, and T. L. Ackerman. 1976. A comparison of seasonal primary productivity of Mojave desert shrubs during wet and dry years. *Am. Midl. Natur.* **95**:398–405.

Barbour, M. G. 1968. Germination requirements of the desert shrub *Larrea divaricata*. *Ecology* **49**:915–923.

Barbour, M. G. 1969. Age and space distribution of the desert shrub *Larrea divaricata*. *Ecology* **50**:679–685.

Barbour, M. G. 1973. Desert dogma reexamined: root/shoot productivity and plant spacing. *Am. Midl. Natur.* **89**:41–57.

Barbour, M. G., G. Cunningham, W. C. Oechel, and S. A. Bamberg. 1977. Growth and development, form and function, pp. 48–91. In T. J. Mabry, J. H. Hunziker, and D. R. Di Feo, Jr. (eds.), *Creosote Bush: Biology and Chemistry of* Larrea *in New World Deserts*. US/IBP Synthesis Series, vol. 6. Dowden, Hutchinson and Ross, Stroudsburg, Pa.

Barbour, M. G., and D. V. Diaz. 1973. *Larrea* plant communities on bajada and moisture gradients in the United States and Argentina. *Vegetatio* **28**:335–352.

Barbour, M. G., J. A. MacMahon, S. A. Bamberg, and J. A. Ludwig. 1977. The structure and distribution of *Larrea* communities, pp. 227–251. In T. J. Mabry, J. H. Hunziker, and D. R. Di Feo, Jr. (eds.), *Creosote Bush: Biology and Chemistry of* Larrea *in New World Deserts*. US/IBP Synthesis Series, vol. 6. Dowden, Hutchinson and Ross, Stroudsburg, Pa.

Barth, R. C., and J. O. Klemmedson. 1978. Shrub-induced spatial patterns of dry matter, nitrogen, and organic carbon. *Soil Sci. Soc. Am. J.* **42**:804–809.

Beatley, J. C. 1970. Perennation in *Astragalus lentiginosus* and *Tridens pulchellus* in relation to rainfall. *Madroño* **20**:326–332.

Beatley, J. C. 1974a. Effects of rainfall and temperature on the distribution and behavior of *Larrea tridentata* in the Mojave Desert of Nevada. *Ecology* **55**:245–261.

Beatley, J. C. 1974b. Phenological events and their environmental triggers in Mojave Desert ecosystems. *Ecology* **55**:856–863.

Beatley, J. C. 1975. Climate and vegetation pattern across the Mojave/Great Basin desert transition of southern Nevada. *Am. Midl. Natur.* **93**:53–70.

Beatley, J. C. 1976. Rainfall and fluctuating plant populations in relation to distributions and numbers of desert rodents in southern Nevada. *Oecologia* **24**:21–42.

Bewley, J. D. 1979. Physiological aspects of desiccation tolerance. *Ann. Rev. Plant Physiol.* **30**:195–238.

Billings, W. D. 1949. The shadscale vegetation zone of Nevada and eastern California in relation to climate and soils. *Am. Midl. Natur.* **42**:87–109.

Björkman, O., R. W. Pearcy, A. T. Harrison, and H. Mooney. 1972. Photosynthetic adaptations to high temperatures: a field study in Death Valley, California. *Science* **175**:786–789.

Black, C. C., Jr. 1973. Photosynthetic carbon fixation in relation to net CO_2 uptake. *Ann. Rev. Plant Physiol.* **24**:253–286.

Boutton, T. W., G. N. Cameron, and B. N. Smith. 1978. Insect herbivory on C_3 and C_4 grasses. *Oecologia* **36**:21–32.

Boyle, A. M. 1949. Further studies of the bacterial necrosis of the giant cactus. *Phytopathology* **39**:1029–1052.

Branson, F. A., R. F. Miller, and I. S. McQueen. 1967. Geographic distribution and factors affecting the distribution of salt desert shrubs in the United States. *J. Range Manage.* **20**:287–296.

Branson, F. A., R. F. Miller, and I. S. McQueen. 1976. Moisture relationships in twelve northern desert shrub communities near Grand Junction, Colorado. *Ecology* **57**:1104–1124.

Brown, J. H. 1975. Geographical ecology of desert rodents, pp. 315–341. In M. L. Cody and J. M. Diamond (eds.), *Ecology and Evolution of Communities*. Belknap Press of Harvard Univ. Press, Cambridge, Mass.

Brown, J. H., and D. W. Davidson. 1977. Competition between seed-eating rodents and ants in desert ecosystems. *Science* **196**:880–882.

Brown, R. W., and B. P. van Haveren (eds.). 1972. *Psychrometry in Water Relations Research*. Utah State Univ., Logan, Utah.

Brum, G. D. 1973. Ecology of the saguaro (*Carnegiea gigantea*): phenology and establishment in marginal populations. *Madroño* **22**:195–204.

Burk, J. H., and D. A. Dick-Peddie. 1973. Comparative production of *Larrea divaricata* Cov. on three geomorphic surfaces in southern New Mexico. *Ecology* **54**:1094–1102.

Cable, D. R. 1977a. Seasonal use of soil water by mature velvet mesquite. *J. Range Manage.* **30**:4–11.

Cable, D. R. 1977b. Soil water changes in creosotebush and bur-sage during a dry period in southern Arizona. *J. Ariz. Acad. Sci.* **12**:15–20.

Caldwell, M. M. and L. B. Camp. 1974. Belowground productivity of two cool desert communities. *Oecologia* **17**:123–130.

Caldwell, M. M., R. S. White, R. T. Moore, and L. B. Camp. 1977. Carbon balance, productivity, and water use of cold-winter desert shrub communities dominated by C_3 and C_4 species. *Oecologia* **29**:275–300.

Campbell, G. S., and G. A. Harris. 1977. Water relations and water use patterns for *Artemisia tridentata* Nutt. in wet and dry years. *Ecology* **58**:652–659.

Campbell, R. S., and J. G. Keller. 1932. Growth and reproduction of *Yucca elata*. *Ecology* **13**:364–374.

Capon, B., and W. Van Asdall. 1967. Heat pre-treatment as a means of increasing germination of desert annual seeds. *Ecology* **48**:305–306.

Carlquist, S. 1975. *Ecological Strategies of Xylem Evolution.* Univ. California Press, Berkeley.

Caswell, H., F. Reed, S. N. Stephenson, and P. A. Werner. 1973. Photosynthetic pathways and selective herbivory: a hypothesis. *Am. Natur.* **107**:465–480.

Chatterton, N. J., and C. M. McKell. 1969. *Atriplex polycarpa*: I. Germination and growth as affected by sodium chloride in water cultures. *Agron. J.* **61**:448–450.

Clark, S. B., J. Letey, Jr., O. R. Lunt, and A. Wallace. 1974. Survival of selected desert shrubs under dry soil conditions. *Calif. Agri.* August 1974:14–15.

Clothier, B. E., D. R. Scotter, and J. P. Kerr. 1977. Water retention in soil underlain by a coarse-textured layer: theory and a field application. *Soil Sci.* **123**:392–399.

Collis-George, N., and J. Williams. 1968. Comparison of the effects of soil matric potential and isotropic effective stress on the germination of *Lactuca sativa*. *Aust. J. Soil Res.* **6**:179–192.

Cornelius, D. R., and L. O. Hylton. 1969. Influence of temperature and leachate on germination of *Atriplex polycarpa*. *Agron. J.* **61**:209–211.

Cronin, E. H. 1965. *Ecological and Physiological Factors Influencing Chemical Control of Halogeton glomeratus.* U.S. Dept. Agr., Agr. Res. Serv. Tech. Bull. No. 1325.

Cunningham, G. L., and J. H. Burk. 1973. The effect of carbonate deposition layers ("caliche") on the water status of *Larrea divaricata*. *Am. Midl. Nat.* **90**:474–480.

Cunningham, G. L., and J. F. Reynolds. 1978. A simulation model of primary production and carbon allocation in the creosotebush (*Larrea tridentata* [DC] Cov.). *Ecology* **59**:37–52.

Cunningham, G. L., and B. R. Strain. 1969. An ecological significance of seasonal leaf variability in a desert shrub. *Ecology* **50**:400–408.

Dasberg, S. 1971. Soil water movement to germinating seeds. *J. Exp. Bot.* **22**:999–1008.

Daubenmire, R. F., and H. E. Charter. 1942. Behavior of woody desert legumes at the wilting percentage of the soil. *Bot. Gaz.* **103**:762–770.

Davidson, D. W. 1977. Species diversity and community organization in desert seed-eating ants. *Ecology* **58**:711–724.

De Pree, E., and J. A. Ludwig. 1978. Vegetative and reproductive growth patterns in desert willow [*Chilopsis linearis* (Cav.) Sweet]. *Southwest. Natur.* **23**:239–246.

De Puit, E. J., and M. M. Caldwell. 1973. Seasonal pattern of net photosynthesis of *Artemisia tridentata*. *Am. J. Bot.* **60**:426–435.

De Puit, E. J., and M. M. Caldwell. 1975a. Gas exchange of three cool semidesert species in relation to temperature and water stress. *J. Ecol.* **63**:835–858.

De Puit, E. J., and M. M. Caldwell. 1975b. Stem and leaf gas exchange of two arid land shrubs. *Am. J. Bot.* **62**:954–961.

Detling, J. K., and L. G. Klikoff. 1973. Physiological response to moisture stress as a factor in halophyte distribution. *Am. Midl. Natur.* **90**:307–318.

Dittmer, H. J. 1969. Characteristics of the roots of some xerophytes, pp. 231–238. In C. C. Hoff and M. L. Riedesel (eds.), *Physiological Systems in Semiarid Environments*. Univ. New Mexico Press, Albuquerque.

Doliner, L. H., and P. A. Jolliffe. 1979. Ecological evidence concerning the adaptive significance of the C_4 dicarboxylic acid pathway of photosynthesis. *Oecologia* **38**:23–34.

Dwyer, D. D., and H. C. De Garmo. 1970. Greenhouse productivity and water-use efficiency of selected desert shrubs and grasses under four soil-moisture levels. *New Mex. St. Univ. Agr. Exper. Sta. Bull.* **570**:1–15.

Dwyer, D. D., and K. Wolde-Yohannis. 1972. Germination, emergence, water use and production of russian thistle. *Agron. J.* **64**:52–55.

Edney, E. B. 1974. Desert arthropods, pp. 311–384. In G. W. Brown, Jr. (ed.), *Desert Biology*, vol. II. Academic Press, New York.

Ehleringer, J., O. Björkman, and H. A. Mooney. 1976. Leaf pubescence: Effects on absorptance and photosynthesis in a desert shrub. *Science* **192**:376–377.

Ehleringer, J., H. A. Mooney, and J. A. Berry. 1979. Photosynthesis and microclimate of *Camissonia claviformis*, a desert winter annual. *Ecology* **60**:280–286.

Ehrler, W. L. 1969. Daytime stomatal closure in *Agave americana* as related to enhanced water-use efficiency, pp. 239–247. In C. C. Hoff and M. L. Riedesel (eds.), *Physiological Systems in Semiarid Environments*. Univ. New Mexico Press, Albuquerque.

Ehrler, W. L. 1975. Environmental and plant factors influencing transpiration of desert plants, pp. 52–66. In W. F. Hadley (ed.), *Environmental Physiology of Desert Organisms*. Dowden, Hutchinson, and Ross, Stroudsburg, Pa.

Eickmeier, W. G. 1978. Photosynthetic pathway distributions along an aridity gradient in Big Bend National Park, and implications for enhanced resource partitioning. *Photosynthetica* **12**:290–297.

Eickmeier, W. G. 1979a. Eco-physiological differences between high and low elevation CAM species in Big Bend National Park, Texas. *Am. Midl. Natur.* **101**:118–126.

Eickmeier, W. G. 1979b. Photosynthetic recovery in the resurrection plant

Selaginella lepidophylla after wetting. *Oecologia* **39**:93–106.

Eickmeier, W. G., and M.S. Adams. 1978. Gas exchange in *Agave lecheguilla* Torr. (Agavaceae) and its ecological implications. *Southwest. Natur.* **23**:473–486.

Eickmeier, W. G., and M. M. Bender. 1976. Carbon isotope ratios of Crassulacean Acid Metabolism species in relation to climate and phytosociology. *Oecologia* **25**:341–347.

Fernandez, O. A., and M. M. Caldwell. 1975. Phenology and dynamics of root growth of three cool semi-desert shrubs under field conditions. *J. Ecol.* **63**:703–714.

Fischer, R. A., and N. C. Turner. 1978. Plant productivity in the arid and semiarid zones. *Ann. Rev. Plant Physiol.* **29**:277–317.

Fonteyn, P. J., and B. E. Mahall. 1978. Competition among desert perennials. *Nature* **275**:544–545.

Freeman, C. E. 1973a. Germination responses of a Texas population of ocotillo (*Fouquieria splendens* Engelm.) to constant temperature, water stress, pH and salinity. *Am. Midl. Nat.* **89**:252–256.

Freeman, C. E. 1973b. Some germination responses of lechuguilla (*Agave lecheguilla* Torr.). *Southwest. Natur.* **18**:125–134.

Freeman, C. E. 1975. Germination responses of a New Mexico population of Parry agave (*Agave parryi* Engelm. var. *parryi*) to constant temperature, water stress, and pH. *Southwest. Natur.* **20**:69–74.

Freeman, C. E., R. S. Tiffany, and W. H. Reid. 1977. Germination responses of *Agave lecheguilla*, *A. parryi*, and *Fouquieria splendens*. *Southwest. Natur.* **22**:195–204.

Freeman, D. C., L. G. Klikoff, and K. T. Harper. 1976. Differential resource utilization by the sexes of dioecious plants. *Science* **193**:597–599.

Frelich, J. R., E. H. Jensen, and R. O. Gifford. 1973. Effect of crust rigidity and osmotic potential on emergence of six grass species. *Agron. J.* **65**:26–29.

Fretwell, S. D. 1977. The regulation of plant communities by food chains exploiting them. *Persp. Biol. Med.* **20**:169–185.

Friedman, J., and W. T. Elberse. 1976. Competition between two desert varieties of *Medicago laciniata* (L.) Mill. under controlled conditions. *Oecologia* **22**:321–339.

Friedman, J., G. Orshan, and Y. Ziger-Cfir. 1977. Suppression of annuals by *Artemisia herba-alba* in the Negev Desert of Israel. *J. Ecol.* **65**:413–426.

Gaff, D. F. 1977. Desiccation tolerant vascular plants of southern Africa. *Oecologia* **31**:95–109.

Gaff, D. F., and N. D. Hallam. 1974. Resurrecting desiccated plants. *Roy. Soc. N. Z. Bull.* **12**:389–393.

Garcia-Moya, E., and C. M. McKell. 1970. Contributions of shrubs to the nitrogen economy of a desert-wash plant community. *Ecology* **51**:81–88.

Ghobrial, L. I., and T. A. Nour. 1975. The physiological adaptations of desert rodents, pp. 413–444. In I. Prakash and P. K. Ghosh (eds.), *Rodents in Desert Environments*. Dr. W. Junk, The Hague.

Gleason, H. A. 1939. The individualistic concept of the plant association. *Am. Midl. Natur.* **21**:92–110.

Glendening, G. F. 1941. Development of seedlings of *Heteropogon contortus* as related to soil moisture and competition. *Bot. Gaz.* **102**:684–698.

Gulmon, S. L., and H. A. Mooney. 1977. Spatial and temporal relationships between two desert shrubs, *Atriplex hymenelytra* and *Tidestromia oblongifolia* in Death Valley, California. *J. Ecol.* **65**:831–838.

Hadas, A., and D. Russo. 1974. Water uptake by seeds as affected by water stress, capillary conductivity, and seed-soil water contact. I. Experimental study. *Agron. J.* **66**:643–647.

Halvorson, W. T., and D. T. Patten. 1974. Seasonal water potential changes in Sonoran Desert shrubs in relation to topography. *Ecology* **55**:173–177.

Halvorson, W. T., and D. T. Patten. 1975. Productivity and flowering of winter ephemerals in relation to Sonoran Desert shrubs. *Am. Midl. Nat.* **93**:311–319.

Hanscom, Z., III, and I. P. Ting. 1977. Physiological responses to irrigation in *Opuntia basilaris*. *Bot. Gaz.* **138**:159–167.

Hanscom, Z., III, and I. P. Ting. 1978. Responses of succulents to plant water stress. *Pl. Physiol.* **61**:327–330.

Harper, J. L. 1977. *Population Biology of Plants*. Academic Press, New York.

Hartsock, T. L., and P. S. Nobel. 1976. Watering converts a CAM plant to daytime CO_2 uptake. *Nature* **262**:574–576.

Hastings, J. R., and S. M. Alcorn. 1961. Physical determinations of growth and age in the giant cactus. *J. Ariz. Acad. Sci.* **2**:32–39.

Hastings, J. R., and R. M. Turner. 1965. *The Changing Mile*. Univ. Ariz. Press, Tucson.

Hegarty, T. W. 1978. The physiology of seed hydration and dehydration, and the relation between water stress and the control of germination: A review. *Plant, Cell, Environ.* **1**:101–119.

Hegarty, T. W., and H. A. Ross. 1978. Differential sensitivity to moisture stress of seed germination and seedling radicle growth in calabrese (*Brassica oleracea* var. *italica*) and cress (*Lepidium sativum*). *Ann. Bot.* **42**:1003–1005.

Hevly, R. H. 1963. Adaptations of cheilanthoid ferns to desert environments. *J. Ariz. Acad. Sci.* **2**:164–175.

Hill, M. O. 1973. The intensity of spatial pattern in plant communities. *J. Ecol.* **61**:225–236.

Hillel, D. 1972. Soil moisture and seed germination. pp. 65–89. In T. T. Kozlowski (ed.), *Water Deficits and Plant Growth*, vol. III. Academic Press, New York.

Hodgkinson, K. C., P. S. Johnson, and B. E. Norton. 1978. Influence of summer rainfall on root and shoot growth of a cold-winter desert shrub, *Atriplex confertifolia*. *Oecologia* **34**:353–362.

Horton, J. S., F. C. Mounts, and J. M. Kraft. 1960. *Seed Germination and Seedling Establishment of Phreatophyte Species*. U.S. Dept. Agr., Forest Service, Rocky Mtn. For. and Range Expt. Sta., Station Pap. No. 48.

Hsiao, T. C. 1973. Plant responses to water stress. *Ann. Rev. Plant Physiol.* **24**:519–570.

Humphrey, R. R. 1974. *The Boojum and Its Home*. Univ. Ariz. Press, Tucson.

Hunter, R. B., E. M. Romney, A. Wallace, H. O. Hill, T. A. Ackerman, and

J. E. Kinnear. 1976. *Responses and Interactions in Desert Plants as Influenced by Irrigation and Nitrogen Applications.* US/IBP Desert Biome Res. Memo. 76-14. Utah State Univ., Logan.

Inouye, R. S., G. S. Byers, and J. H. Brown. Unpublished manuscript. Effects of predation and competition on survivorship, fecundity, and community structure of desert annuals.

Johnson, H. B. 1975. Gas-exchange strategies in desert plants, pp. 105–120. In D. M. Gates and R. B. Schmerl (eds.), *Perspectives of Biophysical Ecology.* Springer-Verlag, New York.

Johnson, H. B. 1976. Vegetation and plant communities of southern California deserts—a functional view, pp. 125–164. In J. Latting (ed.), *Plant Communities of Southern California,* Spec. Publ. #2, Calif. Native Pl. Soc., Berkeley.

Johnson, H. B., F. C. Vasek, and T. Yonkers. 1975. Productivity, diversity and stability relationships in Mohave Desert roadside vegetation. *Bull. Torrey Bot. Club* **102**:106–115.

Juhren, M., F. W. Went, and E. Phillips. 1956. Ecology of desert plants. IV. Combined field and laboratory work on germination of annuals in the Joshua Tree National Monument, California. *Ecology* **37**:318–330.

Kaufmann, M. R. 1969. Effect of water potential on germination of lettuce, sunflower, and citrus seeds. *Can. J. Bot.* **47**:1761–1764.

Kershaw, K. A. 1973. *Quantitative and Dynamic Plant Ecology,* 2d ed. Arnold, London.

King, T. J., and S. R. J. Woodell. 1973. The causes of regular pattern in desert perennials. *J. Ecol.* **61**:761–765.

Klikoff, L. G. 1966. Competitive response to moisture stress of a winter annual of the Sonoran Desert. *Am. Midl. Natur.* **75**:383–391.

Klikoff, L. G. 1967. Moisture stress in a vegetational continuum in the Sonoran Desert. *Am. Midl. Natur.* **77**:128–137.

Klikoff, L. G., D. C. Freeman, and N. Negus. 1975. *Ecology of Cool Desert Annuals.* US/IBP Desert Biome Res. Memo. 75-12. Utah State Univ., Logan.

Kluge, M. 1976. Crassulacean acid metabolism (CAM): CO_2 and water economy, pp. 313–322. In O. L. Lange, L. Kappen, and E. O. Schulze (eds.), Ecol. Stud. 19, *Water and Plant Life.* Springer-Verlag, New York.

Kluge, M., and I. P. Ting. 1979. *Crassulacean Acid Metabolism (CAM).* Ecological Studies, Vol. 30. Springer-Verlag, New York.

Knipe, D., and C. H. Herbel. 1960. The effects of limited moisture on germination and initial growth of six grass species. *J. Range Manage.* **13**:297–302.

Knipe, D., and C. H. Herbel. 1966. Germination and growth of some semidesert grassland species treated with aqueous extract from creosote bush. *Ecology* **47**:775–781.

Knipe, O. D. 1968. Effects of moisture stress on germination of alkali sacaton, galleta, and blue grama. *J. Range Manage.* **21**:3–4.

Knipe, O. D. 1971. Effect of different osmotica on germination of alkali sacaton (*Sporobolus airoides* Torr.) at various moisture stresses. *Bot. Gaz.* **132**:109–112.

Kozlowski, T. T. 1972. Physiology of water stress, pp. 229–244. In C. M.

McKell, J. P. Blaisdell, and J. R. Goodin (eds.), *Wildland Shrubs—Their Biology and Utilization*. USDA For. Ser. Gen. Tech. Rpt. INT-1, 1972.

Kozlowski, T. T. (ed.). 1978. *Water Deficits and Plant Growth*. Vol. 5, *Water and Plant Disease*. Academic Press, New York.

Kramer, P. J. 1969. *Plant and Soil Water Relationships: A Modern Synthesis*. McGraw-Hill, New York.

Levitt, J. 1972. *Responses of Plants to Environmental Stresses*. Academic Press, New York.

Lieth, H. 1976. The use of correlation models to predict primary productivity from precipitation or evapotranspiration, pp. 392–407. In O. L. Lange, L. Kappen, and E. D. Schulze (eds.), Ecol. Stud. 19, *Water and Plant Life*. Springer-Verlag, New York.

Livingston, B. E. 1910. Relation of soil moisture to desert vegetation. *Bot. Gaz.* **50**:241–256.

Lloyd, F. E. 1905. An artificial induction of leaf formation in the ocotillo. *Torreya* **5**:175–179.

Love, L. D., and N. E. West. 1972. Plant moisture stress patterns in *Eurotia lanata* and *Atriplex confertifolia*. *Northwest Sci.* **64**:44–51.

Mabry, T. J., J. H. Hunziker, and D. R. Di Feo (eds.). 1977. *Creosote Bush: Biology and Chemistry of* Larrea *in New World Deserts*. US/IBP Synthesis Series, vol. 6. Dowden, Hutchinson and Ross, Stroudsburg, Pa.

MacDougal, D. T., and E. S. Spalding. 1910. *The Water-Balance of Succulent Plants*. Carnegie Inst. Wash. Publ. No. 141, Washington, D.C.

MacMahon, J. A. 1979. North American deserts: their floral and faunal components, pp. 21–82. In R. A. Perry and D. W. Goodall (eds.), *Arid-land Ecosystems: Structure, Functioning and Management*, Vol. 1. International Biological Programme 16, Cambridge Univ. Press, Great Britain.

MacMahon, J. A., B. E. Norton, and B. M. Capen. 1975. *Growth of Perennials in Response to Varying Moisture and Defoliation Regimes*. US/IBP Desert Biome Res. Mem. 75-14, pp. 151–155.

MacMahon, J. A., and F. H. Wagner. In press. The Mojave, Sonoran and Chihuahuan deserts of North America. In M. Evenari and I. Noy-Meir (eds.), *Hot deserts and Arid Shrublands*. Elsevier, New York.

Mallery, T. D. 1935. Changes in the osmotic value of expressed sap of leaves and twigs of *Larrea tridentata* as influenced by environmental conditions. *Ecol. Monogr.* **5**:1–35.

Mayland, H. F., and T. H. McIntosh. 1966. Availability of biologically fixed atmospheric nitrogen-15 to higher plants. *Nature* **209**:421–422.

McCleary, J. A., and K. A. Wagner. 1973. Comparative germination and early growth studies of six species of the genus *Yucca*. *Am. Midl. Nat.* **90**:503–508.

McDonough, W. T. 1963. Interspecific associations among desert plants. *Am. Midl. Natur.* **70**:291–299.

McDonough, W. T. 1975. Water potential of germinating seeds. *Bot. Gaz.* **136**:106–108.

McIntosh, R. P. 1967. The continuum concept of vegetation. *Bot. Rev.* **33**:130–173.

McLaughlin, A. M. 1934. A *Fusarium* disease of *Cereus schottii*. *Phytopathol-*

ogy **24**:495–506.

McMillan, C., and J. T. Peacock. 1964. Bud-bursting in diverse populations of mesquite (*Prosopis:* Leguminosae) under uniform conditions. *Southwest. Natur.* **9**:181–188.

Moldenke, A. R. 1976. California pollination ecology and vegetation types. *Phytologia* **34**:305–361.

Mooney, H. A., and B. R. Strain. 1964. Bark photosynthesis in ocotillo. *Madroño* **17**:230–233.

Mooney, H. A., O. Björkman, and G. J. Collatz. 1976–77. Photosynthetic acclimation to temperature and water stress in the desert shrub *Larrea divaricata*. *Carnegie Inst. Wash. Yb.* **76**:328–335.

Mooney, H. A., J. Ehleringer, and J. A. Berry. 1976. High photosynthetic capacity of a winter annual in Death Valley. *Science* **194**:322–323.

Moore, R. T., R. S. White, and M. M. Caldwell. 1972. Transpiration of *Atriplex confertifolia* and *Eurotia lanata* in relation to soil, plant, and atmospheric moisture stresses. *Can. J. Bot.* **50**:2411–2418.

Moss, G. I., and L. A. Downey. 1971. Influence of drought stress on female gametophyte development in corn (*Zea mays* L.) and subsequent grain yield. *Crop Sci.* **11**:368–372.

Mott, J. J., and A. J. McComb. 1974. Patterns in annual vegetation and soil microrelief in an arid region of Western Australia. *J. Ecol.* **62**:115–126.

Muller, C. H. 1939. Relations of vegetation and climatic types in Nuevo Leon, Mexico. *Am. Midl. Natur.* **21**:687–728.

Muller, C. H. 1947. Vegetation and climate of Coahuila, Mexico. *Madroño* **9**:33–57.

Muller, C. H. 1953. The association of desert annuals with shrubs. *Am. J. Bot.* **40**:53–60.

Muller, W. H., and C. H. Muller. 1956. Association patterns involving desert plants that contain toxic products. *Am. J. Bot.* **43**:354–361.

Mulroy, T. W., and P. W. Rundel. 1977. Annual plants: adaptations to desert environments. *BioScience* **27**:109–114.

Mutz, K. M. 1979. *Lifeforms and the Environment: A Study of Sonoran Desert Subtrees on Bajadas*. M.S. thesis, Utah State Univ., Logan.

Nash, T. H., G. T. Nebeker, T. Moser, and T. Reeves. 1979. Lichen vegetation gradients in relation to the Pacific coast of Baja California: The maritime influence. *Madroño* **26** *in press*.

Nash, T. H., S. L. White, and J. E. Marsh. 1977. Lichen and moss distribution and biomass in hot desert ecosystems. *Bryologist* **80**:470–479.

Nelson, J. F., and R. M. Chew. 1977. Factors affecting seed reserves in the soil of a Mojave Desert ecosystem, Rock Valley, Nye County, Nevada. *Am. Midl. Natur.* **97**:300–320.

Niering, W. A., R. H. Whittaker, and C. H. Lowe. 1963. The saguaro: a population in relation to environment. *Science* **142**:15–23.

Nobel, P. S. 1976a. Photosynthetic rates of sun versus shade leaves of *Hyptis emoryi*. *Plant Physiol.* **58**:218–223.

Nobel, P. S. 1976b. Water relations and photosynthesis of a desert CAM plant, *Agave deserti*. *Plant Physiol.* **58**:576–582.

Nobel, P. S. 1977a. Internal leaf area and cellular CO_2 resistance: photosynthetic implications of variations with growth conditions and plant species. *Physiol. Plant.* **40**:137–144.

Nobel, P. S. 1977b. Water relations and photosynthesis of a barrel cactus, *Ferocactus acanthodes,* in the Colorado Desert. *Oecologia* **27**:117–133.

Nobel, P. S. 1977c. Water relations of flowering of *Agave deserti. Bot. Gaz.* **138**:1–6.

Nobel, P. S. 1978. Microhabitat, water relations and photosynthesis of a desert fern, *Notholaena parryi. Oecologia* **31**:293–309.

Nobel, P. S., D. J. Longstreth, and T. L. Hartsock. 1978. Effect of water stress on the temperature optima of net CO_2 exchange for two desert species. *Physiol. Plant.* **44**:97–101.

Noy-Meir, I. 1973. Desert ecosystems: environment and producers. *Ann. Rev. Ecol. Syst.* **4**:25–51.

Noy-Meir, I. 1974. Desert ecosystems: higher trophic levels. *Ann. Rev. Ecol. Syst.* **5**:195–214.

Odening, W. R., B. R. Strain, and W. C. Oechel. 1974. The effect of decreasing water potential on net CO_2 exchange of intact desert shrubs. *Ecology* **55**:1086–1095.

Oechel, W. C., B. R. Strain, and W. R. Odening. 1972a. Photosynthetic rates of a desert shrub, *Larrea divaricata* Cav., under field conditions. *Photosynthetica* **6**:183–188.

Oechel, W. C., B. R. Strain, and W. R. Odening. 1972b. Tissue water potential, photosynthesis, ^{14}C-labeled photosynthetic utilization and growth in the desert shrub *Larrea divaricata. Ecol. Monogr.* **42**:127–141.

Oertli, J. J. 1971. A whole system approach to water physiology in plants. *Advan. Frontiers Plant Sci.* **27**:1–200, **28**:1–73.

Oertli, J. J. 1976. The soil-plant-atmosphere continuum (Section C), pp. 32–41. In O. L. Lange, L. Kappen, and E. D. Schulze (eds.), Ecol. Stud. 19, *Water and Plant Life.* Springer-Verlag, New York.

O'Leary, J. W. 1970. Can there be a positive water potential in plants? *BioScience* **20**:858–859.

Orians, G. H., and O. T. Solbrig. 1977. A cost-income model of leaves and roots with special reference to arid and semiarid areas. *Am. Natur.* **111**:677–690.

Otte, D. 1976. Species richness patterns of New World desert grasshoppers in relation to plant diversity. *J. Biogeogr.* **3**:197–209.

Patten, D. T. 1978. Productivity and production efficiency of an upper Sonoran Desert ephemeral community. *Am. J. Bot.* **65**:891–895.

Paulsen, H. A., Jr. 1950. Mortality of velvet mesquite seedlings. *J. Range Manage.* **3**:281–286.

Peacock, J. T., and C. McMillan. 1965. Ecotypic differentiation in *Prosopis* (Mesquite). *Ecology* **46**:35–51.

Pearcy, R. W., and A. T. Harrison. 1974. Comparative photosynthetic and respiratory gas exchange characteristics of *Atriplex lentiformis* in coastal and desert habitats. *Ecology* **55**:1104–1111.

Pearcy, R. W., A. T. Harrison, H. A. Mooney, and O. Björkman. 1974. Seasonal changes in net photosynthesis of *Atriplex hymenelytra* shrubs growing in Death Valley, California. *Oecologia* **17**:111–124.

Phillips, D. L. 1978. *Competition and Spacing Patterns of Shrubs in the Mojave and Sonoran Deserts.* Ph.D. dissertation, Utah State Univ., Logan.

Phillips, D. L., and J. A. MacMahon. 1978. Gradient analysis of a Sonoran Desert bajada. *Southwest. Natur.* **23**:669–679.

Pianka, E. R. 1977. Reptilian species diversity, pp. 1–34. In C. Gans and D. W. Tinkle (eds.), *Biology of the Reptilia, 7.* Academic Press, New York.

Powell, A. M., and B. L. Turner. 1977. Aspects of the plant biology of gypsum outcrops of the Chihuahuan Desert, pp. 315–326. In R. H. Wauer and D. H. Riskind (eds.), *Trans. Sympos. Biological Resources of the Chihuahuan Desert Region, United States and Mexico.* U.S. Dept. Int., N. P. S. Trans. and Proc. Ser. 3.

Reimold, R. J., and W. H. Queen (eds.). 1974. *Ecology of Halophytes.* Academic Press, New York.

Richter, H. 1976. The water status in the plant experimental evidence, pp. 42–58. In O. L. Lange, L. Kappen and E. D. Schulze (eds.), Ecol. Stud. 19, *Water and Plant Life.* Springer-Verlag, New York.

Ritchie, G. A., and T. M. Hinckley. 1975. The pressure chamber as an instrument for ecological research. *Advan. Ecol. Res.* **9**:165–254.

Romney, E. M., A. Wallace, and R. B. Hunter. 1978. Plant response to nitrogen fertilization in the northern Mojave Desert and its relationship to water manipulation, pp. 232–243. In N. E. West and J. J. Skujins (eds.), *Nitrogen in Desert Ecosystems.* US/IBP Synthesis Series, vol. 9. Dowden, Hutchinson and Ross, Stroudsburg, Pa.

Rosenzweig, M. L. 1968. Net primary productivity of terrestrial communities: prediction from climatological data. *Am. Natur.* **102**:67–74.

Rundel, P. W. 1978. Ecological relationships of desert fog zone lichens. *Bryologist* **81**:277–293.

Sánchez-Diaz, M. F., and H. A. Mooney. 1979. Resistance to water transfer in desert shrubs native to Death Valley, California. *Physiol. Plant.* **46**:139–146.

Sankary, M. N., and M. G. Barbour. 1972. Autecology of *Atriplex polycarpa* from California. *Ecology* **53**:1155–1162.

Schall, J. J., and E. R. Pianka. 1978. Geographical trends in numbers of species. *Science* **201**:679–686.

Schmidt-Nielsen, K. 1964. *Desert animals: Physiological Problems of Heat and Water.* Oxford Univ. Press, New York.

Secor, J. B., and D. O. Farhadnejad. 1978. The seed germination of three species of *Gaillardia* that occur in the gypsumland areas of eastern New Mexico. *Southwest. Natur.* **23**:181–186.

Seddon, G. 1974. Xerophytes, xeromorphs and sclerophylls: the history of some concepts in ecology. *Biol. J. Linn. Soc.* **6**:65–87.

Sheps, L. O. 1973. Survival of *Larrea tridentata* S. & M. seedlings in Death Valley National Monument, California. *Isr. J. Bot.* **22**:8–17.

Sherbrooke, W. C. 1977. First year seedling survival of jojoba (*Simmondsia chinensis*) in the Tucson Mountains, Arizona. *Southwest. Natur.* **22**:225–234.

Shreve, E. B. 1914. *The Daily March of Transpiration in a Desert Perennial.*

Carnegie Inst. Wash. Publ. No. 194. Washington, D.C.

Shreve, F. 1910. The rate of establishment of the giant cactus. *Plant World* **13**:235–240.

Shreve, F. 1911. Establishment behavior of the palo verde. *Plant World* **14**:289–296.

Shreve, F. 1923. Seasonal changes in the water relations of desert plants. *Ecology* **4**:266–292.

Shreve, F. 1924. Factors governing seasonal changes in transpiration of *Encelia farinosa. Bot. Gaz.* **77**:432–439.

Shreve, F., and A. L. Hinckley. 1937. Thirty years of change in desert vegetation. *Ecology* **18**:463–478.

Shreve, F., and I. L. Wiggins. 1964. *Vegetation and Flora of the Sonoran Desert,* vol. 1. Stanford Univ. Press, Stanford, California.

Simpson, B. B. 1977a. Breeding systems of dominant perennial plants of two disjunct warm desert ecosystems. *Oecologia* **27**:203–226.

Simpson, B. B. (ed.). 1977b. *Mesquite: Its Biology in Two Desert Ecosystems.* US/IBP Synthesis Series, vol. 4. Dowden, Hutchinson and Ross, Stroudsburg, Pa.

Slatyer, R. O. 1967. *Plant-Water Relationships.* Academic Press, London.

Slatyer, R. O. 1969. Physiological significance of internal water relations to crop yield, pp. 53–83. In J. D. Eastin, F. A. Haskins, C. Y. Sullivan, and C. H. M. Van Bavel (eds.), *Physiological Aspects of Crop Yield.* American Soc. of Agronomy—Crop Sci. Soc. of America, Madison, Wis.

Slatyer, R. O., and S. A. Taylor. 1960. Terminology in plant-soil-water relations. *Nature* **187**:922–924.

Slavik, B. 1974. *Methods of Studying Plant Water Relations.* Ecol. Stud. 9. Springer-Verlag, New York.

Smith, S. D., and J. A. Ludwig. 1976. Reproductive and vegetative growth patterns in *Yucca elata* Engelm. (Liliaceae). *Southwest. Natur.* **21**:177–184.

Smith, S. D., and J. A. Ludwig. 1978. Further studies on growth patterns in *Yucca elata* Engelm. (Liliaceae). *Southwest. Natur.* **23**:145–150.

Smith, W. K. 1978. Temperatures of desert plants: Another perspective on the adaptability of leaf size. *Science* **201**:614–616.

Smith, W. K., and P. S. Nobel. 1977. Influences of seasonal changes in leaf morphology on water-use efficiency for three desert broadleaf shrubs. *Ecology* **58**:1033–1043.

Smith, W. K., and P. S. Nobel. 1978. Influence of irradiation, soil water potential, and leaf temperature on leaf morphology of a desert broadleaf *Encelia farinosa* Gray (Compositae). *Am. J. Bot.* **65**:429–432.

Snyder, J. M., and L. H. Wullstein. 1973. The role of desert cryptogams in nitrogen fixation. *Am. Midl. Natur.* **90**:257–265.

Solbrig, O. T., M. G. Barbour, J. Cross, G. Goldstein, C. H. Lowe, J. Morello, and T. W. Yang. 1977. The strategies and community patterns of desert plants, pp. 67–106. In G. H. Orians and O. T. Solbrig (eds.), *Convergent Evolution in Warm Deserts.* US/IBP Synthesis Series, vol. 3. Dowden, Hutchinson and Ross, Stroudsburg, Pa.

Solbrig, O. T., and G. H. Orians. 1977. The adaptive characteristics of desert plants. *Am. Sci.* **65**:412–421.

Soriano, A. 1953. Estudios sobre germinación. I. *Rev. de Inves. Agric.* **7**:315–340.

Spellenberg, R., and R. K. Delson. 1977. Aspects of reproduction in Chihuahuan Desert Nyctaginaceae, pp. 273–287. In R. H. Wauer and D. H. Riskind (eds.), *Trans. Sympos. Biological Resources of the Chihuahuan Desert Region, United States and Mexico.* U.S. Dept. Int., N. P. S. Trans. and Proc. Ser. 3.

Springfield, H. W. 1966. Germination of fourwing saltbush seeds at different levels of moisture stress. *Agron. J.* **58**:149–150.

Stark, N., and L. D. Love. 1969. Water relations of three warm desert species. *Isr. J. Bot.* **18**:175–190.

Steenbergh, W. F., and C. H. Lowe. 1969. Critical factors during the first years of life of the saguaro (*Cereus giganteus*) at Saguaro National Monument, Arizona. *Ecology* **50**:825–834.

Steenberg, W. F., and C. H. Lowe. 1976. Ecology of the saguaro: I. The role of freezing weather in a warm-desert plant population, pp. 49–92. In *Research in the Parks. Transactions of the National Park Centennial Symposium.* U.S. Dept. Int. Nat. Park Serv. Symp. Ser. No. 1.

Steenberg, W. F., and C. H. Lowe. 1977. *Ecology of the Saguaro: II. Reproduction, Germination, Establishment, Growth, and Survival of the Young Plant.* Nat. Park Serv. Monogr. Ser. No. 8, Washington, D.C.

Stein, R. A., and J. A. Ludwig. 1979. Vegetation and soil patterns on a Chihuahuan Desert bajada. *Am. Midl. Natur.* **101**:28–37.

Sternberg, L. 1976. Growth forms of *Larrea tridentata*. *Madroño* **23**:408–417.

Stowe, L. G., and J. A. Teeri. 1978. The geographic distribution of C_4 species of the Dicotyledonae. *Am. Natur.* **112**:609–623.

Strain, B. R. 1969. Seasonal adaptations in photosynthesis and respiration in four desert shrubs growing in situ. *Ecology* **50**:511–513.

Strain, B. R. 1970. Field measurements of tissue water potential and carbon dioxide exchange in the desert shrubs *Prosopis juliflora* and *Larrea divaricata*. *Photosynthetica* **4**:118–122.

Sturges, D. L. 1977. Soil water withdrawal and root characteristics of big sagebrush. *Am. Midl. Natur.* **98**:257–274.

Syvertsen, J. P., G. L. Cunningham, and T. V. Feather. 1975. Anomalous diurnal patterns of stem xylem water potentials in *Larrea tridentata*. *Ecology* **56**:1423–1428.

Syvertsen, J. P., G. L. Nickell, R. W. Spellenberg, and G. L. Cunningham. 1976. Carbon reduction pathways and standing crop in three Chihuahuan Desert plant communities. *Southwest. Natur.* **21**:311–320.

Szarek, S. R. 1974. *Physiological mechanisms of drought adaptation in* Opuntia basilaris *Engelm. et Bigel.* Ph.D. dissertation, Univ. of California, Riverside.

Szarek, S. R., H. B. Johnson, and I. P. Ting. 1973. Drought adaptation in *Opuntia basilaris*. *Plant Physiol.* **52**:539–541.

Szarek, S. R., and I. P. Ting. 1974. Seasonal patterns of acid metabolism and gas exchange in *Opuntia basilaris*. *Plant Physiol.* **54**:76–81.

Szarek, S. R., and I. P. Ting. 1975. Physiological responses to rainfall in

Opuntia basilaris (Cactaceae). *Am. J. Bot.* **62**:602–609.

Szarek, S. R., and I. P. Ting. 1977. The occurrence of Crassulacean acid metabolism among plants. *Photosynthetica* **11**:330–342.

Szarek, S. R., and R. M. Woodhouse. 1976. Ecophysiological studies of Sonoran Desert plants. I. Diurnal photosynthesis patterns of *Ambrosia deltoidea* and *Olneya tesota. Oecologia* **26**:225–234.

Szarek, S. R., and R. M. Woodhouse. 1977. Ecophysiological studies of Sonoran Desert plants. II. Seasonal photosynthesis patterns and primary production of *Ambrosia deltoidea* and *Olneya tesota. Oecologia* **28**:365–375.

Szarek, S. R., and R. M. Woodhouse. 1978a. Ecophysiological studies of Sonoran Desert plants. III. The daily course of photosynthesis for *Acacia greggii* and *Cercidium microphyllum. Oecologia* **35**:285–294.

Szarek, S. R., and R. M. Woodhouse. 1978b. Ecophysiological studies of Sonoran Desert plants. IV. Seasonal photosynthetic capacities of *Acacia greggii* and *Cercidium microphyllum. Oecologia* **37**:221–229.

Tal, M., I. Rosental, R. Abramovitz, and M. Forti. 1979. Salt tolerance in *Simmondsia chinensis:* Water balance and accumulation of chloride, sodium and proline under low and high salinity. *Ann. Bot.* **43**:701–708.

Taylorson, R. B., and H. A. Borthwick. 1969. Light filtration by foliar canopies: significance for light-controlled weed seed germination. *Weed Sci.* **17**:48–51.

Teeri, J. A., and L. G. Stowe. 1976. Climatic patterns and the distribution of C_4 grasses in North America. *Oecologia* **23**:1–12.

Teeri, J. A., L. G. Stowe, and D. A. Murawski. 1978. The climatology of two succulent plant families: Cactaceae and Crassulaceae. *Can. J. Bot.* **56**:1750–1758.

Tevis, L., Jr. 1958a. A population of desert ephemerals germinated by less than one inch of rain. *Ecology* **39**:688–695.

Tevis, L., Jr. 1958b. Germination and growth of ephemerals induced by sprinkling a sandy desert. *Ecology* **39**:681–688.

Thames, J. L. (ed.). 1974. *Tucson Basin Validation Site Report.* US/IBP Desert Biome Res. Memo. 74-3. Utah State Univ., Logan.

Thames, J. L. (ed.). 1975. *Tucson Basin Validation Site Report.* US/IBP Desert Biome Res. Memo. 75-3. Utah State Univ., Logan.

Tiedemann, A. R., and J. O. Klemmedson. 1973a. Effect of mesquite on physical and chemical properties of the soil. *J. Range Manage.* **26**:27–29.

Tiedemann, A. R., and J. O. Klemmedson. 1973b. Nutrient availability in desert grassland soils under mesquite (*Prosopis juliflora*) trees and adjacent open areas. *Soil Sci. Soc. Amer. Proc.* **37**:107–111.

Tiedemann, A. R., and J. O. Klemmedson. 1977. Effect of mesquite trees on vegetation and soils in the desert grassland. *J. Range Manage.* **30**:361–367.

Ting, I. P., H. B. Johnson, and S. R. Szarek. 1972. Net CO_2 fixation in Crassulacean metabolism plants, pp. 22–53. In C. C. Black (ed.), *Net Carbon Dioxide Assimilation in Higher Plants.* Proc. Symp. S. Sec. Amer. Soc. Pl. Physiol. Cotton Inc., Raleigh, N.C.

Ting, I. P., and S. R. Szarek. 1975. Drought adaptation in Crassulacean acid metabolism plants, pp. 152–167. In N. F. Hadley (ed.), *Environmental*

Physiology of Desert Organisms. Dowden, Hutchinson and Ross, Stroudsburg, Pa.

Tomoff, C. S. 1974. Avian species diversity in desert scrub. *Ecology* **55**:396–403.

Trewartha, G. T. 1968. *An Introduction to Climate,* 4th ed. McGraw-Hill, New York.

Turner, R. M. 1963. Growth in four species of Sonoran Desert trees. *Ecology* **44**:760–765.

Turner, F. B. (ed.). 1975. *Rock Valley Validation Site Report.* US/IBP Desert Biome Res. Memo. 75-2. Utah State Univ., Logan.

Turner, F. B. (ed.). 1976. *Rock Valley Validation Site Report.* US/IBP Desert Biome Res. Memo. 76-2. Utah State Univ., Logan.

Turner, F. B., and J. F. McBrayer (eds.). 1974. *Rock Valley Validation Site Report.* US/IBP Desert Biome Res. Memo. 74-2.

Turner, R. M., S. M. Alcorn, G. Olin, and J. A. Booth. 1966. The influence of shade, soil and water on saguaro seedling establishment. *Bot. Gaz.* **127**:95–102.

Ungar, I. A. 1978. Halophyte seed germination. *Bot. Rev.* **44**:233–264.

Van Devender, T. R., and W. G. Spaulding. 1979. Development of vegetation and climate in the southwestern United States. *Science* **204**:701–710.

Vasek, F. C., H. B. Johnson, and D. H. Eslinger. 1975a. Effects of pipeline construction on creosote bush scrub vegetation of the Mojave Desert. *Madroño* **23**:1–13.

Vasek, F. C., H. B. Johnson, and G. D. Brum. 1975b. Effects of power transmission lines on vegetation of the Mojave Desert. *Madroño* **23**:114–130.

Veihymeyer, F. J., and A. H. Hendrickson. 1961. Responses of a plant to soil-moisture changes as shown by guayule. *Hilgardia* **30**:621–637.

Vest, E. D., and W. P. Cottam. 1953. Some germination characteristics of *Atriplex confertifolia.* (Abstract). *Proc. Utah Acad. Sciences, Arts and Letters* **30**:108–109.

Vollmer, A. T., B. G. Maza, P. A. Medica, F. B. Turner, and S. A. Bamberg. 1976. The impact of off-road vehicles on a desert ecosystem. *Environ. Manage.* **1**:115–129.

Wagenet, R. J., and J. J. Jurinak. 1978. Spatial variability of soluble salt content in a Mancos shale watershed. *Soil Science* **126**:342–349.

Waisel, Y. 1972. *Biology of Halophytes.* Academic Press, New York.

Wallace, A., S. A. Bamberg, and J. W. Cha. 1974. Quantitative studies of roots of perennial plants in the Mojave Desert. *Ecology* **55**:1160–1162.

Wallace, A., and E. M. Romney. 1972. *Radioecology and Ecophysiology of Desert Plants at the Nevada Test Site.* USAEC Office of Information Services, Rep. No. TID 25954.

Wallen, D. R., and J. A. Ludwig. 1978. Energy dynamics of vegetative and reproductive growth in spanish bayonet (*Yucca baccata* Torr.). *Southwest. Natur.* **23**:409–422.

Walter, H. 1962. *Die Vegetation der Erde.* Fischer, Jena.

Walter, H., and E. Stadelmann. 1974. A new approach to the water relations of desert plants, pp. 213–310. In G. Brown (ed.), *Desert Biology,* vol. 2. Academic Press, New York.

Waser, N. M. 1979. Pollinator availability as a determinant of flowering time in ocotillo (*Fouquieria splendens*). *Oecologia* **39**:107–121.

Weatherly, P. E. 1970. Some aspects of water relations. *Adv. Bot. Res.* **3**:171–206.

Wein, R. W., and N. E. West. 1971. Phenology of salt desert plants near contour furrows. *J. Range Manage.* **24**:299–304.

Wells, P. V. 1959. An ecological investigation of two desert tobaccos. *Ecology* **40**:626–644.

Wells, P. V., and J. H. Hunziker. 1976. Origin of the creosote bush (*Larrea*) deserts of southwestern North America. *Ann. Mo. Bot. Gard.* **63**:843–861.

Wendt, C. W., R. H. Maas and J. R. Runkles. 1968. Influence of selected environmental variables on transpiration rate of mesquite [Prosopis glandulosa var. *glandulosa* (Torr.) Cocker.]. *Agron. J.* **60**:382–384.

Went, F. W. 1942. The dependence of certain annual plants on shrubs in southern California deserts. *Bull. Torrey Bot. Club* **69**:100–114.

Went, F. W. 1948. Ecology of desert plants. I. Observations on germination in the Joshua Tree National Monument, California. *Ecology* **29**:242–253.

Went, F. W. 1949. Ecology of desert plants. II. The effect of rain and temperature on germination and growth. *Ecology* **30**:1–13.

Went, F. W. 1955. The ecology of desert plants. *Sci. Am.* **192**:68–75.

Went, F. W. 1973. Competition among plants. *Proc. Nat. Acad. Sci. USA* **70**:585–590.

Went, F. W. 1975. Water vapor absorption in *Prosopis,* pp. 67–75. In F. J. Vernberg (ed.), *Physiological Adaptation to the Environment*. Intext, New York.

Went, F. W., and M. Westergaard. 1949. Ecology of desert plants. III. Development of plants in the Death Valley National Monument, California. *Ecology* **30**:26–38.

West, N. E., and J. Gasto. 1978. Phenology of the aerial portions of shadscale and winterfat in Curlew Valley, Utah. *J. Range Manage.* **31**:43–45.

West, N. E., and J. J. Skujins. 1978. *Nitrogen In Desert Ecosystems*. US/IBP Synthesis Series, vol. 9. Dowden, Hutchinson and Ross, Stroudsburg, Pa.

White, T. C. R. 1976. Weather, food, and plagues of locusts. *Oecologia* **22**:119–134.

White, T. C. R. 1978. The importance of a relative shortage of food in animal ecology. *Oecologia* **33**:71–86.

Whittaker, R. H., S. W. Buol, W. A. Niering, and Y. H. Havens. 1968. A soil and vegetation pattern in the Santa Catalina Mountains, Arizona. *Soil Sci.* **105**:440–450.

Whittaker, R. H., and W. A. Niering. 1964. Vegetation of the Santa Catalina Mountains. I. Ecological classification and distribution of species. *J. Ariz. Acad. Sci.* **3**:9–34.

Whittaker, R. H., and W. A. Niering. 1965. Vegetation of the Santa Catalina Mountains. II. A gradient analysis of the south slope. *Ecology* **46**:429–452.

Wiebe, H. H. 1972. The role of water potential and its components in physiological processes of plants, pp. 194–197. In R. W. Brown and B. P. Van Haveren (eds.), *Psychrometry in Water Relations Research*. Utah Agr. Exp. Sta., Utah State Univ., Logan.

Wiebe, H. H., H. A. Al-Saadi, and S. L. Kimball. 1974. Photosynthesis in the anomalous secondary wood of *Atriplex confertifolia* stems. *Am. J. Bot.* **61**:444–448.

Williams, J., and C. F. Shaykewich. 1971. Influence of soil water matric potential and hydraulic conductivity on the germination of rape (*Brassica napus* L.). *J. Exp. Bot.* **22**:586–597.

Wood, C. W., and T. N. Nash. 1976. Copper smelter effluent effects on Sonoran Desert vegetation. *Ecology* **57**:1311–1316.

Wood, M. K., R. W. Knight, and J. A. Young. 1976. Spiny hopsage germination. *J. Range Manage.* **29**:53–56.

Woodell, S. R. J., H. A. Mooney, and A. J. Hill. 1969. The behavior of *Larrea divaricata* (creosote bush) in response to rainfall in California. *J. Ecol.* **57**:37–44.

Yang, T. W., and C. H. Lowe, Jr. 1956. Correlation of major vegetational climaxes with soil characteristics in the Sonoran Desert. *Science* **123**:542.

Yeaton, R. I. 1978. A cyclical relationship between *Larrea tridentata* and *Opuntia leptocaulis* in the northern Chihuahuan Desert. *J. Ecol.* **66**:651–656.

Yeaton, R. I., and M. L. Cody. 1976. Competition and spacing in plant communities: the northern Mojave Desert. *J. Ecol.* **64**:689–696.

Yeaton, R. I., J. Travis, and E. Gilinsky. 1977. Competition and spacing in plant communities: the Arizona Upland Association. *J. Ecol.* **65**:587–595.

Young, J. A., R. A. Evans, R. O. Gifford, and R. E. Eckert, Jr. 1968. Germination of medusahead in response to osmotic stress. *Weed Sci.* **16**:364–368.

Young, J. A., R. A. Evans, and J. Major. 1972. Alien plants in the Great Basin. *J. Range Manage.* **25**:194–201.

8

Potential Evapotranspiration for Deserts

Lloyd W. Gay

POTENTIAL EVAPOTRANSPIRATION

The potential evapotranspiration (PET) concept, which is widely accepted, appears to have been first proposed by Thornthwaite (1944, 1948) when he concluded that transpiration from vegetation plentifully supplied with water would proceed at a rate governed by the characteristics of the atmosphere. These characteristics also could be used to estimate the maximum potential evapotranspiration that could occur should appropriate vegetative and soil moisture conditions actually be satisfied. This concept has led to a vast amount of research, directed either at classification of climates according to evaporability or techniques for the estimation of PET as a step in evaluation of actual evapotranspiration.

The original definition of PET has received some minor revision. The currently accepted version is that PET is "the rate of evaporation from an extended surface of a short green crop actively growing, completely shading the ground, of uniform height, and not short of water" (Anon., 1956). This statement defines the basic conditions required for PET. The variability of the plant component in the evaporation process is minimized by specifying that the vegetation be low in height, actively growing, and with complete canopy closure. The effect of soil-water content upon the evaporation process is standardized by the requirement that the soil be plentifully supplied with water. In arid zones, these conditions are met in riparian plant communities, in some natural communities for a period after a precipitation event, and in virtually all irrigation projects once the crop canopies have closed.

Indeed, Thornthwaite's (1944) original concept was that PET would be equal to consumptive use in irrigated agriculture. This application has contributed to the continuing interest in the estimation of PET. A substantial research effort has focused upon the development of adjustment factors to relate potential and actual evapotranspiration. The adjustments seek to account for either lack of water or for failure of the plant communities to conform to the surface conditions of the definition.

The PET concept has been severely critized. W. C. Swinbank's (1965) discussion of Stanhill's (1965) paper on this topic is an example: "I would suggest to Dr. Stanhill that the concept of potential evaporation is a useless one, in that it cannot be defined and cannot be measured, and that all he has said this afternoon reinforces this view." Stanhill (1973) recently concluded

172

that "despite the manifold uses to which the concept of potential evapotranspiration has been put in the past, inherent contradictions in the multiplicity of definitions that have been put forward, make it one whose current necessity is open to considerable doubt."

Problems in utilizing the PET concept are related to the imprecise nature of the definition, leading to errors in application and misplaced expectations. There have also been failures to appreciate fully shortcomings inherent in the many different models that have been proposed for estimating PET. The extreme climatic conditions of arid environments have contributed to these problems. This chapter will review the bases for evaluating PET and the relations between PET estimates and the evapotranspiration processes in arid zones. It will conclude with sample applications.

FACTORS AFFECTING PET

The PET concept is an abstraction; PET rates need not necessarily prevail in nature. The factors that affect the relation between potential and actual evapotranspiration can be grouped according to their association with either the atmosphere or with the surface. It is important that these factors be understood in order to minimize difficulties in interpreting PET estimates in arid zones.

Surface Factors

Evaporation is the transformation of water from the liquid to the vapor state. The rate at which evaporation proceeds in nature depends upon the concentration of vapor in the atmosphere and the availability of water to the evaporating surface. The ability of the atmosphere to accept water vapor and the availability of water at the surface combine to produce evapotranspiration rates that are highly variable in time and in space.

The availability of water plays a major role in the rapidity of the evaporation taking place. While a supply of liquid water (such as dew droplets or surface of a lake) is necessary in order for evaporation to proceed, the supply need not be on the surface if it is readily available in the soil within the rooting zone of vegetation. The evaporating surface is within the stomata of the leaves when vegetation is present, and the evaporating area will differ from the area of the ground. In general, the effective evaporating area of a vegetated surface is less than that of the underlying plane surface. Areas with ample subsurface moisture may behave as if they were partially wetted, depending upon the degree of saturation and whether vegetation is present. The wet surface will vary from a value of 1.0 for lakes and ponds, down to lower values that depend upon surface moisture and the density and type of vegetation.

The vegetation density and degree of saturation of the surface and subsurface are particularly variable and difficult to measure in arid zones. If, however, water is added to the surface by precipitation or by irrigation, essentially all variability associated with availability of water is eliminated. Since the effects of vegetation upon the evaporation rate from well-watered surfaces appear to be essentially similar, a vast amount of experimental work has sought to estimate evaporation solely from properties of the atmosphere.

Atmospheric Factors

The effectiveness with which water vapor diffuses into the atmosphere and away from the more saturated regions close to an evaporating surface helps establish the concentration in the atmosphere and hence the rate at which evaporation proceeds. Atmospheric mixing processes affect the diffusion of vapor. At one extreme, vertical mixing is restricted beneath an inversion. The air beneath an inversion is relatively stagnant, cool, and saturated, and evaporation will be relatively lower. At the other extreme, strong winds will generate mechanical turbulence that is greatest over rough surfaces. This turbulence thoroughly mixes water vapor throughout the lower levels of the atmosphere. Evaporation in this situation will tend to be enhanced by the rapid diffusion of vapor away from the evaporating surface.

As the PET concept has become accepted, a variety of models have evolved that are based almost entirely upon atmospheric variables, since the PET definition removes the variability associated with the availability of water. The ability of these models to produce consistent, meaningful PET estimates depends entirely upon their treatment of atmospheric and surface factors.

PET MODELS

The wide variety of models proposed for evaluating PET will not be reviewed in detail here. Doorenbos and Pruitt (1975), for example, identify thirty-one formulas that estimate evapotranspiration from irrigated crops; nine of the formulas estimate PET. Nearly all of these formulas are empirical and depend upon the establishment of a known correlation between evapotranspiration and one or more climate variables such as temperature, radiation, humidity, and wind speed. Other formulas relate evapotranspiration to direct observations from evaporation pans. Almost all of the formulas contain empirical coefficients that calibrate the models for conditions of the regions in which they are used.

There have been many comparisons of different methods for estimating PET, but since the concept is an abstraction, there is no reference standard to determine the true PET value. The lack of a suitable reference has made it difficult to test the various approaches to estimating PET. The models can be grouped into pan evaporation, temperature, radiation, or combination models, depending upon their approach. Each group has disadvantages and advantages.

Pan Evaporation Models

A possible standard for PET is the evaporation rate (E_{pan}) that is measured directly with an evaporation pan. The basic model is simple: $E^* = k_p E_{pan}$

with the constant k_p to be determined empirically. As a matter of convenience, we shall refer to PET as E^*, open water evaporation as E^o, and actual evaporation as E. Stanhill (1965) recommends the class A evaporation pan as the best method of estimating potential evapotranspiration, given consideration of accuracy, simplicity, and cost.

Pruitt (1966) reviewed many studies and concluded that pan evaporation could give an excellent estimate of evapotranspiration from irrigated grass. He emphasized the necessity to standardize the exposure of the pans because rates in agricultural areas may differ as much as 40 percent between dryland sites and irrigated field sites. He further suggested a reduction on the order of 0.75 to bring losses from dryland class A pans down to the levels of those located within irrigated fields.

Pan design also influences the evaporation rate. The exposed class A pan of the U.S. Weather Bureau evaporates at a higher rate than do various sunken or insulated models. Guidelines for choice of an appropriate reduction coefficient are given by Doorenbos and Pruitt (1975) for a variety of climatic and iste conditions.

The relation between adjusted evaporation rates and evapotranspiration from irrigated crops is quite good in temperature regions. The ratio of E to E_{pan} for class A pans over a range of sites was about 0.8 for grass and grass-clover mixtures and 1.0 for alfalfa (Pruitt, 1966). Doorenbos and Pruitt (1975) point out that pan exposure errors increase in arid climates, especially in windy regions. They suggest that other methods, such as those based upon radiation, may be preferable for truly desert areas. They also give excellent application guidelines for the pan method in many types of climates.

Empirical Models

A number of empirical models are used for estimating PET. The agreement between PET predictions by the more common models depends upon the conditions within the area of application, as well as upon the care with which the calibration coefficients are fitted. Several of the more important methods will be discussed briefly here, but the original articles should be consulted for full details.

A Temperature Model

Thornthwaite (1948) recognized the strong correlation between radiation and mean air temperatures. He proposed a model relating PET (E^*) directly to air temperature:

$$E^* = (d/360) \; 1.6 \; (10T/I)^a \; \text{g/cm}^2 \text{ day} \qquad (8.1)$$

where T is the monthly mean temperature (in °C), I is a heat index for the station, derived from long-term monthly air temperature, a is a function of I, and d is the day length (number of hours).

The value of the annual heat index, I, is obtained by summing twelve monthly indexes $i = (T/5)^{1.514}$. The coefficient $a = C_1 I^3 + C_2 I^2 + C_3 I + C_4$ where $C_1 = 6.75\text{E-7}$, $C_2 = -7.71\text{E-5}$, $C_3 = 0.01792$, and $C_4 = 0.49239$.

The term $(d/360)$ in equation 8.1 adjusts the estimated PET for deviations from a standard twelve-hour day $(d/12)$, and thirty-day month $(N/30)$, for a daily basis $(1/N)$ where N is the number of days in the month. Values of d are available in the Smithsonian meteorological tables. The calculations are easily done with a hand calculator or with nomograms that have been developed (Palmer and Havens, 1958).

A Radiation and Temperature Model

The effect of temperature on the evaporation rate has been combined with that of solar radiation by Jensen and Haise (1963). Their model is

$$E^* = C_T(T - T_x)\, K\!\downarrow/L \text{ g/cm}^2 \text{ day} \tag{8.2}$$

where C_T is a temperature coefficient that is approximately equal to the reciprocal of the mean temperature, T is the average daily temperature (°C), T_x is a temperature coefficient, $K\!\downarrow$ is the daily solar radiation (cal/cm² day), and L is latent heat of vaporization (585 cal/g).

The equation is deceptively simple, for the coefficients vary with elevation and atmospheric moisture content, as well as with temperature. The adjustments are summarized by Jensen (1966). The coefficient C_T can be estimated by

$$C_T = \frac{1}{27 + 7.3\, C_H}$$

with

$$C_H = \frac{50\ mb}{e_2 - e_1}$$

where e_2 and e_1 are the saturation vapor pressures at the mean monthly maximum and minimum air temperatures for the warmest month. T_x can be estimated as $T_x = -23 + C_H^2 + 750\, C_T$ for those areas with $C_H < 2.8$. For actual calculations, refer to Jensen and Haise (1963). As an example, the coefficients at Tucson, Arizona (elevation 788m, July maximums of 36.9°C and minimums of 23.3°C), are: $C_T = 0.027/°\text{C}$, $T_x = -3.59°\text{C}$.

A Net Radiation Model

The Priestly and Taylor (1975) model focuses upon available energy ($H = Q^* + G$) as the primary factor controlling potential evapotranspiration from well-watered vegetation. Net radiation (Q^*) is used to represent available energy because the storage term (G) is relatively small at any time, and it is generally negligible when averaged over a twenty-four-hour period. Net radiation is now being measured at a number of locations; it can also be estimated rather easily for those areas where measurements are lacking.

The Priestly-Taylor model is

$$E^* = \alpha W Q^* / L \qquad (8.3)$$

where α is an empirical constant ($\alpha = 1.26$), L is the latent heat of vaporization, and W is a temperature-dependent weighting factor. The flux density of net radiation (Q^*) is expressed as cal/cm² day.

The weighting factor W is equal to $\triangle/(\triangle + \gamma)$, where $\triangle$ is the slope of the saturation vapor curve (in mb/°C) at air temperature Ta, and γ is the psychrometric constant (mb/°C). $\triangle$ can be readily calculated from tabulated values of saturated vapor pressure (e_s, in mb) as a function of temperature (see, for example, the Smithsonian meteorological tables). The psychrometric constant, γ, has a nominal value of about 0.66 mb/°C. This varies with air pressure, p, in the ratio $p/p°$ where $p°$ is sea level pressure ($p° = 1013.25$ mb). W thus varies with both temperature and with pressure (figure 8-1). Typical sea level values of W are 0.55, 0.68, and 0.78 at temperatures of 10°, 20°, 30°C, respectively.

It is interesting to note that since Q^* is linearly related to $K\downarrow$ ($Q^* = a + bK\downarrow$) (Gay, 1971), both the Priestly-Taylor and the Jensen-Haise models have the same basic form: $E^* = \phi K\downarrow$ where ϕ represents the fraction of solar radiation transformed to net radiation, and ultimately, into evapotranspiration.

The Combination Model for PET

The combination model of Penman (1948) is probably the most widely known PET estimator. In contrast to the pan observations and the empirical models, the Penman model is based upon a simplified radiation budget that has been combined with an aerodynamic analysis. The fundamental basis of the model gives it some generality in application over a wide range of conditions.

Penman's Combination Model

Penman's model can be written (after Doorenbos and Pruitt, 1975) as

$$E_o = W \cdot H/L + (1-W) \cdot f(u) \cdot (e_s - e) \qquad \text{g/cm}^2 \text{ day} \qquad (8.4)$$

where E_o is unadjusted (free water) flux density of potential evaporation (g/cm² day), W is a dimensionless weighting factor that accounts for effects of temperature and pressure, H is the flux density of available energy (cal/cm² day) after summing net radiation, Q^*, plus change in storage G, L is latent heat of vaporization (585 cal/g at 21.8°C), $f(u)$ is a wind function that approximates the diffusivity of the atmosphere near the ground (g/cm² day), and $e_s - e$ is the vapor pressure deficit of the atmosphere at 2 m height (in mb).

The weighting coefficient ($W = \triangle/(\triangle + \gamma)$) is the same as in the Priestly-Taylor model (equation 8.3). It expresses the relative importance of the two terms in equation 8.4. The first term is primarily of radiation and the second of aerodynamic processes. The temperature effect is illustrated in figure 8-1 for both sea level and 2,000 meter elevation over a range of temperatures. At sea level, the relative weights of the radiative and the aerodynamic terms are approximately equal at 7°C. As temperatures rise above 30°C, the weight of the radiative term becomes greater than that of the aerodynamic term by a factor of four or more.

The model can be applied over any desired time period. With units above, and for input variables averaged over the period of a day (twenty-four hours), evaporation estimates will be in units of g/cm² day, which are equivalent to evaporation in cm/day. The model is intended to yield mean daily estimates of evaporation, with daily input variables being averaged from weekly or monthly meteorological records.

The model predicts the evaporation expected from an open water surface (E_o) rather than that from vegetation (E^*). Penman related the two estimates by an experimentally determined coefficient, k ($E^* = kE_o$) that varied under English conditions from 0.6 in winter to 0.8 in summer. Few users have distinguished the differences in these estimates; most have accepted E_o as an estimate of E^* (PET).

Wind is an important component of the second term in equation 8.4. The wind function depends upon the units specified, as well as upon the time period over which the estimates are being made. Penman's (1948) wind function (adjusted to g/cm² day mb) was $f(u) = 0.035 (1 + 0.0098U_2)$, with U_2 being the total wind run (miles/day) at a height of 2 m. This was revised slightly (Penman, 1956) to $f(u) = 0.035(0.5 + 0.01U)$. The coefficients are scaled for vapor pressure deficits in mm Hg rather than mb. With U expressed in units of

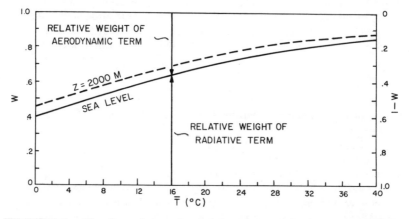

FIGURE 8-1. *The dependence of weighting terms on temperature and pressure.*

km/day and vapor pressure in mb, Penman's original wind function becomes
$f(u) = 0.0262(1 + 0.0061 U_2)$ g/cm² day mb.

Wind values are often measured at a height other than 2 meters; these can be adjusted to the equivalent value at 2 meters by multiplication with an adjustment factor. The approximate adjustment factor is $(2/z_a)^{1/6}$ where z_a is the actual measurement height (in meters).

The Monteith-Penman Combination Model

The wind function of Penman introduced an undesired degree of empiricism into his combination model. A series of improvements has evolved, leading to the definitive analysis of Monteith (1965), which produced a generalized surface-air interaction model that is now known as the Monteith-Penman combination equation.

One of the shortcomings in Penman's wind function was that the coefficients were related to the diffusive characteristics of the atmosphere, as well as to the units chosen for measurement. The original coefficients were determined for average conditions over a relatively smooth grassy surface with a rather small amount of turbulent mixing. Further, the distribution of the wind during the day affected the coefficients. Obviously, wind movement at night is not as effective in evaporation as that movement occurring during the day when the vapor pressure deficits are larger. Tanner and Pelton (1960) examined this problem in some detail.

The effects of different site and environmental conditions upon the diffusive characteristics of the atmosphere can substantially affect the wind function coefficients. Doorenbos and Pruitt (1975) used $f(u) = 0.027 (1 + 0.01 U_2)$ g/cm² day mb, for U_2 in units of km/day. Their function applies to crops during summer conditions in midlatitudes and where about two-thirds of the total wind run occurs during the daylight hours. The difference between this function and Penman's increases with wind. For example, Doorenbos and Pruitt's function is about 33 percent greater than Penman's for light winds of 140 km/day (5 km/hr) and 42 percent greater for moderate winds of 240 km/day.

Interest in estimating actual evaporation from saturated surfaces (a rate approximated by PET) led Businger (1956) to incorporate a refined wind function into the Penman equation. This function could be evaluated from direct measurements at the experimental site. Monteith (1965) rewrote Businger's model of the diffusive properties of the atmosphere as a resistance

$$r_a = \frac{[ln \, (z_a/z_0)]^2}{k^2 \, U_a} \qquad \text{s/cm} \qquad (8.5)$$

where r_a (s/cm) is the aerodynamic resistance to transfer between the surface and the height z_a (cm), z_0 (cm) is the roughness coefficient of the surface, k is Von Karman's constant ($k \simeq 0.41$), and U_a is the wind speed (cm/s) measured at height z_a.

The expression is based upon standard wind profile theory and applies strictly to adiabatic conditions. Adiabatic conditions, however, tend to prevail near the surface of a freely evaporating canopy. The application of equation 8.5 requires that detailed measurements be made of temperature and wind speed, at least initially, in order to evaluate the surface roughness coefficient, z_0.

The aerodynamic resistance can be combined with appropriate constants and written as a function suitable for equation 8.4:

$$f(u) = \frac{\epsilon\rho}{pr_a} = \frac{\epsilon\rho k^2}{p} \cdot \frac{U_a}{[ln(z_a/z_0)]} \quad \text{g/cm}^2\text{/s/mb}, \quad (8.6)$$

where ϵ is the ratio of molecular weight of water to that of air ($\epsilon = 0.622$) ρ is the density of air (g/cm²), and p is the atmospheric pressure (mb). The flux density units for H must, of course, be compatible with the units in equation 8.6. When this is the case, either of the three different forms of $f(u)$ can be used in equation 8.4. These functions range from the relatively crude, semiempirical relation first proposed by Penman to the more general model of Monteith. The increase in generality is accompanied by a corresponding increase in data requirements.

The method was generalized one step further by Monteith (1965), who took into account the reduction in evapotranspiration that is associated with failure of the surface to be saturated effectively. This occurs whenever stomatal openings prevent the vapor from freely moving into the atmosphere or whenever bare ground is no longer saturated at the surface. These are typical conditions for arid zone plant communities. The stomatal resistance will increase due to closure, and transpiration will be reduced if the vegetation is under water stress. However, even well-watered grass plots transpired at 0.8 the potential rate and saturated bare soil at 0.9.

Monteith expressed the resistance to evaporation as a surface or canopy resistance, r_c (s/cm). Rearranging his symbols, equation 8.4 becomes

$$E = \frac{W{\cdot}H/L + (1-W)\ (\epsilon\rho/pr_a)\ (e_s-e)}{W + (1-W)\ (1 + r_c/r_a)} \quad \text{g/cm}^2\text{s} \quad (8.7)$$

yielding the actual evapotranspiration rate (E, g/cm²s) as a function of the state of the environment and the physiological response of the plant.

The canopy resistance can be estimated from profile measurements of temperature and moisture or from the evaporation rate, E, when it is known (Monteith, 1965):

$$r_c = \frac{\rho c_p}{\gamma\,I_.} \left(\frac{e_s-e}{E} \right) \quad \text{s/cm} \quad (8.8)$$

where c_p is the specific heat of air at constant pressure (cal/g°C). Appropriate units are used for the other previously defined terms. This canopy resistance is essentially a stomatal resistance; it should reflect physiological adjustments of the plant to changes in environmental demands for water and changes in water availability.

Equation 8.7 reduces to equation 8.4 whenever $r_c = 0$, as is the case for an open water surface, for a canopy with leaves completely covered with intercepted water, or for soil and plants immediately following a saturating precipitation event. The apparent ease with which equation 8.7 reduces to equation 8.4 with $r_c = 0$ has led to misapplications, however.

Even well-watered vegetation exhibits some resistance to diffusion ($r_c \neq 0$). Typical values for the canopy resistance of well-watered vegetation range from 0.5 to 1.0 s/cm. The effect is to reduce E below E_0. Typical values of aerodynamic resistances are around 1.0 s/cm for low, relatively smooth canopies and 0.05 s/cm for the rougher canopies such as brush and forests. Equation 8.7 shows that as the ratio of the resistances $r_c/r_a \gg 0$ the product of $(1 + r_c/r_a)(1-W)$ in the denominator of equation 8.7 increases, the denominator becomes greater than 1.0, and the actual evapotranspiration is less than Penman's unadjusted, open water evaporation.

Some Considerations in Applying the Combination Equations

Special consideration must be given to PET estimates made with the Monteith-Penman model (equation 8.7) in conditions that differ markedly from those of the definition. Under certain conditions, the aerodynamic term will become disproportionately large, and calculated E_0 will increase to an extraordinarily high rate. This is associated with a corresponding increase in the denominator of equation 8.7 $[W + (1-W)(1 + r_c/r_a)]$ that tends to compensate for the high E_0 and so bring the estimated E rate back down to a reasonable level. However, it would appear inappropriate to compare Monteith-Penman E_0's from two different sites if the conditions at one were at variance with the definition in such a way as to contribute to an excessively large aerodynamic component.

The apparent problem associated with rough surfaces is that they generate sufficient mechanical turbulence to enhance mixing and thus keep the aerodynamic resistance at a low value. For example, aerodynamic resistances over rough canopies are generally small, on the order of 0.05 s/cm, while those over smoother, low vegetation are on the order of 0.5 s/cm. The consequence of $r_a \rightarrow o$ is to "balloon" the aerodynamic term in equation 8.7.

The importance of the r_a term and its effect upon the relation between E_0 and E can be clearly demonstrated with the help of some examples given by Federer (1975). Since studies in rough, arid zone plant communities are lacking, we will examine the data that he selected from studies carried out over pine and Douglas-fir forests: $H = 0.75$ cal/cm^2 min (0.0125 cal/cm^{2}s), $E = 1.08$ E-5 g/cm^{2}s, $e_s - e = 12$ mb, $T_a = 25°$C, $r_c = 1$ s/cm, $r_a = .06$ s/cm. He also selected $r_a = 0.6$ s/cm as an appropriate aerodynamic resistance over a crop. Other constants needed for his example are: $\epsilon = 0.622$, $\rho = 1.293$E-3 g/cm^3, $p = 100$ mb, and $\epsilon\rho/p = 8.04$ E-7. Calculating E_0 (the unadjusted potential evapotranspiration) for the rough canopy by the Monteith-Penman model (equation 8.7 with $r_c = 0$) yields

$$E_0 = 0.74 \cdot 0.0125/585 + 0.26 \cdot 8.04\text{E-7} \cdot 12/0.06$$

$$= 5.76 \text{ E-5 g/cm}^2\text{s} = 0.207 \text{ g/cm}^2 \text{ hr.}$$

This is an unexpectedly high rate of evaporation and it corresponds to a latent energy flux density of 121.1 cal/cm² hr, or 2.02 cal/cm²min. This is unrealistically large with respect to evapotranspiration rates known to exist in well-watered vegetation.

Evaluating Monteith's reduction factor ($T_a = 25°C$) yields

$$W + (1-W)(1 + r_c/r_a) = 5.33,$$

resulting in the actual transpiration of $E = 1.08E\text{-}5$ g/cm²s or 0.039 g/cm²hr. The actual rate predicted for the aerodynamically rough vegetation thus corresponds to a latent energy flux density of 22.8 cal/cm² hr, or 0.38 cal/cm² min.

For the aerodynamically smooth surface, the Monteith-Penman estimate of E_o (equation 8.7, with $r_c = 0$) is

$$E_o = (0.74)\ 0.0125/585 + 0.26 \cdot 8.04E\text{-}7 \cdot 12/0.6$$

$$= 2.0\ E\text{-}5\ \text{g/cm}^2\text{s} = 0.072\ \text{g/cm}^2\ \text{hr}.$$

This potential rate is similar to consumptive use reported elsewhere for well-watered vegetation. This rate is equivalent to 42.1 cal/cm²hr., or 0.70 cal/cm² min. Monteith's reduction factor ($T_a = 25°C$) for the smoother surface example is

$$W = (1-W)(1 + r_c/r_a) = 1.43,$$

resulting in an actual transpiration rate of $E = 1.4\ E\text{-}5$ g/cm²s, or 0.05 g/cm² hr. The equivalent latent energy flux densities are 29.2 cal/cm² hr. or 0.49 cal/cm² min. for the crop.

The example data make it possible to examine the relative importance of the radiative and the aerodynamic terms in the unadjusted potential transpiration rates under similar conditions over two surfaces with different roughness.

For the rough surface, the radiative and aerodynamic terms are in the ratio 1:7.5 before the weights (W, $1-W$) are applied and 1:2.6 after the weights are applied. For the smoother canopy example, the ratios are 1:0.8 and 1:0.3. The aerodynamic component in the Monteith-Penman model is of much greater importance for rough vegetation with small values of r_a than for smooth canopies with large values of r_a.

The importance of the weighting terms varies with temperature. This was evident in figure 8-1. In this example at $T_a = 25°C$, $W = 0.74$ and $1-W = 0.26$. Let us consider a cooler temperature, say $T_a = 16°C$, with the other factors remaining the same. At 16°C, $W = 0.64$ and $1-W = 0.36$; for the rough canopy, E_o becomes 0.258 g/cm² hr. This is an increase in potential evapotranspiration of 25 percent due to a 9°C decrease in temperature. For the smooth canopy, the cooler temperature results in $E_o = 0.07$ g/cm² hr., which is a decrease of 3 percent from the 25°C value.

In estimating actual evaporation, however, the changes in the reduction factor (the denominator in equation 8.7) tend to compensate for the shifts in E_o. The new values of $[W + (1-W)(1 + r_c/r_a)]$ at 16°C are 7.0 for the forest and

1.6 for the crop (versus 5.33 and 1.43 at 25°C). Actual evaporation from the two surfaces thus becomes 0.037 g/cm² hr. for the forest and 0.44 g/cm² hr. for the crop. The increase in the reduction factor at the cooler temperatures more than compensated for the changes in the unadjusted potential, and so the actual evapotranspiration decreased in these two examples.

It is evident that the Monteith-Penman model is a poor choice to use for estimating E_0, with r_c assumed equal to 0 and with measured values of r_a. Either both r_c and r_a must be measured and E estimated, or another model selected. The applicability of several different models will be examined further in the next section.

Comparisons of Models

Inability to identify and develop a standard reference surface has limited tests and verification of the various potential evapotranspiration models. There have, however, been quantitative comparisons of various methods against measurements from irrigated vegetation and, additionally, qualitative comparisons among a number of methods without comparison against a standard.

Many of these studies have been carried out in humid areas with ample precipitation. Some of the studies have been affected by selection of the model or the size of the coefficients used. Not all of the experiments have proven useful in identifying the most general or most accurate PET estimators. Results from several studies that were carried out in arid areas will be discussed with regard to their usefulness.

Stanhill (1961) reported a test of eight methods of calculating potential evapotranspiration, with reference to actual losses from three lysimeters in an irrigated alfalfa crop. The data used covered twelve months (forty-nine weeks) while the crop was fully developed. The methods used included measurements from a class A evaporation pan, the temperature method of Thornthwaite, a solar radiation and air temperature method described by Makkink (1957), and the combination method of Penman.

Monthly comparisons indicated that the unadjusted estimates (E_0) from the Penman equation gave the smallest coefficient of error, the highest correlation coefficient ($r = 0.96$), and the predictions nearest unity ($dE_0/dE = 1.03$). The Makkink and Thornthwaite methods gave similar results in that the correlation coefficients were high ($r = 0.95, 0.94$, respectively), but the model estimates were considerably lower than actual evapotranspiration ($dE^*/dE = 0.67$, 0.68, respectively). Direct measurements of open water evaporation with the class A evaporation pan had a similar degree of suitability but with an overestimate ($dE_0/dE = 1.43, r = 0.95$). Stanhill concluded that the Penman method was the most satisfactory of the ones tested.

Cruff and Thompson (1967) compared a number of methods for estimating potential evapotranspiration in the Southwest, using mean monthly data (ten years of record) from the U.S. Weather Bureau. Their standard of comparison was lake evaporation, which was estimated from evaporation pan measurements that were adjusted for exposure (the adjustment coefficients ranged from

0.60 to 0.78). Methods tested included the temperature methods of Thornthwaite, the temperature plus solar radiation method of Lane (1964) for estimating lake evaporation (E_0), and the U.S. weather Bureau method. The Lane method is of the basic form of the Jensen-Haise model, and the U.S. Weather Bureau method is a minor variant of the Penman combination method.

The combination method gave the best results of those tested. Agreement between mean monthly E_0 and lake (adjusted pan) evaporation was quite close: 1.06 for the seven sites that had adequate data. Other methods with smaller data requirements were tested at as many as twenty-five sites. Results from the Thornthwaite method were much lower (0.61) than the adjusted pan evaporation at twenty-five sites; results at twenty-two sites from the temperature plus solar radiation method of Lane were markedly higher (1.15).

Van Bavel (1966) compared Penman's method with lysimeter measurements of evaporation from open water, saturated soil, and irrigated alfalfa at Phoenix, Arizona. He used a revised wind function, essentially equivalent to that in equation 8.6, to estimate hourly and daily evaporation rates. For thirteen days the ratio of E_0 to E was 1.04, leading Van Bavel to conclude that irrigated alfalfa exhibited essentially no stomatal resistance since it transpired near the potential rate. Further, he concluded that the Penman method satisfactorily evaluated the advective conditions that commonly occur in irrigated fields within arid areas.

CONSIDERATIONS FOR ARID ZONE USE

A major interest in estimating potential evapotranspiration at arid zone sites is to predict water use by irrigated crops, should an irrigation project be established. Although there is interest in applying the potential evapotranspiration concept to evaluate actual water losses, direct methods of measurement are usually required to achieve reasonable accuracy. Application problems considered here are those related to the evaluation of potential evapotranspiration in an arid region where data required for calculating PET do not yet exist.

The influence of an arid surface upon potential evapotranspiration is related partly to the direct effects of the surface and partly to the features of the model being used. The undesired effects of an arid surface can be minimized in some instances by using estimated, rather than measured, variables. This is especially true for radiation.

The net radiation at two different sites will differ because of amounts received (atmospheric transmission), amounts absorbed (albedo), and amounts emitted (surface temperature). The variation can be considerable: net radiation measurements (Gay, 1973) over a pumice desert, a marsh, and a meadow in Oregon were, respectively, 226, 325, and 351 cal/cm² day. These totals are means of two clear days at each site, with measurements being taken between July 17 and September 4. The components of the radiation budgets at these three sites are tabulated in table 8-1. Two factors are evident. First, the albedo values range from 11 to 25 percent; second, the net long-wave loss from the heated pumice surface substantially exceeds the losses from the marsh and the meadow. As a consequence, net radiation over the pumice, marsh, and

TABLE 8-1. *Mean Radiation Budgets at Three Oregon Sites (cal/cm² day)*

	Albedo	Shortwave $K\downarrow$	$- K\uparrow$	$= K^*$	Longwave $L\downarrow$	$- L\uparrow$	$= L^*$	Net Q^*
Pumice	0.23	673	148	489	606	868	−263	226
Marsh	0.11	598	164	529	650	854	−204	325
Meadow	0.25	694	69	529	596	773	−177	351

meadow is in the order of 0.64:93:1.0. Although some of this variation is associated with differences between days at the three sites, the total radiation $(K\downarrow + L\downarrow = Q\downarrow)$ was surprisingly close at each site, about 0.96:0.97:1.0. Most of the variability in net radiation appears to be associated with surface properties, so it would be clearly inappropriate to use measured net radiation values at the pumice site as a basis for estimating potential evapotranspiration there. It would be more satisfactory to use measured values of incoming solar radiation $(K\downarrow)$, with an adjustment for albedo (say $\alpha = 0.25$) and for net long-wave exchange as a function of temperature and vapor content, following the guidelines of Doorenbos and Pruitt (1975).

The failure of the wind-speed measurements to express fully the diffusion capacity of the atmosphere is a shortcoming of both the surface and the form of the models. The rougher the surface, the more effective the turbulent mixing. Although natural vegetation tends to be rough, crop canopies tend to be aerodynamically smooth. Equation 8.6 would therefore be inappropriate to estimate aerodynamic resistances from actual measurements over natural vegetation for use in predicting E_0 or E^* with equation 8.7, the Monteith-Penman model. It would be better to use the Penman equation with an approximation of the aerodynamic resistance expected for the crop surface (say, Penman's original $f(u)$). Measured wind speeds are also affected by characteristics of the vegetated surface. The problems of specifying the measurement point when the vegetation deviates from the required surface characteristics (becoming either tall or discontinuous) have not yet been resolved.

Few of the various comparisons reported have clearly delineated whether the tests were to determine the PET rate of the area if the climatic conditions remained unchanged, or the rate that would be expected if a large area were evaporating. Stanhill (1961), for example, compared his results with unadjusted pan evaporation, assuming that this gave an estimate for the observed climatic conditions. On the other hand, Cruff and Thompson (1967) adjusted pan evaporation data by factors ranging from 0.60 to 0.78 in order to obtain as a comparison standard the "open water" evaporation from an extended, free-water surface.

Even in arid sites originally lacking vegetation, the development of an extensive, low, green canopy will affect the wind speed, temperature, and humidity of the air at the 2 meter level. For example, as the air moves from bare soil into an irrigated area, the wind-speed slows, the temperature decreases, and the humidity increases. The evapotranspiration rate will be very high near the upwind border between the irrigated area and the dry surrounds; it may even be large in the center if the irrigated area is small. The enhanced evapotranspiration in these circumstances is called the *oasis effect*. A theoretical analysis of the variability of evaporation with distance from the border with the desert is given by Vries (1959).

The transpiring oasis surface may utilize sensible heat extracted from the warm air and thus exhibit an actual transpiration rate that is in excess of the energy available from net radiation exchange. The enhanced rate diminishes rapidly with distance from the dry-land border; however, much of the decrease occurs within the first 200 meters, and relatively little beyond that distance (Stanhill, 1965). The amount of the decrease is large. Morton (1975) reasoned that estimates of potential evapotranspiration in a completely humid area should equal precisely one-half the rate in a contiguous, completely arid area. Stanhill (1961) showed that the measured evapotranspiration at a location 100 m inside an irrigated field at Gilat, Israel, was about 0.42 of that measured at the border. Davenport and Hudson (1967) found that evaporation within an irrigated cotton field in the Sudan was 0.53 of that measured at the edge, 300 meters away. Penman, Angus, and Van Bavel (1967) reviewed some exceedingly variable results for downwind distances required for adjustments (from 1 to more than 100 meters); they pointed out that the distance required is affected both by the thickness of the air layer that must come into equilibrium (height of measurement) and by the velocity of the wind. Regardless of the distance required, there is theoretical and observational evidence that transpiration from a large irrigated area will affect the properties of the air sufficiently to reduce the rate to a level of perhaps half that expected from a small test plot.

PET EXAMPLES

The variability between methods of estimating PET at a single point and the spatial variability of a singled method applied to a large arid/semiarid region can be illustrated by reference to some Arizona data.

PET at Tucson, Arizona

The published temperature, wind, humidity, and pan evaporation data (U.S. Department of Commerce, 1966–1975) at Tucson, Arizona, augmented by solar radiation data (Office of the State Climatologist, 1976), were used to estimate PET by the various methods for the ten-year mean 1966–1975.

The net radiation values needed for the Penman and the Priestly-Taylor models were estimated from incoming solar radiation using the procedures of Doorenbos and Pruitt (1975). First the incoming solar radiation was reduced for an assumed albedo of the hypothetical crop canopy (here, $\alpha = 0.25$). Next the long-wave component of net radiation was estimated with reference to percentage possible sunshine and the temperature and the moisture content of the air. Then, the percentage possible sunshine was evaluated from average sky cover. (Refer to Doorenbos and Pruitt, 1975, for the details of the computations).

The Penman estimates were based on equation 8.4, with Doorenbos and Pruitt's (1975) wind function: $f(u) = 0.027 (1 + 0.01 \ U_2)$ g/cm² day. The other methods used the formulas as defined earlier; the adjusted pan evaporation is based upon a pan coefficient of 0.67 for the Tucson area (see figure 8-4).

The mean monthly rates (mm/day) are plotted in figure 8-2. Several methods (Jensen-Haise, adjusted pan, Penman) appeared reasonably consistent. The unadjusted pan evaporation rates were about 150 percent of the PET values predicted by this group. The Jensen-Haise method predicted maximum values of 9.9 mm/day during the midsummer months. The Penman estimates were the next highest of the formula methods; this method predicted 8.0 mm/day, with the evaporation peak also occurring at midsummer. The adjusted pan evaporation rate of 8.8 mm/day fell midway between the two highest formula estimates at the summer peak.

Both the Priestly-Taylor and the Thornthwaite estimates were low in comparison with the other three. The Thornthwaite method also shifted peak evaporation rates from June into July. This phase shift, noted many times by other authors, is associated with heat storage in the soil during the warming season (spring and early summer).

The monthly and annual means produced by the various methods are tabulated in table 8-2 in cm per month and totaled for a year. The Penman estimates exceed adjusted pan evaporation slightly on an annual basis. Otherwise the order is the same as for the midsummer period. The largest estimate from a formula method (Jensen-Haise) is about twice that of the lowest (Thornthwaite).

Considerable variability is evident among the selected methods in figure 8-2 and table 8-2. The Penman method varies with such factors as distribution

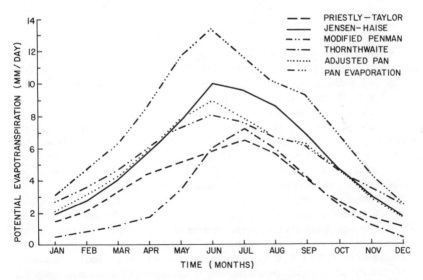

FIGURE 8-2. *Estimates of potential evapotranspiration by several methods at Tucson, Arizona, 1966–1975.*

TABLE 8-2. *Mean Evaporation at Tucson, Arizona, 1966–1975*

Method	J	F	M	A	M	J	J	A	S	O	N	D	Total
Evaporation pan	9.5	12.9	19.1	25.9	36.0	40.0	35.9	30.7	27.6	21.0	12.9	7.9	279.4
Adjusted pan	6.4	8.6	12.8	17.4	24.1	26.8	24.1	20.6	18.5	14.1	8.6	5.3	187.3
Jensen	5.9	7.6	12.4	17.1	23.6	29.7	29.5	26.7	20.4	14.3	8.7	5.3	201.2
Penman	8.4	10.1	14.3	18.3	22.6	24.0	23.3	20.5	18.3	14.0	10.5	7.4	191.7
Priestly	4.2	6.0	10.0	13.1	15.7	17.1	19.9	17.4	12.0	8.9	4.9	3.5	132.7
Thornthwaite	1.6	2.2	3.7	5.1	10.5	18.0	22.0	18.6	12.6	7.4	3.6	1.6	106.9

Note: Amounts are totals (cm/month or cm/year).

of wind between day and night and with choice of wind function. The Thorn-thwaite estimates demonstrate the empirical temperature method's short-comings in arid climates. Rates from the Jensen-Haise method are higher than the adjusted pan evaporation (open water), which itself is directly affected by the selection of a pan coefficient.

The lack of a reference standard makes comparison of methods difficult. Even when evaporation data are available from research plots, the evapotranspiration rate is influenced by the physiological condition of the vegetation, as well as by the size of the plot. These factors tend to support the view that the evaporation pan is the best possibility for a standardized estimate of potential evapotranspiration. The configuration of the pan and condition of exposure can be carefully defined, and the development of reasonable procedures for evaluating pan coefficients is well along (Doorenbos and Pruitt, 1975). The pan method holds the greatest promise for obtaining evaporation estimates that can be compared from one place to another.

Regional PET Estimates

Arizona is a warm, rather dry state in the southwestern United States. It has a maximum length (north-south) of 631 km, a maximum width of 544 km, and an area of about 295,000 km². Approximately half of the state receives less than 25 cm precipitation a year. This area comprises practically all of the northeast and southwest sections. The most arid region along the western border receives less than 13 cm annually. Precipitation distribution is closely linked to physiography, and the abrupt changes in elevation in Arizona can create large differences in precipitation within a short distance. There are certain areas in the northern plateau region and in the central and southeastern mountains that receive more than 65 cm of precipitation.

Pan evaporation data are used to define annual evaporation totals ranging from 380 cm in the extreme west to less than 190 cm in the northeast (figure 8-3). The limited number of observation pans requires considerable conjecture to interpolate the results. Pan coefficients used by the U.S. Weather Bureau are mapped in figure 8-4 (U.S. Department of Commerce, 1968). The coefficients are associated with exposure; they range from 0.60 in the hot, dry west to 0.70 in the cool, more humid central mountain region.

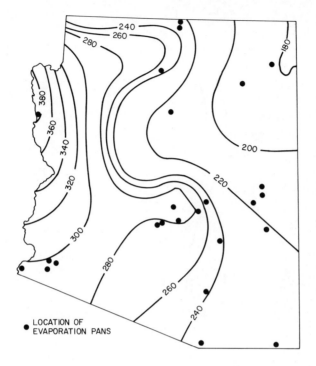

AVERAGE ANNUAL PAN EVAPORATION
(CENTIMETERS)

FIGURE 8-3. *Average annual pan evaporation (cm) in Arizona (after U.S. Department of Commerce, 1968).*

Lake or open water evaporation is obtained by adjusting the pan values. The values across the state are shown in figure 8-5, based upon the pan evaporation in figure 8-3 and the pan coefficients in figure 8-4. Annual values range from 230 cm in the west down to 127 cm in the northeast. Maximum values are in the arid western lowlands, and the minimum values are in the higher, cooler northeast.

Annual pan evaporation totals for a large region such as Arizona are of general interest but are not necessarily indicative of actual evapotranspiration, even from irrigated crops that meet the conditions of the PET definition. Problems with the models have already been identified. The period during which plants meet the PET conditions is another reason for discrepancy. Most irrigated crops do not maintain closed canopies and full growth throughout the year, even in warm regions. Grains, for example, cease growth at maturity, and a considerable period may elapse in the spring before crown closure occurs in some crops. Further, below-freezing temperatures effectively limit transpiration. Tucson, Arizona, for example, has a growing season from February 16 to November 28 between the normal occurrence of the last severe frost ($-2.2°C$,

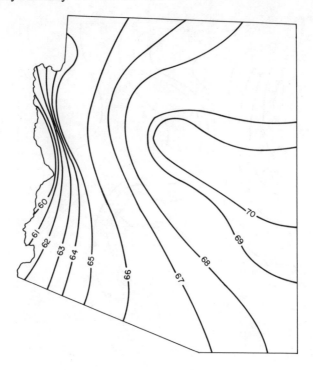

PAN COEFFICIENT
(PERCENT)

FIGURE 8-4. *Coefficients (%) to adjust pan evapora-tion measurements for microclimate variations (after U.S. Department of Commerce, 1968).*

or 28°F) in the spring and the first in the fall. Yuma, in the southwest corner of Arizona, is normally frost free throughout the year, while Flagstaff, in the central mountains, is normally free of −2.2°C frosts only from May 22 to October 10 (Sellers and Hill, 1974).

Regional evaporation estimates can be adjusted to indicate totals for the frost-free season. Buol (1964), for example, prepared such maps for Arizona using the Thornthwaite model for the basic calculations, however, his totals appear questionably low.

CONCLUSIONS

This review of the development and use of potential evapotranspiration estimates in arid zones suggests that the concept may have a great deal of usefulness in comparing the evaporative demand of different environments.

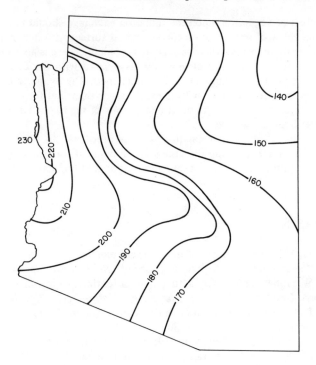

AVERAGE ANNUAL LAKE EVAPORATION
(CENTIMETERS)

FIGURE 8-5. *Annual lake evaporation (cm) in Arizona (after U.S. Department of Commerce, 1968).*

The concept isolates evaporation from the variability encountered in water availability, physiological factors, and canopy structure. The concept has not proven as useful in estimating actual transpiration.

The PET concept has not led to a precise formulation that will accurately predict actual water loss rates from an appropriate plant community. The surface evaporation pan offers considerable promise as an evaporation reference because it can be effectively standardized in construction and exposure. The PET models that appear to give good results, with regard to either irrigated fields or adjusted pan readings, are those that emphasize the major evaporation processes. The Jensen-Haise radiation model and the combination model have given good results in many arid zone tests.

The combination model can be used for either PET or for actual ET. When the Monteith-Penman form for ET is used to estimate PET with canopy resistance (r_c) assumed to be zero, exceptionally large estimates of PET may occur. This is a problem when measured aerodynamic resistances over rough canopies are applied in the model. Obviously, r_c cannot equal zero in these situations, although little work has been done on this problem.

The effect of vegetation upon the radiation exchange should not be over-looked. Estimates of net radiation for vegetated surfaces, rather than measurements over desert soils, will minimize this problem. There is also a problem in accounting for the reduced evaporation associated with the cooler, more humid environment when large areas are moistened. The evaporation from a small plot in arid surroundings will be much larger than that from one in the midst of a large, moist area. Practical evaluations of the expected reductions have not yet been developed.

Despite the problems in evaluation and interpretation, the PET concept is a useful means for evaluating the atmospheric demand for water. Upon this basis it will continue to receive research attention and popular application.

REFERENCES

Anonymous. 1956. Proceedings of the informal meeting on physics in agriculture, Wageningen 7–13 September, 1955. *Neth. J. Agric. Sci.* **4**:1–162.

Buol, S. W. 1964. Calculated actual and potential evapotranspiration in Arizona. *Univ. Ariz. Tucson Agric. Exper. Station Tech. Bull. 162*, p. 48.

Businger, J. A. 1956. Some remarks on Penman's equation for evapotranspiration. *Neth. J. Agric. Sci.* **4**:77–80.

Cruff, R. W., and T. H. Thompson. 1967. A Comparison of Methods of Estimating Potential Evapotranspiration from Climatological Data in Arid and Subhumid Environments. U.S. Geol. Survey Water Supply Paper 1839-M.

Davenport, D. C., and J. P. Hudson. 1967. Meteorological observations and Penman estimates along a 17 km transect in the Sudan Gezira. *Agric. Meteorol.* **4**:405–414.

Doorenbos, J., and W. O. Pruitt. 1975. Guidelines for predicting crop water requirements. *Irrigation and Drainage Paper 24*. FAO, Rome, 179 pp.

Federer, C. A. 1975. Evapotranspiration. *Rev. Geophys. Space Phys.* **12**:442–445, 487–494.

Gay, L. W. 1973. Energy exchange studies at the earth's surface. I. Energy budgets of desert, meadow, forest and marsh sites. *Tech. Report 73-1*. Dept. Atmosph. Sci., Oregon State Univ., Corvallis, Ore.

Jensen, M. E. 1966. Empirical methods of estimating or predicting evapotranspiration using radiation, pp. 49–53. In *Evaporation and Its Role in Water Resources Management Proceedings*. Am. Soc. Agric. Eng., St. Joseph, Mich.

Jensen, M. E., and H. R. Haise. 1963. Estimating evapotranspiration from solar radiation. *J. Irrig. Drain. Div., Am. Soc. Civil Eng. Proc.* **89** (IR4):15–41.

Lane, R. K. 1964. Estimating evaporation from insulation. *J. Am. Soc. Civil Eng. Hydraul. Div.* **90**(HY5):33–41.

Makkink, G. F. 1957. Ekzameno de la formula de Penman. *Neth. J. Agric. Sci.* **5**:290–305.

Monteith, J. L. 1965. Evaporation and environment. *Symp. Soc. Exper. Biol.* **19**:205–234.

Morton, F. I. 1975. Estimating evaporation and transpiration from climatological observations. *J. Appl. Meteorol.* **14:**488–497.

Office of the State Climatologist. 1976. *Solar Radiation Data for Arizona.* Mimeographed report. Lab. Climatol., Arizona State Univ., Tempe, Ariz.

Palmer, W. C., and A. V. Havens. 1958. A graphical technique for determining evapotranspiration by the Thornthwaite method. *Monthly Weather Rev.* **86:**123–128.

Penman, H. L. 1948. Natural evaporation from open water, bare soil and grass. *Proc. Roy. Soc. (London),* Ser. A, **193:**120–145.

Penman, H. L. 1956. Evaporation, an introductory survey. *Neth. J. Agric. Sci.* **4:**9–29.

Penman, H. L., D. E. Angus, and C. H. M. Van Bavel. 1967. Microclimatic factors affecting evaporation and transpiration, pp. 483–505. In *Irrigation of Agricultural Lands,* Am. Soc. Agronomy Monogr. 11, Madison, Wisc.

Priestly, C. H. B., and R. J. Taylor. 1975. On the assessment of surface heat flux and evaporation using large-scale parameters. *Monthly Weather Rev.* **100:**81–92.

Pruitt, W. O. 1966. Empirical method of estimating evapotranspiration using primarily evaporation pans, pp. 57–61. In *Evaporation and Its Role in Water Resources Management Proceedings.* Am. Soc. Agric. Eng., St. Joseph, Mich.

Pruitt, W. O. 1971. Factors affecting potential evapotranspiration, pp. 82–102. In E. J. Monke (ed.), *Biological Effects in the Hydrologic Cycle.* Proc. 3d Internat. Seminar Hydrol. Prof. Purdue Univ.

Sellers, W. D., and R. H. Hill. 1974. *Arizona Climate, 1931–1972.* Univ. Arizona Press, Tucson.

Stanhill, G. 1961. A comparison of methods of calculating potential evapotranspiration from climatic data. *Isr. J. Agric. Res.* **11:**159–171.

Stanhill, G. 1965. The concept of potential evapotranspiration in arid zone agriculture, pp. 109–117. In *Arid Zone Research,* v. 25. Proc. Montpellier. Symp. UNESCO, Paris.

Stanhill, G. 1973. Evaporation, transpiration and evapotranspiration: A case for Ockham's razor, pp. 207–220. In A. Hadas, D. Swartzendruber, P. E. Rijtema, M. Fuchs, and B. Yaron (eds.), *Physical Aspects of Soil Water and Salts in Ecosystems.* Springer-Verlag, New York.

Swinbank, W. C. 1965. Discussion of "The concept of potential evapotranspiration in arid zone agriculture," p. 116. In *Arid Zone Research,* v. 25. Proc. Montpellier Symp. UNESCO, Paris.

Tanner, C. B., and W. L. Pelton. 1960. Potential evapotranspiration estimates by the approximate energy balance method of Penman. *J. Geophys. Res.* **65:**3391–3413.

Thornthwaite, C. W. 1944. Report of the Committee on Transpiration and Evaporation, 1943–44. *Trans. Am. Geophys. Union* **25:**686–693.

Thornthwaite, C. W. 1948. An approach toward a rational classification of climate. *Geogr. Rev.* **38:**55–94.

U.S. Department of Commerce. 1966–1975. *Local Climatological Data, Arizona.* Published monthly. Govt. Printing Off., Washington, D.C.

U.S. Department of Commerce. 1968. *Climatic Atlas of the United States.* Govt. Printing Off., Washington, D.C.

Van Bavel, C. H. M. 1966. Potential evaporation: the combination concept and its experimental verification. *Water Resour. Res.* **2**:455–467.

Vries, P. A. de. 1959. The influence of irrigation on the energy balance and the climate near the ground. *J. Meteorol.* **16**:256–270.

9

Actual Evapotranspiration under Desert Conditions

Daniel D. Evans, Theodore W. Sammis, and *Dwight R. Cable*

Actual evapotranspiration, in contrast to potential evapotranspiration, which was covered in chapter 8, refers to the amount of water actually transferred from the soil to the atmosphere through evaporation and transpiration processes during a specified time. For desert conditions, actual evapotranspiration is a small percentage of the potential, except perhaps immediately following a rainfall event. Water availability and extent of plant cover are not usually sufficient to meet the requirements for potential rates.

Although the controlling processes and parameters governing evapotranspiration for desert conditions are the same as for more humid regions or irrigated lands, the magnitude of the controlling factors may differ greatly. Biotic, climatic, and soil controls are most often significantly different for desert versus other environments.

In general, the total annual evapotranspiration for desert conditions is equal to the cumulative water infiltration into the soil for the year, or it is equal to the total annual precipitation minus surface runoff. At least once during any year, the soil-water content consistently becomes very low at all depths, with immeasurable differences from year to year. Also, deep drainage is usually negligible relative to total annual evapotranspiration. Therefore the principal interest is the temporal distribution of evapotranspiration during the year.

Many studies have been conducted to measure or predict evapotranspiration rates for irrigated and nonirrigated croplands, grasslands, and forests. In contrast, very few studies were made for deserts prior to the initiation of the Desert Biome Program. Deserts have been considered of low economic value, and the result has been little incentive for research. However, recent increased incentives have developed because of greater interests in preservation of the desert in its near-natural state and for predicting water yields from desert areas. Evapotranspiration is an important hydrologic process in desert regions.

Evapotranspiration and related data presented in this chapter are primarily from Desert Biome studies performed at various field sites in the western United States. Some additional information from studies other than those related to the program was included, but available quantitative data were very limited. No attempt was made to include transpiration results for individual plants or plant parts as determined by gas exchange systems, such as reported by Caldwell et al. (1977). Although transpiration is important to the understanding of desert ecosystems, the results are commonly expressed in mass of water transpired per unit mass of plant during a specified time and are not readily interpretable in terms of total loss of water from a given area, the emphasis of this chapter.

Many problems are encountered in the measurement of evapotranspiration, particularly in the desert. The principal method employed is to measure the total soil water in a given depth of soil at selected intervals of time. The change in stored water during a time interval is algebraically added to the precipitation amount during the same time period to determine the total water loss to the atmosphere. Usually the total water loss is divided by the number of days to obtain an average rate for the time period, for example, mm/day. A common assumption is that there is no surface runoff during a precipitation event, mainly because runoff is not measured. This assumption can introduce a sizable error during periods when rainfall occurs with intensities greater than the infiltration capacity. In addition, soil-water measurement techniques are not adequate to yield a reliable estimate of water loss for a short time period, especially when the evapotranspiration rate is low. Also, sampling errors may be large due to spatial variation in soil properties and rooting characteristics and restrictions on the number of sampling sites at any given time. Hence the total measurement error associated with the estimated evapotranspiration rate may be large, and results should be viewed as order of magnitude estimates.

At all Desert Biome measurement sites, evapotranspiration was estimated using time periods of two weeks or longer. The neutron method has been the principal technique for measuring soil-water content at selected depths and times. Data from a weighing lysimeter were collected at one site adjacent to an area where evapotranspiration was determined by the neutron technique. Results are presented for four sites:

1. Silverbell site, 70 km northwest of Tucson, Arizona.
     Dominant plants: *Larrea tridentata* (creosote bush), *Ambrosia deltoidea* (bursage).
2. Santa Rita site, 50 km southeast of Tucson.
     Dominant plants: *Prosopis juliflora* (mesquite), *Celtis pallida* (desert hackberry), *Heteropogon contortus* (tanglehead grass), *Aristida glabrata* (Santa Rita threeawn)
3. Washtucna site, near Lind, Washington.
     Dominant plants: *Artemisia tridentata* (sagebrush) and associated grasses.
4. Curlew site, northwestern tip of the Great Salt Lake, Utah.
     Dominant plants: *Atriplex confertifolia* (shad-scale), *Eurotia lanata* (winter fat), *Argopyron desertorum* (crested wheatgrass).

The first two sites are considered warm desert sites, and the latter two are cold ones. The annual precipitation means for the sites are 280, 294, 262, and 250 mm, respectively. Data for sites 1 and 2 extend over more years and are more complete than for sites 3 and 4. Evapotranspiration results are expressed graphically in mm per day over the period of measurement for each site. Precipitation data and other site characteristics are included as available to assist in interpreting the evapotranspiration results.

SILVERBELL SITE, ARIZONA

The Silverbell site was a validation site for the Desert Biome Program. The site is at an elevation of 730 m. Mean annual precipitation of 280 mm approximates that for Tucson. Vegetation is typical of the middle elevation Sonoran Desert, with dominant species being creosote bush (*Larrea tridentata*), bursage (*Ambrosia deltoidea*), paloverde (*Cercidium microphyllum*) and mesquite (*Prosopis juliflora*) (figure 9-1).

Two study areas were selected about 1.5 km apart for installation of 5-cm diameter aluminum access tubes for the measurement of soil-water content by the neutron method. The tubes were installed to depths of 75 to 200 cm under or near selected creosote bush and bursage plants and in open areas.

In area I, the soil type is Tubac gravelly, sandy loam on a 1 to 3 percent slope with good drainage. Eleven access tubes were installed in the open, four near creosote bush plants (or clumps of plants), and three near bursage plants. To minimize root activity at the open locations, all plants within a radius of 10 m from access tubes were removed. A detailed description of the location of tubes with respect to plants was given by Evans et al. (1976). Measurements were started on February 27, 1973, and continued to October 20, 1975, at two-week intervals or longer (depending on plant activity) and at 15-cm depth intervals.

In area II, the soil type is Tres Hermanos fine, gravelly, sandy loam on a slope similar to area I. Access tubes were located near creosote bush and bursage plants (Cable, 1977) in such a way as to sample a range of plant distributions:

Location 1, on crown perimeter where crowns of adjacent plants touch.
Location 2, on crown perimeter facing adjacent plant whose crown is 2 m away (1 m for bursage).
Location 3, on crown perimeter facing 4 m minimum opening (2 m for bursage).
Location 4, in opening 2 m from plant crown and with no other plant crown closer than 2 m (1 m for bursage).
Location 5, in open area, isolated from all shrub roots by trenching and plastic lining the block of soil to 1 m depth.

For creosote bush, tubes in the first four locations were keyed to four individual plants (four replications), and four location 5 tubes were placed in an adjacent isolated plot. For bursage, the four replications were keyed to only nine plants because individual plants meeting all four specifications were not available. Again, four location 5 tubes were installed in an adjacent plot. Tubes in the open and around creosote bush plants extended to 2-m depth, while

FIGURE 9-1. *General view of vegetation at the Silverbell site.*

those for bursage extended to 1.5 m. Readings were taken at 25-cm depth intervals, starting on June 7, 1974, and continuing at nearly two-week intervals to December 1975.

Close to area II, a weighing lysimeter was installed, which enclosed a single clump of creosote bush plants (Young et al., 1976; Sammis et al., 1976). The installation was made with minimal soil and plant disturbance during construction. A representative plant was selected on the basis of size, condition, and proximity to neighboring plants. The installed lysimeter is shown in figure 9-2.

The cylindrical lysimeter contained a volume of soil 4 m in diameter by 1 m deep. The three strain gauges supporting the 16.3-plus metric tons of soil indicated a measurable weight difference of 2.7 kg, or the equivalent of 0.2 mm depth of water over the contained surface. Weight measurements were started in June 1975 and were made periodically through 1976.

Evapotranspiration from Water Balance

Calculated evapotranspiration rates for the Silverbell site by the water balance approach are shown in figure 9-3. No significant differences were apparent between plant species, between locations in area II, or between plots with and without plants (Sammis and Weeks, 1977). Therefore, data for all tubes were averaged and plotted in the figure. The length of the vertical lines indicates the extremes of the averages for individual locations with respect to plants. Variations about the mean appeared to be random and were probably due to measurement errors.

Evapotranspiration rates were dominated by rainfall patterns (figure 9-4). Periods of relatively high evapotranspiration rates correspond to periods of rainfall. During periods without rainfall, rates drop to very low levels (table 9-1). Most of the increase in evapotranspiration rate following a rainfall event is probably due to increased evaporation at the soil surface immediately following the event rather than to an increase in transpiration rate.

The low rates of less than 0.1 mm per day emphasize the ability of desert plants to exist under extreme water stress environments. The final soil-water contents of 0.10 to 0.06 (table 9-1) correspond to soil suction values of -10 to -50 bars.

TABLE 9-1.   *Average Evapotranspiration Rates (mm/day) for Selected Periods with No Rainfall and Range of Soil Water Contents (Θ) for Each Period*

Dates	Bare soil	Creosote bush	Bursage	Average	Θ cm³/cm³
3/30 to 5/2/73	1.29	1.36	1.15	1.26	0.14–0.10
9/15 to 11/10/73	0.04	0.05	0.04	0.04	0.07–0.06
3/20 to 6/26/74	0.01	0.01	0.01	0.01	0.08–0.06
1/23 to 2/20/74	0.13	0.19	0.11	0.14	0.08–0.07

FIGURE 9-2. *Lysimeter containing creosote bush plant.*

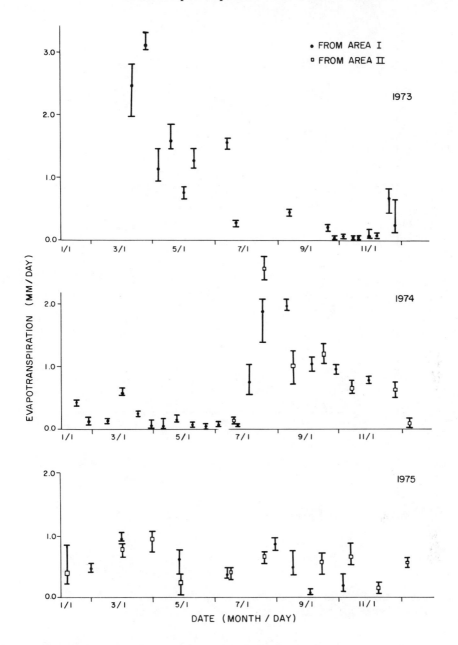

FIGURE 9-3. *Evapotranspiration results for Silverbell site.*

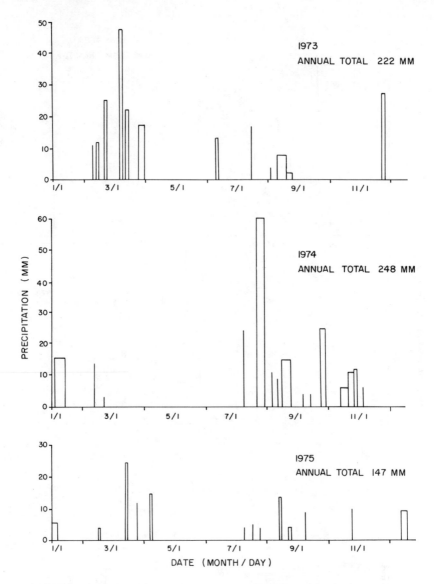

FIGURE 9-4. *Total precipitation during period shown by width of bar at the Silverbell site.*

The Silverbell site is further characterized by a mean monthly temperature and relative humidity pattern during 1973 (figure 9-5). The pattern shows the characteristic mild winters, hot summers, and long periods of low relative humidity that yield potential evapotranspiration rates as high as 20 mm per day during the summer months. Actual evapotranspiration may be only 0.05 percent of potential rates at certain times.

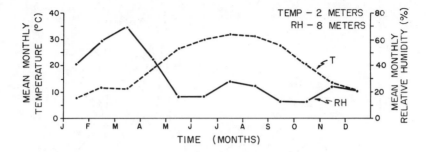

FIGURE 9-5. *Mean monthly temperature and relative humidity for 1973 at the Silverbell site.*

In an earlier study, Sellers and Dryden (1967) used a specially designed fluxometer system to estimate evaporation from bare soil at a site near Tucson, Arizona. Measurements were made every thirty minutes for various lengths of time on selected dates between June 11 and August 20, 1965. The soil was extremely dry from June 11 to July 7, with no measurable evaporation. Following July 8, there was intermittent rainfall, and the evaporation rate between times 0600 and 2000 ranged from 0.12 to 4.3 mm per day for fifteen different days without rainfall. The observed variation was due to time after rainfall events and climatic condition. However, the range of values was of the same order of magnitude as measured at the Silverbell site.

Evapotranspiration by Lysimeter

Evapotranspiration data from the lysimeter and from the water balance approach for 1976 are shown in figure 9-6. Lysimeter readings were made more frequently than were soil moisture measurements, which resulted in more data points from the lysimeter and inconsistencies in the time period over which evapotranspiration was averaged. Because there were no significant differences between types of plant and vegetated versus nonvegetated plots for the water balance approach, all results were combined to form the plotted averages.

Generally there is good agreement between results by the two methods. Discrepancies may be explained by the different time intervals and time of measurements in relation to rainfall events (figure 9-6), spatial variability between the measurement sites, and measurement errors. Total evapotranspiration from February 6 to November 10 differed by only 1 mm (235 to 236 mm) for the two methods. Total precipitation during the same period was 218 mm, from which there was a net loss of only 18 mm from soil storage. Evapotranspiration rates for 1976 varied from a high of 4 to 5 mm per day to less than 1 mm per day.

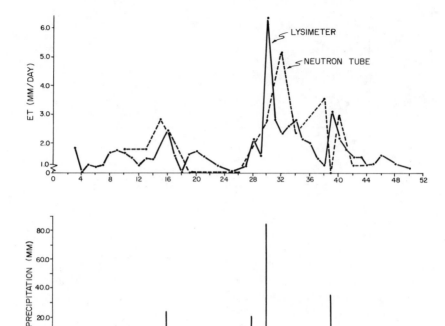

FIGURE 9-6. *Evapotranspiration data by the lysimeter and water balance methods and precipitation for 1976 at the Silverbell site.*

SANTA RITA SITE, ARIZONA

The Santa Rita site near Tucson at 1,000 m elevation has middle-elevation Sonoran Desert vegetation. The major plant species are mesquite (*Prosopis juliflora*), paloverde (*Cercidium microphyllum*), cholla (*Opuntia fulgida*), prickly pear (*Opuntia engelmannii*), desert hackberry (*Celtis pallidas*), and several grasses. The mean annual precipitation near the site is 294 mm, with 65 percent occurring during the late summer.

Evapotranspiration rates were determined by the water balance method for three types of vegetation: desert hackberry, mesquite, and five grasses. Also, evaporation from a bare soil plot was determined, and climatic variables were measured at the study site.

Desert Hackberry

A clump of fifteen individual desert hackberry plants was selected for study (figure 9-7) (Sammis, 1974). A rectangular trench, 1.5 m deep enclosing a square area of 18 m², was dug around the plants. The plant canopy covered an

FIGURE 9-7. *Desert hackberry study plant at the Santa Rita site.*

area of 12 m². A plastic liner was installed along the side of the trench next to the plants, and the trench was then backfilled. Observations have shown that desert hackberry roots extend laterally no more than 1 m and downward about the same distance, with concentration of roots between 0.2 and 0.6 m. Therefore, the lined volume of soil was believed to enclose the root mass of the study plants. The soil at the site is Sonoita sandy loam, which is nearly uniform to a depth of 0.9 m, where only a slight change in texture occurs.

Nine neutron access tubes were installed to a depth of 1.5 m under and around the desert hackberry plants. Three tubes were also installed to the same depth in a nearby denuded plot of similar size. Soil-water potential and soil temperature were measured in both plots, using thermocouple psychrometers at 0.15, 0.3, 0.5, 0.75, and 1.0 m depths. Several climatic variables were measured but are not reported here (see Sammis, 1974, for data). Measurements were made from October 1972 to September 1973 at approximately two-week intervals during periods of active uptake of water and less frequently when plant activity was low.

A summary of the results is included in figure 9-8. Evapotranspiration rates varied from 3 mm per day to 0.1 mm per day for the desert hackberry plot. Nearly the same rates were measured for the bare plot, except during the spring when the plants were fully leafed and soil water potential was greater than −20 bars. During the measurement period, the average soil-water content in the top 1.2 m of soil ranged from 4 to 13 percent by volume, corresponding to soil-water potential values of −40 bars to −1 bar. Psychrometers used were not sensitive at potentials greater than −1 bar. After May 1, the soil-water potential gradually decreased to −50 bars by July 15 at the 0.3 m depth and by September 15 at the 0.6 m depth. The relatively small rains during the summer months had little or no effect on the soil water potential at 0.3 m.

Mesquite

Soil at the mesquite study site is a gravelly, sandy loam, changing to a gravelly clay at 2 to 5 m depth. Four mesquite trees, each located at the edge of an opening 20 to 30 m across, were selected for study trees. The trees were 5 to 6 m tall, with crowns 8 to 9 m in diameter. Figure 9-9 shows one of the measurement sites.

At each of the four trees, six neutron access tubes were installed to 6 m depth. The tubes were located on a radial line from the tree trunk near the trunk, midway between the trunk and the edge of the crown, at the edge of the crown, and at 5, 10, and 15 m beyond the edge of the crown in the adjacent opening.

Soil-water content was measured at thirteen depths from 0.25 to 6 m starting in July 1971 and continuing to December 1973. On some dates, no measurements were made below 3 m because essentially static conditions existed at the greater depths.

Calculated evapotranspiration rates, using all depths and distances from the tree trunk for the four trees, are shown in figure 9-10, along with the precipitation record. The rate reached a maximum of 6 mm per day during a

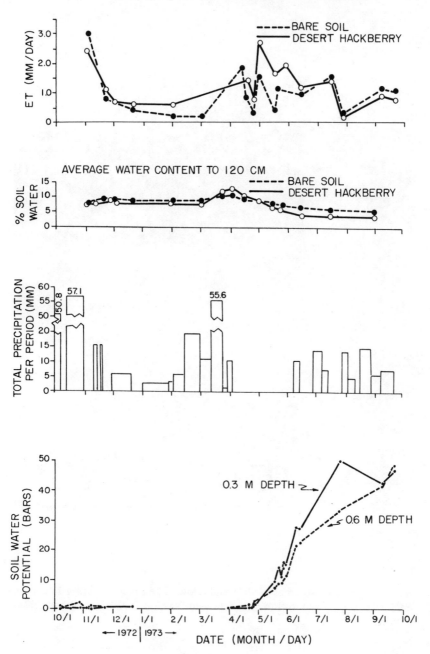

FIGURE 9-8. *Evapotranspiration for desert hackberry plants, associated average soil moisture content and potential, and precipitation at the Santa Rita site.*

FIGURE 9-9. *One of the mesquite study trees at the Santa Rita site.*

rainy period in the summer of 1971 and a low of nearly zero during December 1973. In general, evaporation rates followed the rainfall distribution and season of year.

Grasses

Five native perennial grass species, located near the mesquite study site, were studied for soil moisture extraction patterns and evapotranspiration rates. The species were *Aristida glabrata* (Santa Rita threeawn), *Aristida ternipe*

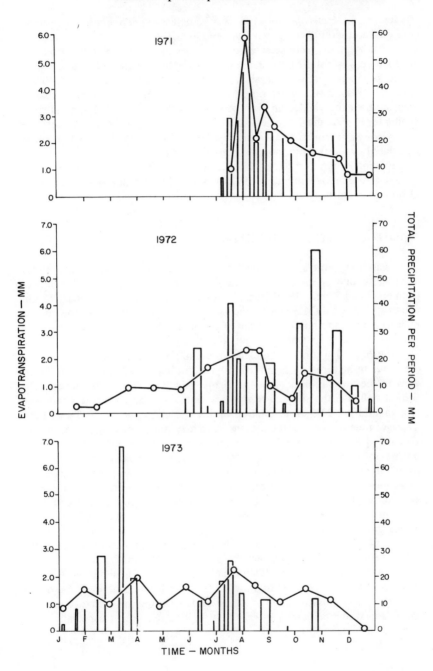

FIGURE 9-10. *Evapotranspiration for mesquite and associated precipitation data for the Santa Rita site.*

(spider grass), *Heteropogon contortus* (tanglehead), *Trichachne californica* (Arizona cottontop), and *Bouteloua eriopoda* (black grama). Four medium-size, healthy plants were selected of each species (see figure 9-11). A neutron access tube was installed within a few cm of the base of each plant to a depth of 3.0 m. Readings were taken at about two-week intervals from June 28, 1972, to May 15, 1975. Evapotranspiration rates were calculated assuming that the measurement site yielded an average value for the root zone. The results were similar for the five grass species, so data for only two species will be presented: *Heteropogon contortus* and *Aristida glabrata*. Figures 9-12 and 9-13 show the calculated evapotranspiration and precipitation record.

Evapotranspiration varied from a high of 10 mm per day during a prolonged period in the summer of 1972 to essentially zero during several periods of no rain or during the winter.

WASHTUCNA SITE, WASHINGTON

Evapotranspiration rates were measured for sagebrush (*Artemisia tridentata*) and a mixture of sagebrush and grasses at a site in western Washington (Campbell and Harris, 1975). Mean annual precipitation at the site is 262 mm, occurring mainly in the winter and spring. Precipitation during the summer months amounts to only 12 percent of the annual total. The soil at the site has been classified as Esquatzel silt loam.

The 20 × 20 m study site included areas of primarily grass, small sagebrush (up to 0.5 m high), large sagebrush (about 2 m high), and bare soil. A general view of the vegetation is shown in figure 9-14. Eleven neutron access tubes were installed at the site and readings were taken at approximately two-week intervals during 1973. Precipitation during the early part of 1973 was below average; thus the results for the one year may not be descriptive of the site. Calculated evapotranspiration rates are shown in figure 9-15, along with the precipitation record. The data line for small sagebrush and grass was obtained from four access tubes located in a mixture of small sagebrush and grasses; the other line is for four tubes located in stands of large sagebrush. Data from the two vegetative covers are similar; the differences are probably due to measurement errors. As expected, evapotranspiration rates were relatively high during the spring and early summer and became lower later in the summer. A maximum rate of 2.3 mm per day was measured in May, a value lower than would be expected for a year with average precipitation.

In a similar study, Belt (1969) measured an evapotranspiration rate of 3.4 mm per day from May 29 to June 9, 1969 for a low sagebrush (*Artemisia arbuscula*) and grass range in southern Idaho. During the period of measurement, soil-water content was relatively high at all times, especially in the subsoil.

CURLEW VALLEY, UTAH

Evapotranspiration rates for a mixed stand of two cold desert halophytes, *Atriplex confertifolia* (shad-scale) and *Ceratoides lanata* (winter fat), were ob-

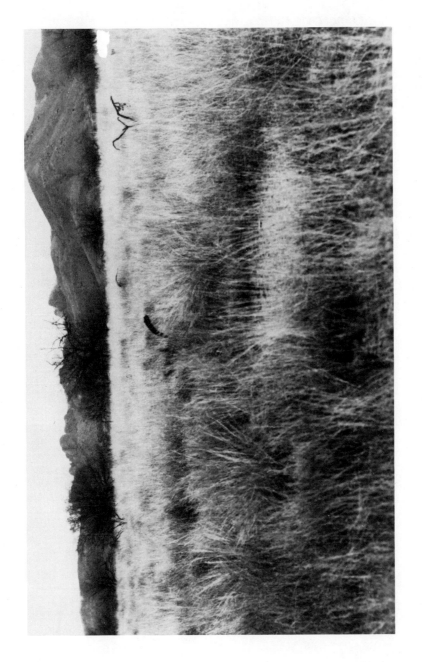

FIGURE 9-11. *Grass study area at the Santa Rita site.*

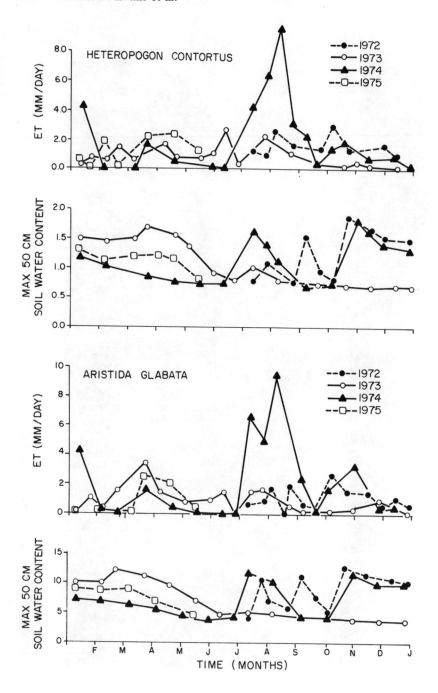

FIGURE 9-12. *Evapotranspiration for two grass species and related soil moisture data at Santa Rita site.*

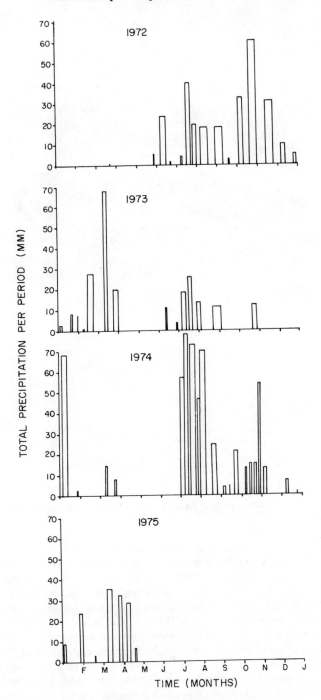

FIGURE 9-13. *Precipitation record for grass study at Santa Rita site.*

FIGURE 9-14. *Washtucna study site.*

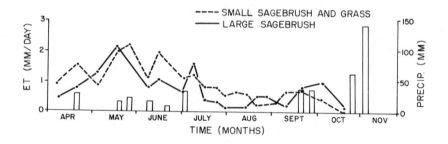

FIGURE 9-15. *Evapotranspiration and precipitation data for the Washtucna study site.*

tained during 1970 (Caldwell et al., 1971; Moore and Caldwell, 1972). Figure 9-16 depicts the study site that is north of the northwestern tip of the Great Salt Lake in Utah at approximately 1,350 m elevation. Soils at the site are lacustrine deposits of reasonably uniform silt to sand loam texture and are low in organic matter below the 0.02 m depth. At depths below 0.6 m, the soil is saline. The average annual precipitation is about 250 mm, with 60 percent occurring from April through October. Soil-water content measurements were made by the neutron method to depths of 1.5 m from March through September 1970.

Results are shown in figure 9-17. Evapotranspiration rates dropped off rapidly from a high of 2 mm per day in June to a low of 0.3 mm per day in August. During the same period, soil-water potential at depths of 0.3 and 0.6 m dropped nearly linearly from less than −10 bars in April to about −70 bars in September. The water potential at the 0.15 m depth fluctuated with rainfall and

FIGURE 9-16.   *Curlew Valley study site.*

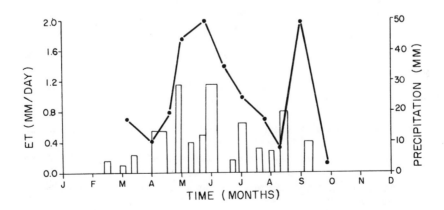

FIGURE 9-17.   *Evapotranspiration and precipitation for the Curlew Valley study site.*

was never lower than −40 bars. The large increase in evapotranspiration rate in September appears to be a reflection of rainfall decreasing the soil moisture potential in the surface 0.15 m layer.

Jurinak et al. (1976) presented evapotranspiration data for crested wheat-grass (*Argopyron desertorum*) at the same Curlew Valley site. Measurements were made during 1974 and 1975, two years that differed consistently in precipitation distribution. In 1974, a wet winter was followed by an extremely dry spring and summer. In 1975, a relatively dry winter was followed by a wet spring. Soil moisture depletion to 0.75 m depth was measured between April 2 and July 1, 1974, and between April 1 and August 6, 1975. Precipitation was also recorded for the same periods. For 1974, soil-water depletion was 87 mm and precipitation was 28.5 mm; during the 1975 period these values were 80 mm and 122 mm, respectively. Again assuming no surface runoff and no deep seepage, the amounts of water evapotranspired were 115 mm per year in 1974 and 202 mm per year in 1975. The average rate was 1.3 mm per day for a shorter period in 1974 and 1.6 mm per day in 1975. From climatic data, they estimated that the average potential evapotranspiration rate during the 1975 period was 26.4 mm per day.

DISCUSSION

The data presented on evapotranspiration rates for desert conditions offer the best available estimates. In fact, no other data sufficiently complete have been found in the literature for other sites and conditions. There are results on transpiration rates for individual desert plants (or parts of plants), but these are not immediately useful in determining a hydrologic balance for an area.

Individual data points shown on the graphs are averages for several days between measurement dates. Thus, the maxima shown may be lower than short-term maxima for certain days within the averaging period. The average rate was greatly influenced by the amount and timing of precipitation during the period. If surface runoff had occurred during a rainfall event, the calculated values would be too high since no runoff was assumed. In contrast, if water had accumulated at the measurement sites due to low microrelief, the calculated values would be low. These possible errors would apply only to a few measurement periods because runoff occurs only for a small percentage of rainfall events for the study areas. Data on runoff occurrence are not available for any of the sites, except for the lysimeter site, where no runoff occurred during the data collection period. Estimates of runoff from natural desert areas have ranged from 3 to 10 percent of the total annual precipitation.

Unfortunately, the data do not allow statistical analyses because of the limited number of measurements and lack of replications. Therefore comparisons between species and vegetated versus bare soil can only be judged visually. Comparisons among sites are even more tenuous because of lack of uniformity in experimental design, such as dates of measurements, length of averaging period, number and placement of access tubes, and depths of soil moisture content measurements.

TABLE 9-2. *Maximum Measured Evapotranspiration Rate at Different Locations*

Site	Cover	ET rate (mm/day)
Silverbell (Ariz.)	Creosote bush	3.0
Silverbell	Creosote bush (lysimeter)	5.0
Tucson (Ariz.)	Bare soil	4.3
Santa Rita (Ariz.)	Desert hackberry	3.0
Santa Rita	Grass	10.0
Washtucna (Wash.)	Sagebrush and grass	2.3
Southern Idaho	Sagebrush and grass	3.4
Curlew Valley (Utah)	Salt bush	2.0

All of the results presented are for sites that are semiarid (annual precipitation over 250 mm); thus the results are not applicable to extreme deserts. All sites are normally used as rangeland but are lightly grazed.

In no case was there an appreciable difference between a bare soil and an adjacent vegetated plot for any extended period of time. Any possible difference appeared to be masked within the range of measurement error. However, differences would not be expected to be large since evapotranspiration rates were closely associated with rainfall events, and most of the events were of such magnitude that only the top few centimeters of soil were wetted. Any infiltrated water is rapidly removed by either evaporation or transpiration. Water that reaches greater depths is removed at a low rate by evapotranspiration, and differences between bare soil and vegetated areas may not be measurable. In addition, there were no measurable differences between plant species at any of the sites where more than one species was studied.

The maximum calculated evapotranspiration rate varied from location to location (table 9-2) and ranged from 2.0 to 10.0 mm per day. Maximum rates were generally higher for the warm desert sites, as would be expected. Minimum rates dropped to less than 0.1 mm per day at most sites. In general, the rates were less than 1 mm per day for extended periods of time when there was no precipitation.

Although the results presented may be considered only as approximate values for evapotranspiration rates, they do give a reasonable estimate of expected rates and demonstrate the ability of desert plants to exist at extremely low rates of transpiration.

REFERENCES

Belt, G. H. 1969. *Spring Evapotranspiration from Low Sagebrush Range in Southern Idaho*. Res. Proj. Tech. Compl. Rept. A-014-IDA. Univ. Idaho, Moscow, Idaho.

Cable, D. R. 1974. *Seasonal Use of Soil Moisture by Mature Velvet Mesquite* (Prosopis juliflora var. velutina). US/IBP Desert Biome Res. Memo. 74-18. Utah State Univ., Logan, Utah.

Cable, D. R. 1977. Soil water changes in creosote and bur-sage. *J. Aria. Acad. Sci.* **12**:15–20.

Caldwell, M. M., N. E. West, and P. J. Goodman. 1971. *Autecology Studies of* Atriplex confertifolia *and* Eurotia lanta. US/IBP Desert Biome Res. Memo. 71-13. Utah State Univ., Logan, Utah.

Caldwell, M. M., R. S. White, and R. T. Moore. 1977. Carbon balance, productivity and water use of cold-winter desert shrub communities dominated by C_3 and C_4 species. *Oecologia* **29**:275–300.

Campbell, G. S., and G. S. Harris. 1975. *Effect of Soil Water Potential on Soil Moisture Absorption, Transpiration Rate, Plant Water Potential and Growth of* Artemisia tridentata. US/IBP Desert Biome Res. Memo 75-44. Utah State Univ., Logan, Utah.

Evans, D. D., T. W. Sammis, and J. Ben Asher. 1976. *Plant Growth and Water Transfer Interactive Processes under Desert Conditions.* US/IBP Desert Biome Res. Memo. 76-33. Utah State Univ., Logan, Utah.

Jurinak, J. J., D. W. James, and A. Van Luik. 1976. *Nitrogen and Phosphorus Constraints on Primary Productivity in the Great Basin Desert.* US/IBP Desert Biome Res. Memo. 76-17. Utah State Univ., Logan, Utah.

Moore, R. T., and M. M. Caldwell. 1972. The field use of thermocouple psychromoters in desert soils, pp. 165–169. In R. W. Brown and B. P. Van Heveren (eds.), *Proc. Symp. Thermocouple Psychrometers,* March 17–19, 1971. Utah State Univ., Logan, Utah.

Sammis, T. W. 1974. *The Microenvironment of a Desert Hackberry Plant* (Celtis pallida). Ph.D. dissertation. Univ. Arizona.

Sammis, T. W., D. W. Young, and C. W. Constant. 1976. Construction, calibration and operation of a monolith weighing lysimeter. *Proc. Hydrology and Water Resources of Arizona and the Southwest* **6**:227–231.

Sammis, T. W., and D. L. Weeks. 1977. Variations in soil moisture under natural vegetation. *Proc. Hydrology and Water Resources in Arizona and the Southwest* **7**:235–240.

Sellers, W. D., and P. S. Dryden. 1967. *An Investigation of Heat Transfer from Bare Soil.* Rept. Meteorol. Dept. U.S. Army Electronic Proving Ground, Fort Huachuca, Arizona.

Young, D. W., D. D. Evans, and C. Constant. 1976. *Measurement of Evapotranspiration with a Monolith Lysimeter.* US/IBP Desert Biome Res. Memo. 76-34. Utah State Univ., Logan, Utah.

10
Precipitation in the Desert

Martin M. Fogel

Desert precipitation may be characterized by a single descriptive phrase: highly variable in both time and space. This variability increases as the annual total precipitation decreases. Precipitation in desert regions usually occurs during either one or two periods within a year rather than scattered throughout the entire year. For example, precipitation in the Great Basin of the North American desert and the Arabian Desert generally occurs in the winter season, while the Sonoran Desert in the southwestern United States and Mexico has two precipitation seasons, winter and summer. Prolonged dry spells usually precede or follow a precipitation season.

The characteristics that describe the particular precipitation occurring in one season are often markedly different from those of the other season. Summer precipitation in the Sonoran Desert is the result of high-intensity, short-duration, localized convective thunderstorms in contrast to the winter frontal storms, which produce precipitation of an entirely different character. Under extreme conditions, both storm types may produce disastrous flooding, or extended dry periods may result from the continued nonoccurrence of precipitation-producing storms. This great variability has spawned a considerable amount of hydrologic research concerned with the driving dynamic force of natural hydrologic and water resource systems, precipitation. The material that follows is a summary of the event-based, stochastic precipitation models researched in the last ten years.

PROCESS DESCRIPTION

Intermittent Data

For reasons of convenience or tradition, hydrologic data are usually taken at or averaged over equally spaced time intervals. Although such data constitute useful information, it is of less than optimal value for desert conditions in which ephemeral or intermittent flows are the rule. This limitation is principally the result of the small sample size due to the relatively infrequent occurrence of hydrologic phenomena in arid to semiarid regions. As an example, according to Wiesner (1970), at least thirty years of data are required to obtain stable frequency hydrologic distributions. Even with this minimum amount of data, the occurrence of an extreme event, which may not be included in the data set, can drastically affect frequency distributions (Reich, 1973).

Although the analyses of intermittent or event-based data are subjected similarly to the same uncertainty from extreme events, each year may produce ten to forty or more data points rather than the one used for obtaining the conventional annual maximum distributions. For precipitation analyses, these data points are usually the daily precipitation amounts or any other definition that is used to describe an event.

Stochastic Process

For summer-type rainfall characterized by local, scattered thunderstorms, the underlying assumption in developing event-based stochastic models has been that thunderstorm rainfall is a sequentially independent phenomenon. Smith and Schreiber (1973) have questioned this assumption, but the fact remains that the use of certain probabilistic distributions that are based on it cannot be rejected by statistical tests (Fogel and Duckstein, 1969; Fogel et al., 1971; Duckstein, Fogel, and Kisiel, 1972; Fogel, Duckstein, and Sanders, 1974).

Thunderstorm rainfall at a point is not a pure random or independent process nor is it a pure Markov (dependent) process. The question to be answered concerns which process better lends itself to solving hydrologic problems without jeopardizing any reliability of the eventual solution. Coupling the event-based stochastic model with deterministic models has resulted in a viable methodology for analyzing water-related activities (Fogel, Duckstein, and Kisiel, 1974a, b; Fogel et al., 1975; Fogel, 1975; Fogel et al., 1976; Hekman et al., 1976; Smith et al., 1977; Hanes et al., 1977; Fogel et al., 1977).

Definition of an Event

In event-based modeling, the first step concerns defining an event. This could be simply the occurrence of daily precipitation that exceeds a certain threshold value. For spatial conditions or consideration of an entire watershed, a definition may be one in which the mean precipitation from a number of precipitation gauges exceeds a given amount or one in which a single gauge records precipitation greater than a certain value.

Basic Probability Distributions

Event-based models are characterized by at least two random variables and their distributions. First, there is the random number of events per unit of time (month, season, year) or, as an alternate, the interarrival time between events (the time between the beginning of an event and the start of the next event). The second class of random variables comprises the variables of interest, such as the depth of precipitation, the duration of precipitation or the maximum fifteen-minute intensity of rainfall.

SUMMER PRECIPITATION MODEL

Events per Season

Precipitation during the summer months in North American deserts is generally of the convective storm type such that the events appear to occur in an independent manner in time and space. This suggests that the variable for the number of events per season can be described by a Poisson distribution, which can be mathematically expressed as

$$f_N(n) = \frac{e^{-m}m^n}{n!} \qquad n = 0, 1, 2, \ldots, \tag{10.1}$$

where m is estimated by the mean number of events per season using the method of moments. Results attesting to this have been obtained by Fogel and Duckstein (1969) and Todorovic and Yevjevich (1969). For example, the observed number of storm centers per season located over the Atterbury Experimental Watershed near Tucson, Arizona, for the period 1956–1976 is shown in figure 10-1.

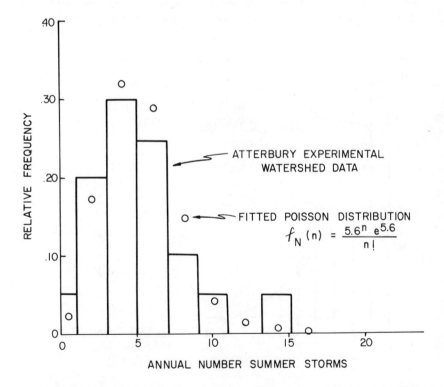

FIGURE 10-1. *Observed number of storm centers per season located over Herbury Experimental Watershed.*

If the number of events per season are in fact described by a Poisson distribution, then interarrival times are defined by an exponential variate (Feller, 1967). This distribution is defined as

$$f_T(t) = ue^{-ut} \quad t > 0, \tag{10.2}$$

where u is the distribution parameter that can be estimated as the inverse of the mean interarrival time by the method of moments. Figure 10-2 illustrates the distribution of storm interarrival times for Tucson, Arizona. In this instance, a storm is defined as a day of rain during the July to October thunderstorm season in which the amount of precipitation exceeds 10 mm.

Inasmuch as the occurrence of summer storms is seldom a pure Poisson process, the distribution for interarrival times may in many situations best be described by a gamma rather than an exponential variate. The former is a two-parameter distribution in which

$$f_T(t) = \frac{b^a \, t^{a-1} \, e^{-bt}}{(a-1)!} \quad \text{for } t > 0, \tag{10.3}$$

where a and b are distribution parameters. Using the method of moments, a is equal to b times the sample mean, and b is the mean divided by the variance.

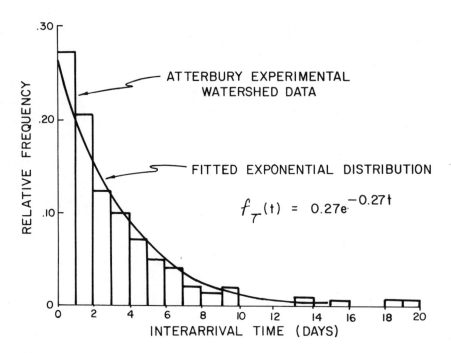

FIGURE 10-2. *Distribution of summer storm interarrival times for Tucson, Arizona.*

Compared to the one-parameter exponential distribution, the gamma can be made to fit a greater variety of conditions.

Depth and Duration of Storm Rainfall

Hot season precipitation is often characterized by short-duration, localized thunderstorms. In the Sonoran Desert, at least 80 percent of total storm rainfall will fall in less than one hour and cover an area of less than 30 km^2 (Fogel, 1969; Osborn and Lane, 1972). There are occasions, however, such as during the late summer months, when the occurrence of a tropical disturbance will result in storms lasting several hours and falling on hundreds of square kilometers. Modeling summer precipitation requires quantification of either storm duration or intensity, its spatial distribution, and its relation to the amount of storm rainfall.

Under the hypothesis that the occurrence of thunderstorms and the maximum depth of rainfall within that storm are independent variables, a geometric distribution for point rainfall depths was derived (Fogel and Duckstein, 1969). In a later paper, Fogel, Duckstein, and Sanders (1974) showed that the distribution for mean areal rainfall could be described by a negative binomial function. Analysis of desert precipitation data suggests that rainfall depths can better be fitted to the two-parameter gamma distribution, a continuous version of the negative binomial, rather than to the derived geometric distribution.

One of the earlier attempts at modeling the storm depth-duration phenomemon was to obtain independent distributions for storm depths and the maximum fifteen-minute intensity (Fogel, 1969). Independence was assumed, as very little correlation was obtained between total storm depth and the intensity occurring in a short burst of heavy rainfall. Naturally, the longer the time period for calculating intensity, the greater the correlation. Another, perhaps more accurate, method for modeling storm rainfall is the bivariate gamma distribution proposed by Crovelli (1971).

Spatial Distribution of Storm Rainfall

There have been several attempts at modeling depth-area relationships for air mass thunderstorms, the predominant type of summer storms in the Sonoran Desert. Fogel and Duckstein (1969) adopted the univariate bell-shaped normal distribution or Gaussian curve as their model, which is given by

$$R = R_o \exp\left(-\pi x^2 b\right), \tag{10.4}$$

where R is storm rainfall depth at a distance x from the storm center assumed to be at the point of maximum rainfall, R_o, and b is a shape factor. Using experimental data in which rainfall depths are in inches and distances are in miles, b was found to be related to R_o by

$$b = 0.27 \exp\left(-0.67\, R_o\right). \tag{10.5}$$

Based on probably the most intensive set of hydrologic data in the south-western United States, Osborn and Lane (1972) developed a different depth-area relationship, also assuming symmetry around storm center depths. Their model can be expressed as

$$R = R_o (0.9 - 0.2 \ln A),$$ (10.6)

where R and R_o are expressed in inches and A is area covered by R and greater rainfall, in square miles, for $1 \leq A \leq 90$. Both sets of investigators recognize that univariate models are simplistic and that a bivariate model, which would result in elliptical isohyets, would be a more accurate representation for thunderstorm rainfall. Also, while the two models are somewhat similar for a 50 mm storm, differences in rainfall volume increase with depth of rainfall (Osborn and Renard, 1977).

WINTER PRECIPITATION MODEL

Winter precipitation is generally the result of frontal storms affecting fairly large areas, perhaps thousands of square kilometers. Duckstein et al. (1975) developed two probabilistic winter precipitation models for the Sonoran Desert. The first model assumes that the arrival of winter storms is a Poisson process, which implies that the number of events in any time interval is independent of the number in any other interval of time. With the assumption that there is some persistence in the weather and that the occurrence of a particular event or sequence of events is somewhat dependent on past events, a second model is developed, which employs a mixed distribution to describe the number of events in an interval of time.

Poisson Model

With the assumption that winter storms arrive in an independent manner, the probabilistic model for such storms is similar in form to the convective-storm model (Duckstein, Fogel, and Sanders, 1972). In the case under consideration, an event is defined as a sequence of consecutive wet days for which each day a measurable (equal or greater than 0.25 mm) amount of precipitation is recorded. The test for such an assumption is whether the interarrival time for events can be described by an exponential distribution. The model attempts to simulate a set of meteorologic events, each of which is assumed to be the aforementioned sequence of wet days.

Mixed Model

The rationale for using the mixed distribution model is based on observations that reveal that under certain meteorological conditions, winter storms often come in sequences in which one storm follows another within a short time interval. At other times, a winter storm appears to arrive in an independent manner. Random variables used in this model are schematically shown in figure 10-3 and are defined as follows:

> Event or storm group: The consecutive days of precipitation in which an amount of 0.25 mm or more was recorded for each day.
> Storm sequence: Storm groups separated by three or fewer days. Persistence in the weather system is thus described by a dependent arrival of precipitation groups within a sequence.
> Interarrival or renewal time: The time between the beginning of one sequence and the beginning of the next one.

The number of sequences per unit of time are generally distributed as a Poisson variate because the interarrival time between sequences is exponentially distributed. The number of dry days between groups, one, two, or three days, is usually uniformly distributed. A gamma distribution can be used to define the amount of precipitation per storm group.

DERIVED DISTRIBUTIONS

Maximal Distribution

Where hydrologic data are limited, it is of considerable advantage to use the event-based approach for determining the return period of a given event or the probability that a given event will be equaled or exceeded in a year or any

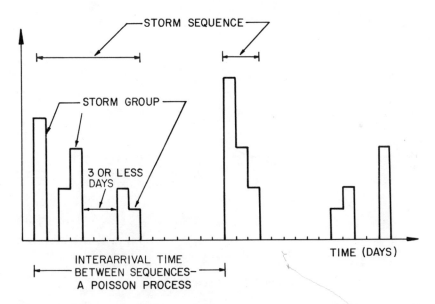

FIGURE 10-3. *Schematic representation of event-based winter rainfall model.*

other time period. While engineers require such information for the design of water control structures, it is also of value to determine the hydrologic effects of man's activities on the environment.

To determine the distribution of the annual maximum precipitation event, two basic distributions are required: the amount of precipitation per event and the number of events per time period. If this latter distribution can be described by a Poisson process, as it generally can be for desert regions, it has been shown by Fogel and Duckstein (1969) that the maximal distribution function is

$$\phi_R(r) = e^{-m[1-F_R(r)]}, \tag{10.7}$$

where m is the mean in the Poisson distribution and $F_R(r)$ is cumulative distribution of R conditioned on an event occurring. According to Feller (1967), equation 10.7 is a compound Poisson distribution. Figure 10-4 compares the above derived distribution with the annual maximum series for thunderstorms in Tucson fitted to a Gumbel distribution.

Total Precipitation

For certain purposes, it may be desirable to determine the distribution for the total amount of precipitation that would fall in a given time period, such as a year or a season. During one season, either summer or winter, of duration n days, there are $N(n)$ events, so that $S(n)$ is the sum of a random number $N(n)$

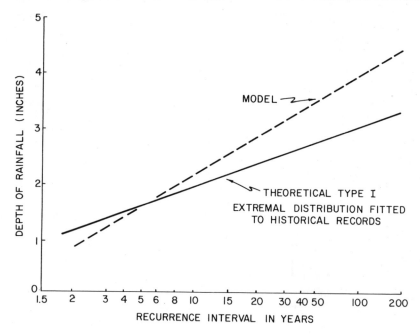

FIGURE 10-4. *Distribution of storm runoff: a comparison between event-based models and annual maximum series.*

of random variables R, precipitation per event. Difficulties may arise, however, in evaluating $S(n)$ because the number of events and ther duration may not be independent. If they are assumed to be independent, then

$$S(n) = R_1 + R_2 + \ldots + R_n, \tag{10.8}$$

in which $R_1, R_2, \ldots, R_n$ are independent, identically distributed variates where the random variables $N(n)$ and R are taken as independent.

The mean or expected value $E[S(n)]$ and the variance Var $[S(n)]$ can be calculated directly without determining the probability distribution function through the relationships

$$E[S(n)] = E(N) E(R)$$

$$\tag{10.9}$$

$$\mathrm{Var}[S(n)] = E(N)\ \mathrm{Var}\ (R) + [E(R)]^2\ \mathrm{Var}\ (N)$$

To obtain frequency values for $S(n)$, the statistical parameters calculated in equation 10.9 can be used to determine the parameters for an assumed particular distribution such as the log normal, the extremal, or the gamma. More directly, the maximal distribution for $S(n)$ can be obtained by successive differentiations of the generating function as mentioned by Fogel, Duckstein, and Sanders (1974).

Effect of Elevation

It is generally well known that precipitation increases with elevation. In contrast with simple regression or correlation models, the event-based modeling approach provides several phenomenological options to explain this behavior.

For summer convective storms, the elevation effect may be caused by an increase in the rate of arrival of events $E(N)$ or equivalent decrease of expected interarrival time $E(T)$, an increase in the mean rainfall per event $E(R)$, or a combination of these two. The discussion of such a model is found in Duckstein, Fogel, and Thames (1972) where data from the Santa Catalina Mountains near Tucson, Arizona, were used to demonstrate the applicability of the method.

Essentially, the model consists of assuming

$$E(N) = m_0 + ah$$

$$\tag{10.10}$$

$$E(R) = r_0 + bh$$

where m_0 is the mean number of events per season at a datum, r_0 is the mean amount of rainfall per event at the datum, a and b are constants, and h is elevation. Using equation 10.9, the expected total amount of rainfall per season is

$$E[S(n)] = m_0 r_0 + (ar_0 + bm_0)h + abh^2. \tag{10.11}$$

Experimental results indicated that the assumed linear models (equation 10.10), which lead to the expressions,

$$E(N) = 12.44 + 3.12h$$

$$E(R) = 0.187 + 0.0116h$$

$$E[S(n)] = 2.33 + 0.727h + 0.0362h^2, \tag{10.12}$$

were satisfactory (see figures 10-5, 10-6, and 10-7) where depths are in inches and elevation is in thousands of feet between 2.5 and 8.6, the limits of the data.

A measure of confidence in this approach was gained when the event-based model was compared to a regression of total summer rainfall on elevation. In an independent study, Osborn and Davis (1977) incorporated longitude and latitude into a regional model that determines the effect of elevation on the number of summer rainfall occurrences. When the specific coordinates of the Santa Catalina (Tucson) study are applied to their model, the results compare favorably to those obtained from the Tucson study, considering that the two studies were based on two different periods of record. That is, the seven-year period for the Tucson study (1957–1962 and 1964) was about 20 percent drier than the fifteen-year period (1958–1972) upon which the regional model was based.

In the case of the winter frontal storm, the effect of elevation may be accounted for as in the case for summer storms but with the following additional features specific to the definition of a sequence: the mean number of events per sequence may increase with elevation, the mean duration of sequences may increase, and the mean dry spell duration between events in a sequence may presumably decrease.

Simulations

Distributions of either storm or seasonal precipitation can also be obtained from a synthetic time series generated from simulated data. From previous discussions, it is evident that the total seasonal rainfall can come from various combinations of point rainfall depths per event and the number of events during a season. A table can be prepared to produce these combinations for the parameters $m = 5.33$ and $p = 0.48$, values obtained in the original analysis of the Tucson experimental data, in which the rows correspond to the number of events per year, while the columns refer to the total seasonal rainfall (Fogel, Duckstein, and Sanders, 1974). Cell (j,k) thus represents the joint probability of j units of rain and k events per year. For example, the probability of seven units of rain occurring in four events is

$$P(Z = 7, N = 4) = P(Z = 7/N = 4) \, p \, (N = 4) -$$

$$= (0.0531) \, (0.163) = 0.00835.$$

Within each cell, different occupancy distributions of storms are possible.

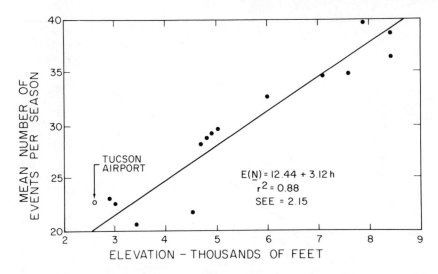

FIGURE 10-5. *Effect of elevation on the occurrence of summer storms.*

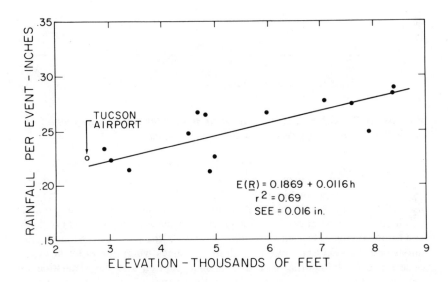

FIGURE 10-6. *Effect of elevation on storm rainfall.*

Continuing with the above example, without regard to the order in which the rains occur, the seven units can be combined into four events in three possible ways: 4-1-1-1, 3-2-1-1, and 2-2-2-1. Using classical combinatorial analysis techniques, the probability of each of these occupancies can be calculated.

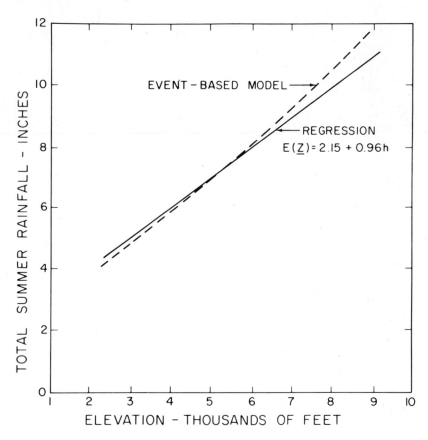

FIGURE 10-7. *Effect of elevation on total summer rainfall: a comparison between event-based models and regression analysis.*

A Monte Carlo simulation can now be set up to generate an unordered succession of yearly combination of events. This synthetic rainfall set may be useful for determining the seasonal or annual water yield, for evaluating runoff modification and water conservation practices (urbanization, water harvesting, and artificial recharge), and for studing separately the effect of random fluctuations and the effect of control. In those instances where the order of event occurrence is of importance, it can be incorporated into the simulation to generate a time series of events. Also a time series of runoff events can be generated by transforming rainfall into runoff.

APPLICATIONS

The discussion that follows on the applications of event-based models is presented in greater detail in Fogel et al. (1976).

Design of Water Control Structures

It is often surprising to some that floods occur in desert areas. This is, however, consistent with the fact that desert precipitation (and, hence, runoff) is highly variable.

In arid regions, floodwater retarding structures are often designed for ungauged watersheds, even though hydrologic data are limited, or where the characteristics of the basin itself are changing. To overcome these difficulties, a stochastic analysis of rainfall events may be used to serve as inputs into a deterministic rainfall-runoff formula, which, if data are available, is calibrated from experimental watersheds. Thus, the suggested procedure for determining the optimum size of a water control structure for an ungauged watershed consists first of obtaining parameter estimates from precipitation data for the event-based stochastic rainfall model. Then rainfall is converted to runoff by means of appropriate rainfall-runoff relations such as Soil Conservation Service (SCS) equations (Soil Conservation Service, 1972a), and, finally, a form of benefit risk analysis is made.

Two approaches can be used to convert distributions of rainfall into runoff. One uses the Monte Carlo simulation of rainfall events, each of which is transformed into runoff by the SCS equations or similar formulas. Although the necessary parameters may be estimated from site inspection, the use of experimental watershed runoff data is naturally preferred, although not always available. A conventional frequency analysis can then be made from the simulated time series of runoff volumes. Similarly a distribution of peak discharge rates can be obtained by using an appropriate formula that relates rainfall characteristics to peak flow rates.

In the second method, the distribution function of rainfall is transformed directly into storm runoff volumes and to peak discharge rates. These distribution functions are then combined with a distribution that describes the arrival of a given number of runoff events in a specified time interval to give extreme value distributions.

With distributions of storm runoff obtained from a simulated set of runoff events or from the transformation of actual rainfall data, benefits resulting from flood prevention and associated construction costs can be examined for structures of varying sizes. Associated with each size of structure is an expected net benefit, which is derived by weighting the net benefits for each possible flow with the probability of that flow's occurrence. The purpose of this analysis would be to determine the design that maximizes the expected net benefits. Since a damage-frequency analysis is usually made for these structures, the only additional effort would be to estimate the cost for several economically feasible structures of different capacities. In effect, the suggested analysis does not design for a single event, such as the 100-year storm, but includes all possible runoff-producing events and selects the size of the structure based on maximizing the expected net benefits from all such events.

Forecasting Snow-Melt Runoff

This section illustrates a procedure for generating a probability distribution for a basin's total water yield to be derived from the melting of accumulated snow and subsequent precipitation following the date of the forecast. One of the problems of current methods is this latter aspect. Studies indicate that precipitation after the forecast date can account for between 10 to 60 percent of the variance in runoff (Soil Conservation Service, 1972b).

The generated total water yield requires first simulating a number of sets of winter precipitation to take into consideration the various combinations and sequences of precipitation events that may follow the forecast date. The event-based stochastic precipitation model serves as inputs into a deterministic watershed model, which routes the precipitation through the watershed. The result is a probability distribution of snow-melt runoff for various forecast dates.

Evaluating Watershed Changes

In response to concern for the environment, land managers need procedures for predicting the effect of man's activities. Land use changes are often contemplated where little or no data are available for evaluating the hydrologic effects of these actions. The basic objective of this section is to present a methodology for predicting the hydrologic effects of land modification.

The proposed precedure utilizes the event-based precipitation model as an input to a rainfall-runoff relationship that transforms the inputs into probabilistic distributions of such desired hydrologic variables as water yield, peak discharge rate, and sediment yield. The Soil Conservation Service formulas presented earlier can be used for gauged watersheds. That is, procedures are available for estimating the parameters from on-site observations. Without doubt, there are problems in using relationships that are not directly based on actual data. Since the current discussion is just for those cases, there is not much choice in selecting a procedure for evaluating watershed changes. At the very least, this procedure could be viewed as an initial approximation.

REFERENCES

Crovelli, R. A. 1971. *Stochastic Models for Precipitation*. Ph.D. dissertation. Colorado State Univ.

Duckstein, L., M. M. Fogel, and C. C. Kisiel. 1972. A stochastic model of runoff-producing rainfall for summer type storms. *Water Resour. Res.* **8**:237–350.

Duckstein, L., M. M. Fogel, and J. L. Thames. 1972. Elevation effects on rainfall: a stochastic model. *J. Hydrol.* **19**:21–35.

Duckstein, L., M. M. Fogel, and D. F. Davis. 1975. Mountainous winter precipitation: a stochastic event-based approach, pp. 172–188. In *Proc. Am. Geophys. Union Symp. Precipitation Analysis for Hydrologic Modeling, June 26–28*. Univ. California, Davis, Calif.

Feller, W. 1967. *An Introduction to Probability Theory and Its Applications*, v. 1. Wiley, New York, 509 pp.

Fogel, M. M. 1969. The effect of storm rainfall variability on runoff from small semi-arid watersheds. *Trans. Am. Soc. Agric. Eng.* **12**:808–812.

Fogel, M. M., and L. Duckstein. 1969. Point rainfall frequencies in convective storms. *Water Resour. Res.* **5**:1229–1237.

Fogel, M. M., L. Duckstein, and C. C. Kisiel. 1971. Space-time validation of a thunderstorm rainfall model. *Water Resour. Bull.* **7**:309–316.

Fogel, M. M., L. Duckstein, and C. C. Kisiel. 1974a. Modeling the hydrologic effects of land modifications. *Trans. Am. Soc. Agric. Eng.* **17**:1006–1010.

Fogel, M. M., L. Duckstein, and C. C. Kisiel. 1974b. Optimum control of irrigation water application. *Automatica* **10**:579–586.

Fogel, M. M., L. Duckstein, and J. L. Saunders. 1974. An event-based stochastic model of areal rainfall and runoff, pp. 247–261. In *USDA Agric. Res. Service Misc. Publ. No. 1275.* Proc. Symp. Stat. Hydrol.

Fogel, M. M. 1975. Vegetation management guidelines for increasing water yields in a semi-arid region: an Arizona case study, pp. 73–84. In *FAO Conservation Guide No. 3, Conservation in Arid and Semi-arid Zones.* FAO, Rome.

Fogel, M. M., I. Bogardi, and L. H. Hekman. 1975. Design of floodwater retarding structures under uncertain watershed conditions, pp. 681–690. In *Proc. Internat. Assoc. Sci. Hydrol., Tokyo, Publ. No. 1.*

Fogel, M. M., L. Duckstein, and A. Musy. 1976. An event-based formulation of watershed management, pp. 349–373. In *Proc. Irrigation and Drainage Division of Am. Soc. Civil Eng. Spec. Conf., July 21–23, Ottawa, Ontario.*

Fogel, M. M., L. H. Hekman, and L. Duckstein. 1977. A stochastic sediment yield model using the modified universal soil loss equation, pp. 226–233. In *Soil Erosion: Prediction and Control.* Soil Conservation Society of America, Ankeny, Iowa.

Hanes, W. T., M. M. Fogel, and L. Duckstein. 1977. Forecasting snowmelt runoff: a probable stochastic model. *J. Irrigation and Drainage Div. Am. Soc. Civil Eng.* **103**(IR3):343–356.

Hekman, L. H., M. M. Fogel, and L. Duckstein. 1976. *Efficient Hydrologic Design Using Simulated Data.* Paper no. 76-2036 presented at Annual Meeting of the American Society of Civil Engineers, 28–30 June 1976, Lincoln, Neb.

Osborn, H. B., and D. R. Davis. 1977. Simulation of summer rain occurrence in Arizona and New Mexico, pp. 153–162. In *Hydrology and Water Resources in Arizona and the Southwest,* v. 7.

Osborn, H. B., and L. J. Lane. 1972. Depth area relationships for thunderstorm rainfall in southwestern Arizona. *Trans. Am. Soc. Agric. Eng.* **15**: 670–673.

Osborn, H. B., and K. G. Renard. 1977. Discussion: stochastic consideration in thunderstorm modeling. *J. Hydraul. Div. Am. Soc. Civil Eng.* **103** (HY6):667–670.

Reich, B. M. 1973. *Effect of Agnes Floods on Annual Series in Pennsylvania.* Inst. Res. Land and Water Resources, Penn State Univ., State College, Penna., 74 pp.

Smith, R. E., and H. A. Schreiber. 1973. Point processes of seasonal thunderstorm rainfall distribution of rainfall events. *Water Resour. Res.* **9**:871–884.

Smith, J. H., D. R. Davis, and M. M. Fogel. 1977. Determination of sediment yield by transferring rainfall data. *Water Resour. Bull.* **13**:529–541.

Soil Conservation Service. 1972a. *Hydrology. Sec. 4 SCS National Engineering Handbook.* U.S. Dept. Agric., Washington, D.C.

Soil Conservation Service. 1972b. *Snow Survey and Water Supply Forecasting. SCS National Engineering Handbook.* Dept. Agric., Washington, D.C.

Todorovic, P., and V. Yevjevich. 1969. Stochastic process of precipitation. *Hydrology Paper No. 35.* Civil Eng. Dept., Colorado State Univ., Ft. Collins., Colo.

Wiesner, C. J. 1970. *Hydrometeorology.* Chapman and Hall, London, 232 pp.

11
Modeling Desert Soil Water Systems

R. J. Hanks

In a desert ecosystem the nature of water distribution in the soil profile is a basic property needed to evaluate most biological and physical processes. Water infiltrates into the soil during rainfall or snow melt from overland flow. If the infiltration rate is lower than the rainfall rate, runoff may occur. Most of the water entering desert soils will be stored in the soil for some time but may move through the soil to underground storage below the root zone. The water that is stored in the soil may be returned to the atmosphere as direct evaporation from the soil or as transpiration by plants. Thus, the soil-water system is influenced not only by soil properties but also by plant and climatic factors. The model described here attempts to organize these complex interactions into a logical system that obeys known physical laws.

MODEL DESCRIPTION

The model was modified by Nimah and Hanks (1973) from an earlier model of Hanks and Bowers (1962). The model was tested for desert applicability by Griffin et al. (1974).

The basic soil-water flow equation is

$$\frac{\partial \Theta}{\partial t} = \frac{\partial}{\partial z} \left(K(\Theta) \frac{\partial H}{\partial z} \right) + A(z), \tag{11.1}$$

where Θ is the volumetric water content, t is time, z is depth, $K(\Theta)$ is hydraulic conductivity (which is assumed to be a function of water content only), and H is hydraulic potential. The root extraction term, $A(z)$, is defined as

$$A(z) = \frac{[H\text{root} + (1 + Rc) \cdot (z) - h(z) - S(z)] \cdot RDF(z) \cdot K(\Theta)}{\Delta z}, \tag{11.2}$$

where Hroot is the effective water potential of the root system at the soil surface where z is taken as a zero, Rc is a flow coefficient in the roots taken to

235

be about 0.05, h is the soil matric potential, S is the soil solution osmotic potential, RDF is the root density function, and Δz is the depth increment.

The osmotic component may or may not be negligible. If it is not, salt flow must be considered with the water. The equation describing this flow is (Bresler, 1973)

$$\frac{\partial(\Theta C)}{\partial t} = \frac{\partial}{\partial z} \left(D(\Theta,v) \frac{\partial C}{\partial z} + qC \right) + S, \qquad (11.3)$$

where C is solute concentration, S is a source-sink term, q is volumetric flux of solution. The combined diffusion and hydrodynamic dispersion coefficient $D(\Theta,v)$ is defined as

$$D(\Theta,v) = Do \cdot a \cdot e^{b\Theta} + \lambda(v) \qquad (11.4)$$

where v is average flow velocity, Do is the diffusion coefficient in pure water, a and b are diffusion constants, and λ is a dispersion constant. The source-sink term is often ignored (Childs and Hanks, 1975) but may be very important (Melamed et al., 1976).

Assumptions

Flow is treated as one-dimensional, which may be a serious limitation in some desert situations. As used in the desert ecosystem studies, the model does not consider hysteresis in the soil-water parameters or layered soils, but both have been considered earlier by Bresler et al. (1969) and by Hanks and Bowers (1962). Another assumption that may be a serious limitation in some desert situations is isothermal flow. Condensation is not considered.

The soil parameters used are assumed to be known and not to change with time. Thus, the soils are considered homogeneous and have no structural change with time. This is a serious limitation because few soils are homogeneous. Nimah and Hanks (1973) minimized this error by using average field data and making a calibration run in the area of interest.

Inputs

The inputs can be classified as soil properties, plant properties, and climate. The soil properties include the following:

1. Data to show the relation of water content to matric potential and hydraulic conductivity. Table 11-1 is an example of data from the Curlew Valley site in Utah.
2. Initial conditions, which include water content and soil solution concentration at the beginning of the computation. Table 11-2 shows an example for the Curlew Valley site.

TABLE 11-1. *Relation of Soil-Water Content to Matric Potential and Hydraulic Conductivity for Curlew Valley, Utah*

Water Content (cm³/cm³)	Matric potential (cm of water)	Hydraulic conductivity (cm/hour)
0.02	-2.0×10^5	1.5×10^{-6}
.04	-8.0×10^4	2.8×10^{-6}
.06	-3.8×10^4	5.2×10^{-6}
.08	-2.4×10^4	8.8×10^{-6}
.10	-2.1×10^4	1.7×10^{-5}
.12	-1.7×10^4	3.2×10^{-5}
.14	-1.5×10^4	6.0×10^{-5}
.16	-9.0×10^3	1.1×10^{-4}
.18	-4.0×10^3	2.1×10^{-4}
.20	-2.0×10^3	3.8×10^{-4}
.22	-1.4×10^3	7.8×10^{-4}
.24	-1.0×10^3	1.4×10^{-3}
.26	-9.0×10^2	2.5×10^{-3}
.28	-7.3×10^2	4.2×10^{-3}
.30	-5.8×10^2	8.0×10^{-3}
.32	-4.7×10^2	1.7×10^{-2}
.34	-3.8×10^2	3.2×10^{-2}
.36	-3.0×10^2	5.9×10^{-2}
.38	-2.5×10^2	8.0×10^{-2}
.40	-2.0×10^2	1.2×10^{-1}
.42	-1.9×10^2	1.8×10^{-2}
.44	-1.1×10^2	2.6×10^{-2}
.46	-8.0×10	3.9×10^{-2}
.48	-4.0×10	5.6×10^{-2}
.50	-1.0×10	8.0×10^{-1}
.52	0	1.2

The plant properties needed are as follows:

1. Rooting depth relation ($RDF(z)$ of equation 11.2) as a function of time. Nimah and Hanks (1973) assumed that this relation does not change with time, but Childs and Hanks (1975) described a situation where this relation changes with time. Table 11-2 shows data used for a model verification comparison at Curlew Valley that assumed no change in root distribution with time.
2. Above-ground-cover properties to determine how to divide potential evapotranspiration into potential evaporation and potential transpiration. For the example of Curlew Valley from a sagebrush site, this cover property was assumed not to change with time.
3. The value of the root water potential below which the plant will not be able to meet potential transpiration demands of the climate. A value of 20,000 millibars was used for the Curlew Valley example.

TABLE 11-2.   *Initial Conditions for the*
Curlew Valley Site

Depth (cm)	Fraction	C (meq/l)	RDF (fraction)
0	0.012	0.9	0
3	0.060	50.3	0.334[a]
15	0.103	30.3	0.300
28	0.173	73.0	0.272
40	0.190	406.4	0.094
70	0.153	630.8	0
90	0.151	878.8	0
108	0.163	810.9	0
135	0.150	956.5	0
160	0.140	1189.0	0

a. The depth increment associated with this value is halfway between the above and lower depth or in this example from 1.5 to 9 cm.

The climatic data needed are as follows:

1. Rainfall amount, intensity, and time of occurrence. Table 11-3 shows data used for the Curlew Valley example.
2. Derived values of potential evaporation and potential transpiration. There are many methods for obtainig potential evapotranspiration as discussed by Jensen (1973). The method used to separate potential evapotranspiration to potential evaporation and potential transpiration is discussed by Childs and Hanks (1975). For the Curlew Valley example, shown in table 11-3, potential evaporation was assumed to be 75 percent of the potential evapotranspiration. Potential transpiration is the difference between potential evapotranspiration and potential evaporation.

Computational Procedure

Numerical approximations of the basic equation and a program to solve the equations were given in detail by Griffin et al. (1974). The computation flow is as follows:

1. Read input data.
2. Transform input data to a form compatible with programs and print out input data.
3. Based on the known water content profile, a value of hydraulic conductibility, K, and specific water capacity, $6\Theta/\triangle h$, is computed for each depth and is assumed to hold for a small time increment, $\triangle t$.

TABLE 11-3. *Climatic Data from Curlew Valley Site, August 18–September 15, 1971*

Period (0–1 day)	Potential evaporation (cm/hour)	Potential evapotranspiration (cm/hour)	Rain intensity (cm/hour)
1–4 days	0.02C	0.026	0
1–4	.017	.022	0
4–5	.018	.024	0
5–6	.016	.021	0
6–8	.015	.020	0
8–9	.016	.021	0
9–10	.017	.022	0
10–10.05	0	0	0.26
10.05–10.24	0	0	0.56
10.24–15	.015	.020	0
15–15.10	0	0	0.36
15.10–17	.0024	.0030	0
17–18	.011	.015	0
18–19	.013	.017	0
19–20	.014	.018	0
20–20.10	0	0	0.09
20.10–22	.012	.016	0
22–28	.014	.019	0

4. The surface values of Θ and h are found by a hunting technique to correspond to the surface boundary conditions. For evaporation, if the surface soil value of Θ is above the air dry value, the computed evaporation will equal the potential evaporation. The surface boundary condition is the known potential flux. If this condition cannot be attained for a matric potential above the air dry value, the computed evaporation will be less than the appropriate potential.
5. New boundary conditions are then chosen for the new time, the values of h, Θ, and C just computed are taken as new initial values, and the process is repeated from step 3 above until the end time is reached.

Outputs

There is a wide variety of data available for output if desired, such as h, Θ, and C profiles, infiltration, evaporation, transpiration, runoff, and root water potential all as a function of time. Many other computations are readily available, such as water or salts flux, at any depth or time.

VALIDATION

The model has been validated for alfalfa under irrigated conditions for a season by Nimah and Hanks (1973). Also, somewhat limited validation of the model for osmotic effects has been done under laboratory conditions by Childs and Hanks (1973). Griffin et al. (1974) ran a limited validation test of the model for the Curlew Valley data. Their results are used here for an example.

The data used for illustration purposes in tables 11-1, 11-2, and 11-3, were taken from a validation run of twenty-eight days from August 8 to September 15, 1971.

Rainfall events occurred on the eleventh, twelfth, sixteenth, and twenty-first days of the run, as shown in table 11-3. Figure 11-1 shows the initial water content profile at the beginning of the run. Figure 11-2 shows the response of the model predictions to the light rainfall that occurred on the sixteenth day.

Figure 11-3 shows good agreement of the computed and measured water content profile on the twenty-fifth day. Thus, it appears that the model predicts water content profiles fairly well.

Figure 11-4 shows the initial electrical conductivity of the soil solution as measured and used in the computation. Figure 11-5 shows that the predicted electrical conductivity after twenty-five days agreed closely with the measured values. Further work has shown, however, that the salt prediction of this model may be inadequate for some situations because of chemical changes occurring within the soil solution that are not considered.

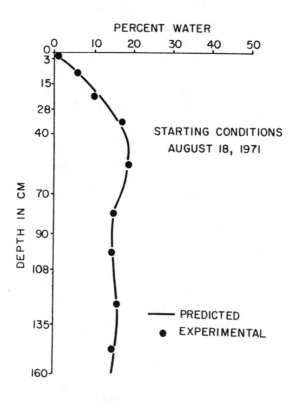

FIGURE 11-1. *Moisture content as a function of depth in the soil profile.*

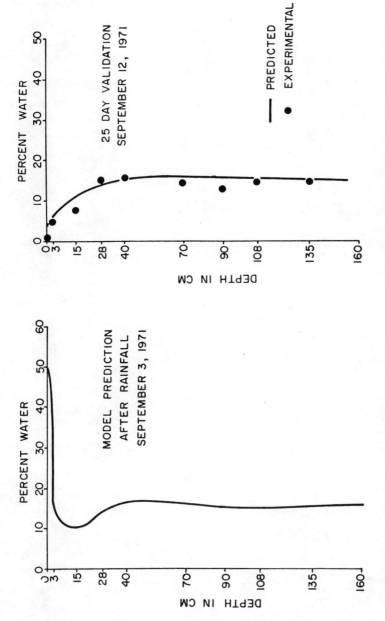

FIGURE 11-3. *Moisture content as a function of depth in the soil profile.*

FIGURE 11-2. *Moisture content as a function of depth in the soil profile.*

241

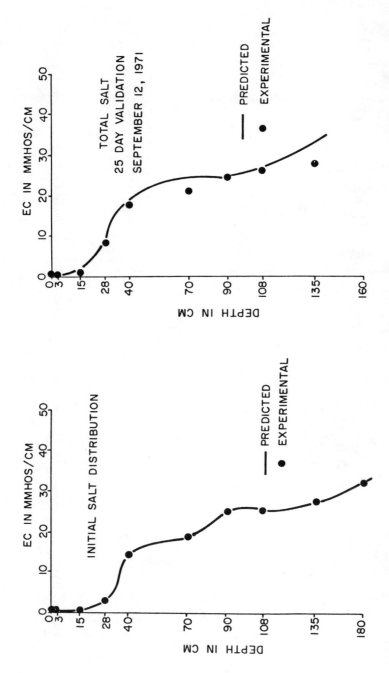

FIGURE 11-5. *Total salt content as a function of depth in the soil profile.*

FIGURE 11-4. *Total salt content as a function of depth in the soil profile.*

242

In summary, the model I have described, which was originally developed for agricultural situations, has been shown to yield good predictions of salt and water flow for a desert ecosystem. The model is quite generally applicable and uses basic, easily identified input variables of climate (potential evapotranspiration and rainfall), plant (cover), and soil properties (initial soil water and salt concentration and soil-water characteristics). Predictions of soil-water content, soil-water potential, and soil solution concentration as a function of time and depth are available. The flow of water and salt at any depth and time can also be predicted. The model is limited to one-dimensional flow for uniform soils with no chemical reactions.

REFERENCES

Bresler, E. 1973. Simultaneous transport of solute and water under transient, unsaturated flow conditions. *Water Resour. Res.* **9**:975–986.

Bresler, E., W. D. Kemper, and R. J. Hanks. 1969. Infiltration, redistribution and subsequent evaporation of water from soil as affected bv wetting rate and hysterisis. *Proc. Soil Sci. Soc. Am.* **33**:832–840.

Childs, S. W., and R. J. Hanks. 1975. Model of soil salinity effects on crop growth. *Proc. Soil Sci. Soc. Am.* **39**:617–622.

Griffin, R. A., R. J. Hanks, and S. Childs. 1974. *Model for Estimating Water, Salt, and Temperature Distribution in Soil Profile.* US/IBP Desert Biome Res. Memo. 61-74.

Hanks, R. J., and S. A. Bowers. 1962. Numerical solution of the moisture flow equation for infiltration into layered soils. *Proc. Soil Sci. Soc. Am.* **26**:530–534.

Jensen, M. E. 1973. *Consumptive Use of Water and Irrigation Water Requirements.* Am. Soc. Soc. Civil Eng., New York, 215 pp.

Melamed, D., R. J. Hanks, and L. S. Willardson. 1977. Model of salt flow in soil with a source-sink term. *J. Soil Sci. Soc. Am.* **41**:29–33.

Nimah, M. N., and R. J. Hanks. 1973. Model for estimating soil and atmospheric interrelation: I. Description and sensitivity. II. Field test of the model. *Proc. Soil Sci. Soc. Am.* **37**:522–532.

12
Modeling Desert Runoff

Louis H. Hekman, Jr., and *Wayne R. Berkas*

In desert ecosystems, stream flow occurs infrequently and is derived almost exclusively from surface runoff. The contributions of subsurface and groundwater flows to stream flow are characteristically minimal. The desert climate with its meager annual precipitation, warm daytime temperatures, and low relative humidity elicits high potential evapotranspiration rates that serve to keep the soil generally dry. Crusting of the desert soil surface is a generally prevalent condition fostered by sparse vegetative cover, overland flow, and soil-water chemical reactions. Although surface crusting reduces the infiltration rate, the paucity of precipitation and the low intensities associated with winter frontal storms serve to limit the number of runoff events. Desert runoff, when it occurs, is associated primarily with high-intensity, short-duration summer thunderstorms.

The infrequence of desert runoff should not belie the importance of this phenomenon within the desert ecosystem. As overland flow becomes increasingly concentrated in a diminishing array of larger and larger channels, it can become a highly erosive force, cutting and shaping desert topography into arroyos, gullies, and canyons. As man's activities encroach on desert regions through urbanization, livestock operations, and irrigated agriculture, to name just a few, large flows also pose an increasingly greater threat to life and property. Although the available moisture is usually too limited and the water table is too far beneath the land surface for overland flow to contribute directly to groundwater storage, the infiltration occurring in major channels during runoff events is the primary source of groundwater recharge in desert ecosystems (Renard 1970). Surface water infiltrating channel banks provides moisture to support a wide variety of desert vegetation. Natural and man-made catchments trap surface runoff and provide temporary supplies of vital fresh water for desert wildlife and domestic stock. Although limited in quantity, surface runoff is a critical element of desert ecosystems.

The modeling of desert runoff has three general purposes:

1. To improve understanding of the desert runoff system with its components and their interactions.
2. To increase knowledge of the hydrologic character of a specific desert area, thereby expanding the information base from which decisions regarding man's activities can be made. For example, the design and sizing of flood-retarding structures, detention dams, stock tanks, bridges, and culverts may be benefited by modeling the impacting hydrologic system and simulating a synthetic time series of hydrologic

events. Modeling and simulation is particularly helpful in cases where historical records are limited (see chapter 10).
3. To provide a predictive tool whereby future conditions can be mapped based on estimates of naturally occurring and/or man-caused changes within the system. The simulation of desert hydrologic response to increasing urbanization is an example of this.

The selection of an existing model to be used in full, part, or modified form or the decision to develop a new model will be strongly influenced by the type of information desired and the nature of the models and data available. All models are, of necessity, simplified representations of natural processes. Generally, model complexity is directly related to the number of factors for which information is desired. Greater complexity does not, however, ensure greater accuracy. Often as complexity increases with the incorporation of additional model components, subtle offsetting interactions arise among components, enabling the tracing of specific cause-effect or input-output relationships to be achieved only with great difficulty. Uncertainties due to weaknesses in modeling, data sampling, and parameter estimation may be compounded, thereby greatly reducing a model's effectiveness.

The major portion of this chapter is devoted to the presentation of a fairly complex model depicting surface runoff phenomena. This model is essentially a hybrid, composed of modified portions of existing models of soil water (see chapter 11) and overland flow routing (Huggins and Monke, 1968, 1970). Routines for handling evapotranspiration and interception are also included. For illustration and validation purposes the model is applied to a small desert watershed (1.17 square kilometers) near Tucson, Arizona. The surface runoff model is then linked to an event-based stochastic precipitation model (see chapter 10), and twenty-five synthetic summer thunderstorm seasons are generated and analyzed. As an alternative to the use of the complex watershed model, a simple Soil Conservation Service (SCS) rainfall-runoff relationship is described and applied to the same desert watershed. The performances of these two approaches are compared.

MODEL DESCRIPTION

The watershed model is essentially that described by Berkas (1978) and is composed of four basic process components: evapotranspiration, interception, soil moisture movement, including infiltration and evaporation, and surface runoff routing.

Evapotranspiration

Average monthly potential evapotranspiration rates representative of the area to be modeled are used to determine potential evaporation and potential transpiration. Potential transpiration rates are estimated by multiplying potential evapotranspiration rates by the vegetative ground-cover percentage. The ground-cover percentage may vary with time or may be held constant. The potential evaporation rate is simply the difference between the potential evapotranspiration and potential transpiration rates. A sinusoidal function is used to vary potential evapotranspiration rates from 8:00 A.M. to 8:00 P.M. with peak rates occurring at 2:00 P.M. During evening and early morning, the potential rates are maintained at constant minimum levels. Actual transpiration and evaporation rates are calculated in the soil moisture component of the model and are not allowed to exceed the potential amounts.

Interception

Interception losses, representing that portion of precipitation stored on and subsequently evaporated from vegetation surfaces, is a function of vegetation type and density. The model requires the estimation of plant interception capacity (depth) and the percentage of vegetative cover on the watershed. Upon encountering vegetation, only that portion of precipitation in excess of existing unsatisfied interception capacities can contribute to runoff or infiltration. The precipitation amount actually available for runoff or infiltration is averaged over the entire watershed: i.e.

$$P_{ROI} = P_S \times OPEN + (P_S - I_D) \times COVER, \quad P_S > I_D, \tag{12.1}$$

and

$$P_{ROI} = P_S \times OPEN, \quad P_S \le I_D$$

where P_{ROI} is precipitation available for runoff or infiltration (depth), P_S is storm precipitation (depth), $OPEN$ is fraction of watershed with no vegetation cover, I_D is current interception demand (depth), and $COVER$ is fraction of watershed covered with vegetation.

At the end of a precipitation event, the moisture in interception storage is evaporated at the potential evaporation rate. Interception losses may be insignificant on desert watersheds that have very low vegetation densities.

Soil Moisture Movement

The soil-water movement component of the hydrologic model is a modified version of the model described by Hanks in chapter 11. Essentially the procedures for computing the amount of moisture extracted from the soil by roots have been vastly simplified. This alteration was made to make the model less cumbersome and to increase computational speed. The limiting assumptions discussed in chapter 11 also apply to the current model.

Soil moisture transfer between adjoining soil layers is described by the following relationship:

$$I = (h_i - h_{i+1} + G) \, K/\triangle X \tag{12.2}$$

where I is the movement rate (cm/hr), h is the suction of the soil (cm), $\triangle X$ is the length of the depth increment (cm), K is the unsaturated hydraulic conductivity (cm/hr), G is the gravitational factor ($\triangle X$), and i refers to the depth increment.

Moisture flows from areas of low suction to areas of high suction, with a positive I corresponding to downward moisture flow, and a negative I corresponding to upward moisture flow. When there is no difference in suction, moisture moves downward at the unsaturated hydraulic conductivity rate.

Equation 12.2 only repositions moisture within the soil profile. An equation is therefore needed to remove soil moisture when evaporation occurs and add soil moisture when infiltration occurs. The rate that water enters or leaves a soil is governed by the soil hydraulic conditions at the surface. Equation 12.2 is modified to account for infiltration or evaporation as follows:

$$EOI = (S - h + G)\ K/\triangle X \qquad (12.3)$$

where EOI is the evaporation or infiltration rate (cm/hr), S is the surface suction (cm), h is the suction at 1 cm depth (cm), G is the gravitational factor (1 cm), $\triangle X$ is the surface "depth" (1 cm), and K is the hydraulic conductivity at the surface.

The amount evaporated is subtracted from the moisture at the surface, while the infiltrating water is added. If the calculated evaporation rate is greater than the potential evaporation rate, the potential evaporation rate is used. Similarly if the infiltration rate is greater than the precipitation rate and antecedent surface runoff is not occurring, the infiltration is set equal to the precipitation rate.

Two assumptions govern the soil moisture movement process. First, the maximum amount of water leaving a depth increment is half the difference between the moisture contents of the sending and receiving layers. In this way, the layer receiving the water is not allowed to become wetter than the layer from which the water came. Second, when infiltration is occurring, water moving downward from the surface soil layer is not allowed to exceed the infiltration rate.

Actual transpiration rates are calculated from the water content of the soil, rooting density, and potential transpiration. The amount of moisture extracted by the roots is assumed to be linearly related to the soil moisture content.

Rooting density for each depth increment is needed to estimate transpiration. The potential transpiration for a time interval is multiplied by the percentage of roots in each depth increment to get the amount of possible transpiration originating in each soil layer. This amount is then multiplied by the ratio of average soil moisture in the depth increment to the saturated soil moisture to estimate the actual amount of water lost from each increment. The soil moisture in each layer is reduced by the calculated transpiration. The transpiration amounts from all layers are summed, yielding an estimate of total actual transpiration for the current time interval. The actual transpiration is equal to the potential transpiration only when the soil is completely saturated.

The basic steps of soil moisture routing are:

1. Values of suction and hydraulic conductivity are calculated for the soil moisture conditions at each depth increment.
2. Transpiration losses are calculated for each depth increment and subtracted from the soil moisture content.

3. Soil moisture movement for each depth increment is calculated, and soil moisture is redistributed.
4. Evaporation/infiltration is calculated and subtracted/added to surface soil moisture.

Soil moisture conditions for each depth are updated by this procedure for each modeled time step.

Routing of Surface Runoff

All precipitation in excess of interception and infiltration demands becomes surface runoff and must be routed down slope. The basic method employed is similar to that developed by Huggins and Monke (1968, 1970). The watershed is divided into square elements, the slope and aspect of which must be specified. The elements are kept sufficiently small to ensure topographic uniformity within each element.

All surface flow over an element will travel parallel to that element's aspect. The least elevated corner of each element is intersected by a straight line, which divides the element into two areas, thereby determining the proportion of total runoff that will go to each of the two adjacent downslope elements. These percentages are computed using the following functions:

$$\text{fraction}_S = (\text{tangent (aspect}'))/2, \text{aspect}' \leq 45°,$$

$$\text{fraction}_S = (\text{tangent } (90° - \text{aspect}'))/2, \text{aspect}' > 45°, \text{ and} \tag{12.4}$$

$$\text{fraction}_L = 1 - \text{fraction}_S,$$

where fraction_L = is fraction of total element runoff going in major outlfow direction, aspect' is element aspect modulus 90, and fraction_S is fraction of total element runoff going in minor outflow direction.

The total amount of water leaving each element is a function of flow rate and element length. The rate of flow is calculated using Manning's equation modified for overland flow (Musgrave and Holtan 1964):

$$V = \frac{4.65}{n} (S)^{1/2} (R)^{2/3} \tag{12.5}$$

where V is flow velocity (cm/sec), S is slope, R is hydraulic radius, here equal to depth of flow (cm), n is Manning's roughness coefficient, and 4.65 is the coefficient for metric units. An example of surface routing follows.

One cm of water is to be routed from a 50 meter by 50 meter element. Assume the slope and aspect of this element are 0.05 and 231°, respectively, and that the duration of runoff is 0.02 hours. The aspect dictates that water will flow to adjacent elements on the west and south (assuming 0° is due north) with the largest percentage of flow being routed west (see figure 12-1). Aspect' equals 51°, fraction_S equals 40.5%, and fraction_L equals 59.5%. Using a rough-

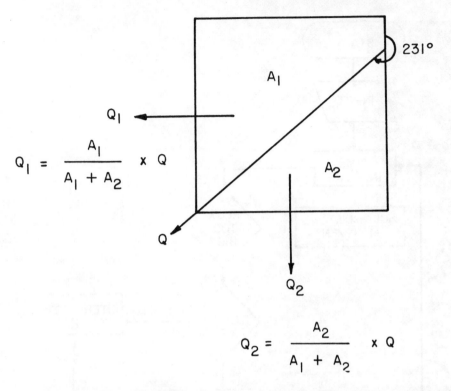

FIGURE 12-1. *The distribution of flow leaving a bisected watershed element.*

ness coefficient of 0.08, Manning's equation yields a velocity of 13.0 cm/sec, which translates into a runoff travel distance of 9.36 meters during the 0.02 hour time interval. Because the element is 50 meters square, only 18.7% of the 1 cm surface water will run off in the time period. Therefore, 0.111 cm of water (0.187 × 0.595 × 1.0) is transfered to the adjacent element on the west, and 0.076 cm of water (0.187 × 0.405 × 1.0) is transferred to the adjacent element on the south.

Model Operation

Listed below is the operating sequence of the watershed model. The flow-chart of this process is given in figure 12-2.

1. Read input data into the program.
2. Calculate a time interval.
3. Calculate potential transpiration and potential evaporation for the time interval.
4. Calculate soil moisture movement.
5. Calculate infiltration or evaporation.
6. If the soil moisture movement is too large, go to step 2.

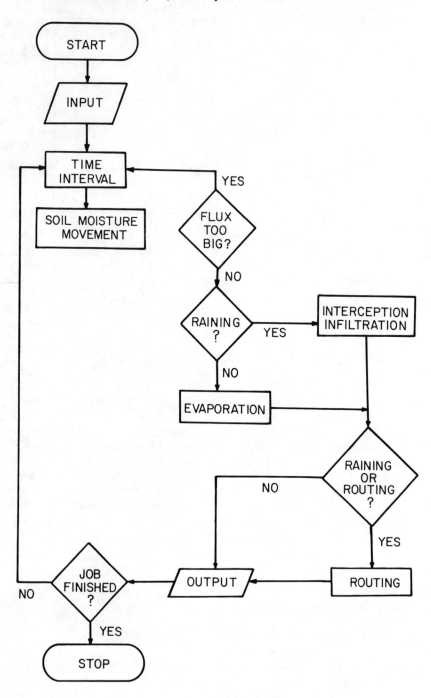

FIGURE 12-2. *Flowchart of the watershed model.*

7. Calculate interception losses if raining, or evaporate intercepted water if vegetation is wet.
8. Calculate transpiration and redistribute soil moisture.
9. Subtract/add evaporation/infiltration amount from the surface soil moisture conditions.
10. Routing sequence: (a) if it is not raining and water is not being routed, then go to step 11; (b) if rainfall exceeds infiltration, add the depth of water available for runoff to each element; (c) route the water on each element.
11. Print output.
12. Check time to see if event has ended; if it has, read in new precipitation data.
13. If job is finished, stop; otherwise, return to step 2.

Model outputs include:

1. Precipitation and infiltration rates or potential evaporation and actual evaporation rates over each time interval.
2. The total amount of evaporation and transpiration for the time interval.
3. Runoff over time.
4. Total runoff (area-cm), total outflow (m^3), and peak flow (m^3 sec^{-1}).
5. Soil moisture with depth.

MODEL ILLUSTRATION AND VALIDATION

Watershed Description

The W-3 subwatershed of the Atterbury Experimental Watershed located near Tucson, Arizona, was chosen to illustrate and validate the hydrologic model of surface runoff. The watershed encompasses 1.17 square kilometers and is oblong in shape with a major channel length of slightly more than 3,000 meters. Average land slope is 3.7 percent, and channel slope is 1.20 percent. The watershed ranges from about 950 to 975 meters above sea level. Vegetation cover is thin, consisting primarily of cresote bush (*Larrea tridentata*), palo verde (*Cericidium microphyllum*), mesquite (*Prosopis juliflora*), and ocotillo (*Fouquieria splendens*). Soil surfaces range from sandy or gravelly materials on the rounded, gently sloping ridges to loams on the nearly level water courses that separate the ridges. The main drainage ways consist of either broad swales or gullies with sandy bottoms. During the summer thunderstorm months of July, August, and September, the watershed receives approximately 15.5 centimeters of rainfall. Storm runoff volume for the watershed is determined from a volumetrically calibrated reservoir.

Model Calibration

To apply the surface runoff model to a particular watershed, estimates of the following site specific characteristics must be made:

1. Potential evapotranspiration.
2. Plant cover characteristics and rooting densities with depth.
3. Relationship of hydraulic conductivity and soil suction to volumetric soil moisture content.
4. Manning's roughness coefficient.
5. Slope and aspect of each grid element.

Thirty-five years of monthly pan evaporation measurements recorded at the University of Arizona in Tucson (Green and Sellers, 1964) served as the basis for estimating potential evapotranspiration. A pan coefficient of 0.69 was used in the conversion. Average maximum daily potential evapotranspiration rates determined for July, August, and September were 0.058, 0.046 and 0.042 cm/hr, respectively.

Vegetative ground cover was estimated at 20 percent and was assumed to be constant during the three-month thunderstorm season. The average interception storage capacity of the vegetation was estimated to be 0.07 cm. For modeling soil moisture movement, the soil profile was conceptually divided into six layers, each 10 cm thick. Root densities used for each of these layers were based on reported research findings of the US/IBP Desert Biome at the Tucson Basin Validation Site (Thames et al. 1974). These densities are presented in table 12-1.

The relations of hydraulic conductivity and soil suction to volumetric soil moisture were approximated from general curves (figures 12-3 and 12-4) presented by Hillel (1977). The values used in modeling soil moisture movements are listed in table 12-2.

Manning's equation (12.5) was developed for use in estimating flow rates in channels, but the roughness coefficient, n, cannot be measured directly. Although tables and methods exist for estimating values for the coefficient, these primarily apply to channel flow conditions. The method described by Cowan (1956) and outlined in Chow (1959) for estimating Manning's roughness coefficient for very small channels was used to approximate an average n value of 0.08 for the Atterbury watershed.

The watershed was partitioned into seventy-eight square elements, each of which measured 121.9 meters on a side. Slope and aspect values for each element were estimated from a contour map of the watershed. Although much

TABLE 12-1. *Summary of Precipitation, Actual Runoff, and Modeled Runoff for Five Storms on the Atterbury W-3 Watershed*

Date	Total precipitation (cm)	Precipitation duration (hrs)	Runoff (depth) Actual (cm)	Runoff (depth) Model (cm)	Peak flow (model) (m^3sec^{-1})	Runoff duration (hrs)
7/29/56	4.27	2.00	0.71	0.79	1.52	5.97
8/23/58	3.10	0.80	0.46	0.46	1.04	4.57
7/22/64	2.41	0.45	0.18	0.18	0.45	3.56
8/18/67	2.77	0.80	0.48	0.46	1.00	4.77
8/7/69	2.13	0.50	0.10	0.10	0.23	3.19

TABLE 12-2. *Summary of Simulation Run for Twenty-five Summer Seasons Using Watershed Model*

Season	Precipitation			Runoff depth			Peak event	
	Total (cm)	N	$\bar{x}$ (cm)	Total (cm)	N	$\bar{x}$ (cm)	Flow (m^{3}sec^{-1})	Depth (cm)
1	19.74	29	0.68	1.60	20	0.080	0.90	0.439
2	19.76	33	0.60	0.21	21	0.010	0.18	0.086
3	18.85	34	0.55	0.42	20	0.021	0.30	0.150
4	19.25	32	0.60	1.26	20	0.063	1.95	0.909
5	10.19	22	0.46	0.08	10	0.008	0.17	0.079
6	13.46	27	0.50	0.41	15	0.028	0.49	0.234
7	14.53	30	0.49	0.24	11	0.022	0.44	0.183
8	16.33	34	0.48	0.09	14	0.007	0.15	0.074
9	21.01	37	0.57	2.66	21	0.127	4.41	2.032
10	19.41	23	0.84	3.55	17	0.209	3.44	1.595
11	14.73	30	0.49	0.49	15	0.033	0.56	0.236
12	15.70	23	0.68	2.81	13	0.216	5.27	2.395
13	14.78	32	0.46	1.99	13	0.153	3.52	1.615
14	16.61	34	0.49	0.45	18	0.025	0.89	0.427
15	14.76	27	0.55	0.28	17	0.017	0.63	0.264
16	20.19	24	0.84	2.67	16	0.167	2.75	1.283
17	13.97	26	0.54	1.90	11	0.172	1.79	0.861
18	16.74	31	0.54	1.20	15	0.080	2.01	0.879
19	13.26	27	0.49	0.26	16	0.017	0.58	0.251
20	19.02	38	0.50	0.05	20	0.003	0.07	0.023
21	13.06	27	0.49	0.21	13	0.017	0.43	0.206
22	18.03	39	0.46	0.28	18	0.015	0.47	0.218
23	11.66	29	0.40	0.03	10	0.003	0.05	0.013
24	14.91	29	0.51	0.28	13	0.022	0.36	0.157
25	15.70	31	0.51	2.03	17	0.120	2.27	0.988
$\bar{x}$	16.23	29.92	0.54	1.02	15.76	0.065	1.36	0.625
s	2.90	4.63		1.07	3.47		1.48	0.679

leeway exists in the choice of element size, a few important considerations must be kept in mind. Element size must be large enough to ensure that the distance traveled by water in one routing time step does not exceed the length of the element. On the other hand, element size must not be so large as to mask important variations in site topography. Element size, routing time step, and execution time requirements are all interdependent. Thus, a decrease in element size must be accompanied by a shortening of the routing time step. The smaller time step coupled with the necessary increase in the number of elements results in significantly increased time requirements for computer processing. A routing time step of 0.04 hours was used in the model.

Model Validation

The hydrologic model was initially developed to model the dynamics of soil moisture and surface runoff on reclaimed strip-mine lands in semiarid

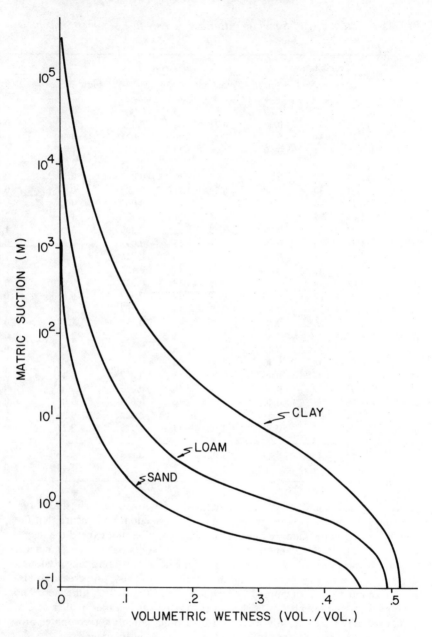

FIGURE 12-3.   *Soil moisture content versus soil matrix suction for three general soil types (Hillel, 1977).*

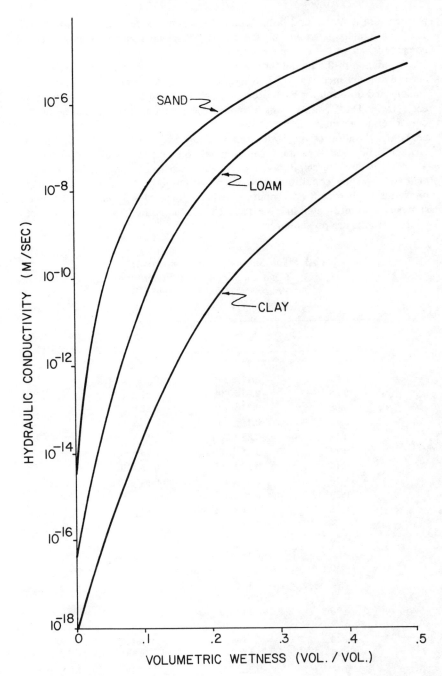

FIGURE 12-4. *Soil moisture content versus hydraulic conductivity for three general soil types (Hillel, 1977).*

northeastern Arizona, and in this context it has had some degree of success. The hydrographs generated by the model for selected historical rain events compared well with the actual hydrographs.

Validation of the model for the Atterbury W-3 watershed is severely hindered by the absence of actual hydrograph records. Available data only include amount and duration for each precipitation event and total runoff volume for each storm. Thus, comparisons of modeled versus actual runoff can be made only in terms of runoff volume. However, subjective comparisons of the shape, peak, and duration of the hydrographs produced by the model with known characteristics of desert runoff can be made to evaluate model acceptability.

Five historical precipitation events were processed by the model. Antecedent soil moisture conditions were estimated based on the actual antecedent precipitation record. Storm inputs together with modeled and actual runoff summaries are presented in table 12-3. The simulated hydrographs for four of the five storms are presented in figure 12-5.

TABLE 12-3. *Soil Suction (h) and Hydraulic Conductivity (K) as a Function of Volumetric Water Content (Θ) for Atterbury Watershed W-3*

Θ	h (cm)	k (cm/hr)
0.02	-0.70×10^5	0.32×10^{-9}
0.04	-0.17×10^5	0.72×10^{-8}
0.06	-0.65×10^4	0.11×10^{-6}
0.08	-0.27×10^4	0.22×10^{-5}
0.10	-0.15×10^4	0.13×10^{-4}
0.12	-0.85×10^3	0.58×10^{-4}
0.14	-0.55×10^3	0.18×10^{-3}
0.16	-0.37×10^3	0.43×10^{-3}
0.18	-0.30×10^3	0.94×10^{-3}
0.20	-0.25×10^3	0.22×10^{-2}
0.22	-0.21×10^3	0.43×10^{-2}
0.24	-0.18×10^3	0.77×10^{-2}
0.26	-0.15×10^3	0.14×10^{-1}
0.28	-0.13×10^3	0.21×10^{-1}
0.30	-0.11×10^3	0.32×10^{-1}
0.32	-0.10×10^3	0.50×10^{-1}
0.34	-0.88×10^2	0.72×10^{-1}
0.36	-0.78×10^2	0.10
0.38	-0.68×10^2	0.14
0.40	-0.54×10^2	0.18
0.42	-0.38×10^2	0.22
0.44	-0.26×10^2	0.29
0.46	-0.14×10^2	0.36
0.48	-0.14×10^1	0.45
0.50	0	0.50

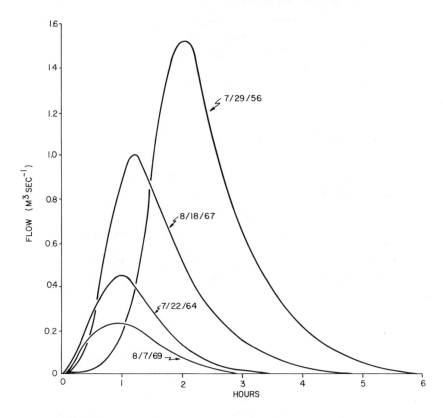

FIGURE 12-5. *Simulated hydrographs for Atterbury W-3 watershed based on four actual storms.*

The match between actual and modeled storm runoff depths is very close. The shapes of the hydrographs conform to the general runoff patterns produced by convective thunderstorms observed at other desert sites. Particularly characteristic are the high peak flows and the short durations of runoff. The simulated peak flows for these five storms are also in close agreement with those estimated using the Soil Conservation Service method presented at the end of this chapter.

SIMULATION OF LONG-TERM RECORDS

Knowledge concerning the runoff regime expected from a watershed is vital for estimating the consequences of man-ecosystem interactions. This knowledge is often hindered by the absence of adequate hydrologic data. In such cases, the stochastic simulation of synthetic time series of runoff events can be used to extend the data base. The procedure consists of using an event-based stochastic model of precipitation (see chapter 10) to generate a long-term synthetic precipitation record, which, in turn, is used to drive a deterministic watershed model. The watershed model, having been calibrated for a specific site, transforms the precipitation record into a corresponding time series of runoff events reflecting current or projected watershed conditions. For illustrative purposes, twenty-five summer thunderstorm seasons were simulated for the W-3 watershed.

Precipitation Model

Standard Monte Carlo techniques were used to generate values randomly for rainfall depths per storm (event), storm interarrival times, and storm beginning times. No more than one event was assumed to occur per day. Nineteen years of precipitation records for the months of July, August, and September were analyzed. The mean and variance of event rainfall depths were 0.617 cm and 0.497 cm^2, respectively, and the mean interarrival time was 3.0 days.

The two-parameter gamma distribution was used to describe mean areal rainfall per event. The probability density function of this distribution is given by

$$f_R(r) = \frac{b^a \, r^{a-1} \, e^{-br}}{\Gamma(a)} \, . \tag{12.6}$$

Using the method of moments, with r being rainfall depth in millimeters, values for a and b that yielded the best fit were 0.766 and 0.1241, respectively. Figure 12-6 illustrates the fit between the gamma distribution and the cumulative frequency distribution of the actual rainfall data. A geometric distribution was fitted to the storm interarrival time, the probability mass function of which is

$$f_T(t) = (1-p)^{t-1}p \, , \, t \geq 1. \tag{12.7}$$

A value of 0.33 was used for parameter p, with t being expressed in days. Figure 12-7 compares the actual and theoretical distributions for storm interarrival times. The goodness of fit between the theoretical and actual distributions for both event rainfall and event interarrival time could not be rejected at the 10 percent level of significance using the Kolmogorov-Smirnov test.

The beginning time of an event was described by a uniformly distributed random variable ranging in value from 13.0 (1:00 P.M.) to 19.0 (7:00 P.M.). Storm durations were estimated as a function of rainfall depths with the following equation:

$$D = 10 \left(\frac{R - 4.67}{6.15} \right) , \tag{12.8}$$

where R is storm depth in centimeters and D is the duration in hours of 90 percent of the total storm depth. This relationship is described by Fogel and Duckstein (1970) and is based on studies of Atterbury precipitation records.

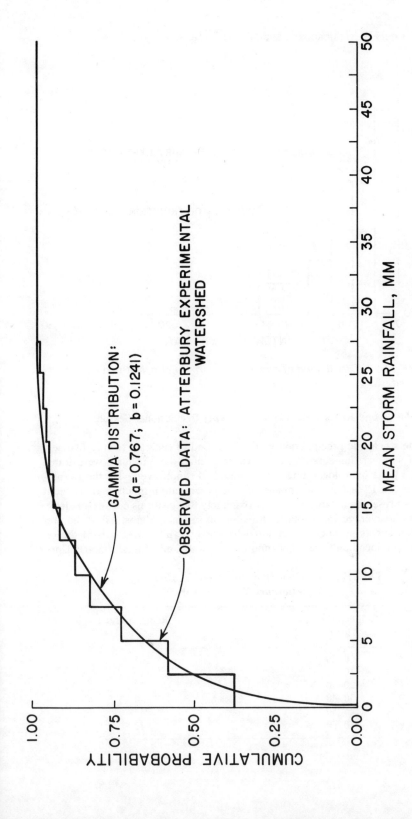

FIGURE 12-6. *Frequency distribution of mean convective storm rainfall, Atterbury watershed.*

259

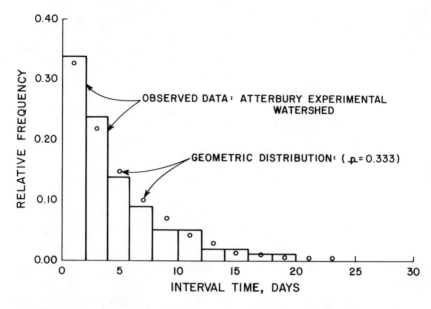

FIGURE 12-7.   *Distribution of convective storm interarrival time, Atterbury watershed.*

Precipitation and Runoff: Simulation of Twenty-five Summer Seasons

The stochastic precipitation model was used to generate twenty-five seasons of summer thunderstorm data. These rainfall data, in turn, were transformed by the hydrologic model into individual runoff events for the twenty-five simulated seasons. A summary of the precipitation inputs and resultant runoff is presented in table 12-4. Approximately thirty storms per season delivered on the average 16.23 total centimeters of rainfall. Almost half of all precipitation events produced no runoff whatsoever, while two-thirds of the remainder produced only traces of runoff (0.001 to 8.5 m³ of total runoff). Thus,

TABLE 12-4.   *Root Densities Used in Modeling Atterbury Watershed W-3*

Soil depth zone (cm)	Root density (%)
0–10	5
10–20	10
20–30	30
30–40	30
40–50	15
50–60	10

only about a sixth of all precipitation events produced runoff volumes in excess of 8.5 m³. The average watershed runoff efficiency was roughly 6 percent. As would be expected, the precipitation patterns and timing within a season were extremely important in determining total seasonal runoff. A wet season did not guarantee large runoff volumes. The twenty-five-year runoff event produced a peak flow of 5.27 m³ sec⁻¹.

AN ALTERNATIVE METHODOLOGY

The watershed model, with its many component processes interacting over small time steps, is both detailed and complex. As is typical with such models, its computer time requirements are relatively large. The twenty-five-season (three months per season) simulation run required 125 seconds of central processor time on the University of Arizona's CDC CYBER 175 computer, at a cost of thirty dollars.

The answer to the question of whether to use such a model is dependent upon the type of information desired and the worth of that information to the investigator. In many cases such extensive and detailed modeling would not be needed. For example, the sizing of a culvert may be based on estimates of the expected twenty-five- or fifty-year peak flow event, with no need to monitor soil moisture conditions closely. In another instance, information concerning expected total seasonal runoff volumes may be desired, with no need to study individual storm hydrographs directly. Costs also must be considered. The costs of simulating long periods of record may be prohibitive in many cases.

An alternative to the use of comprehensive process-oriented models of surface runoff from small desert watersheds is the use of simple empirical rainfall-runoff relationships. Information derived in this manner is generally limited to estimates of total storm runoff volumes and peak flow rates. One such set of empirical rainfall-runoff relationships is presented by the Soil Conservation Service (SCS) (Soil Conservation Service, 1972).

SCS Rainfall-Runoff Relationships

The SCS method relates storm rainfall and runoff with the following expression:

$$V = \frac{(R-A)^2}{(R-A) + S} \quad , \tag{12.9}$$

where V is runoff, R is storm precipitation, S is the potential maximum retention, and A is the initial abstraction. All terms are expressed as depths.

The peak discharge equation used by the SCS is

$$Q = \frac{2.0832 \times A \times V}{0.5D + 0.6T_c} \quad , \tag{12.10}$$

where Q is the peak discharge (m^3sec^{-1}), A is the watershed area (km^2), V is runoff depth (cm), D is duration of excess rainfall (hrs.), and T_c is the watershed time of concentration (hrs.).

Application of SCS Approach to the W-3 Watershed

The SCS equations were applied to the Atterbury W-3 watershed to compare the performance of the SCS rainfall-runoff methodology with that of the watershed model. Standard SCS procedures were used to obtain values for S corresponding to three classes of antecedent moisture conditions. If the previous five-day rainfall total exceeded 3.81 cm, S was set equal to 1.07 cm. If the five-day antecedent rainfall totaled less than 1.52 cm, S was set equal to 8/03 cm. S equaled 3.15 cm for the intermediate antecedent moisture range. The initial abstraction term A was assumed to equal 0.15 x S rather than 0.2 x S as normally is used by the SCS. Previous studies in Arizona (Fogel, 1969) indicate that 0.15 is more representative of semiarid conditions.

Due to limited information on intrastorm rainfall intensities, the duration of excess rainfall, D, was assumed to equal the duration of the total precipitation event. The time of concentration, T_c, was estimated to be 1.23 hours using the upland method as presented by the SCS (Soil Conservation Service, 1972).

Using these parameter values, the SCS equations were then applied to the same five historic events presented earlier in this chapter. Table 12-5 lists the actual runoff and that simulated with the SCS equations and the watershed model. Results obtained with the SCS approach appear to be less accurate with regard to runoff depths for the five storms than those obtained using the watershed model. However, with the possible exception of the event on August 18, 1967, both runoff depths and peak flows determined by the two methods are generally comparable.

For all but the first storm, the SCS estimates of peak flows, when based on storm depths produced by the watershed model, are almost identical to those generated by the watershed model (table 12-6).

TABLE 12-5. *Runoff Summary for Five Storms on the Atterbury W-3 Watershed as Determined by the Watershed Model and the SCS Methodology*

	Runoff (cm)			Peak flow (m^3sec^{-1})	
Date	Actual	Model	SCS	Model	SCS
7/29/56	0.71	0.79	0.86	1.52	1.21
8/23/58	0.46	0.46	0.36	1.04	0.76
7/22/64	0.18	0.18	0.15	0.45	0.38
8/18/67	0.48	0.46	0.25	1.00	0.54
8/7/69	0.10	0.10	0.10	0.23	0.25

TABLE 12-6. *Comparisons of Peak Flows Generated by the Watershed Model and the SCS Equation for Five Storms*

Date	Modeled runoff depth (cm)	Modeled peak flow (m³sec⁻¹)	SCS peak flow (m³sec⁻¹)
7/29/56	0.79	1.52	1.10
8/23/58	0.46	1.04	0.98
7/22/64	0.18	0.45	0.45
8/18/67	0.46	1.00	0.98
8/7/69	0.10	0.23	0.25

Note: The runoff depths used with the SCS method are those generated by the watershed model.

TABLE 12-7. *Statistics for Twenty-five Season Runoff Simulation as Generated by the Watershed Model and the SCS Equations*

Category	SCS	Model
Mean number of runoff events per season	7.04	15.76
Mean runoff depth per season (cm)	1.02	1.02
Mean runoff depth per event (cm)	0.14	0.07
Mean yearly maximum peak flow (m³sec⁻¹)	1.31	1.36
Standard deviation of yearly maximum Peak flows (m³sec⁻¹)	1.22	1.48

To complete the comparison of the two approaches, the SCS expressions were used to transform the same twenty-five-season simulated precipitation record into a corresponding record of runoff events. The statistics of the runoff data obtained from the two approaches are presented in table 12-7.

In terms of seasonal runoff totals and peaks, the two approaches yield impressively similar results. Since approximately half of all runoff events generated by the watershed model were negligible, the events-per-season and runoff-per-event categories also are almost identical for the two methodologies.

Computer execution time for the SCS simulation was 0.34 seconds at a cost of sixty cents.

CONCLUDING COMMENT

Within limits, both the watershed model and the SCS rainfall-runoff relationships successfully transform precipitation data into runoff estimates for desert watersheds. Both approaches are deterministic, are predicated on numerous assumptions, and in comparison with the actual hydrologic system are highly simplistic. This relative simplicity is understandable, considering the extreme complexity of the natural system. There is a tendency for models to become unwieldy as they are expanded to include more and more facets of the natural system. It is unlikely that a totally comprehensive watershed model will ever be made that will answer all questions. However, if used with discretion, models can be extremely useful tools for aiding understanding of desert hydrology.

REFERENCES

Berkas, W. R. 1978. *Deterministic Watershed Model for Evaluating the Effects of Surface Mining on Hydrology.* M.S. thesis. Univ. Arizona.

Chow, V. T. 1959. *Open Channel Hydraulics.* McGraw-Hill, New York, 680 pp.

Cowan, W. L. 1956. Estimating hydraulic roughness coefficients. *Agric. Eng.* 37:473–475.

Fogel, M. M. 1969. The effect of storm variability on runoff from small semiarid watersheds. *Trans. Am. Soc. Agric. Eng.* 12:808–812.

Fogel, M. M., and L. Duckstein. 1970. Prediction of convective storm runoff in semiarid regions, pp. 465–478. In *Proc. IASH-UNESCO Symp. on the Results of Research on Representative and Experimental Basins, Wellington, New Zealand.*

Green, C. R., and W. D. Sellers. 1964. *Arizona Climate.* Univ. Arizona Press, Tucson, 503 pp.

Hillel, D. 1977. *Computer Simulation of Soil-Water Dynamics: A Compendium of Recent Work.* International Development Research Center, Ottawa, Canada, 214 pp.

Huggins, L. F., and E. J. Monke. 1968. A mathematical model for simulating the hydrologic response of a watershed. *Water Resourc. Res.* 4:329–339.

Huggins, L. F., and E. J. Monke. 1970. *Mathematical Simulation of Hydrologic Events on Ungauged Watersheds.* Water Resourc. Res. Center, Purdue Univ., Lafayette, Ind., 46 pp.

Musgrave, G. W., and H. N. Holtan. 1964. Infiltration, pp. 12–15. In V. T. Chow (ed.), *Handbook of Applied Hydrology.* McGraw-Hill, New York.

Renard, K. G. 1970. *The Hydrology of Semiarid Rangeland Watersheds.* USDA, Agric. Res. Service, ARS-41-162, Washington, D.C., 26 pp.

Soil Conservation Service. 1972. *Hydrology. Sec. 4 SCS National Engineering Handbook.* U.S. Dept. Agric., Washington, D.C.

Thames, J. L., E. Arvizo, J. Kramer, and L. Hekman. 1974. *Tucson Validation Site.* J. Thames, Coordinator. US/IBP Desert Biome Res. Memo. 74-3, 33 pp.

13
Desert Hydrologic Systems

Daniel D. Evans and *John L. Thames*

Water availability to plants is a principal component of any definition of a desert. Water can be related directly or indirectly to most properties and processes of desert ecosystems. The pronounced spatial and temporal diversity of plant species composition and spacings, and even animal species and behavior, is primarily a reflection of precipitation characteristics in relation to evapotranspiration rates as they influence water availability. Because of the extreme temporal variation of available soil moisture, desert ecosystems are among the most diverse natural systems.

An understanding of desert ecosystems must be based, therefore, on knowledge of the hydrologic properties of desert regions. In essence, the previous chapters have presented various components of the hydrologic system, both on a microscale and a macroscale. This chapter briefly integrates what has been covered earlier, utilizing the hydrologic cycle concept.

Conceptually, desert hydrologic systems are subsystems of the global hydrologic system, which in turn is strongly interactive with global energy distribution and flow. Therefore, any macroscale treatment of deserts must consider global water and energy systems. However, deserts may be simply viewed on a microscale as open systems with inflow and outflow at specified boundaries. With this perspective, desert hydrologic systems are in some respects simpler than most other hydrologic systems. Water entering the system is mostly lost from the system near where it enters, with only a small percentage of annual precipitation moving as runoff to another location. Also deep percolation of water is usually negligible in typical desert regions. Hence, the horizontal boundaries of the system may be taken as just above the plant canopy and just below the root zone in the soil. The system components are, then, the processes and storages within this relatively narrow band near the earth's surface. However, runoff cannot be completely ignored because the amount and effects can be sizable during an occasional event.

The hydrologic processes involved are precipitation entering the system, interception, retention and detention on the soil surface, infiltration and evaporation at the soil surface, transpiration by plants, transport of vapor out of the system, and runoff. Each of these processes will be discussed in light of the information presented in the previous chapters.

Although precipitation normally follows a seasonal pattern with one or more periods of heavy precipitation, the variations within the pattern are usually extreme. The variability tends to increase with decreasing annual precipitation. Present statistical techniques using historical data provide estimates of means and other statistical parameters, but forecasting of precipitation with the extreme variations and most-often short-term and scattered data lacks precision even for expected annual magnitudes. However, considerable research has been done on the character of stochastically variable rainfall in arid and semiarid regions using event-based data.

In the western United States, the characteristics of summer convectional storms usually are different from winter frontal storms. Summer storms are generally higher in intensity, shorter in duration, and cover less area than do winter storms. Also, they tend to occur in an independent manner in time and space. Therefore, frequency distributions are more nearly of the Poisson type. Event-based data have been analyzed using stochastic models based on number of events per unit of time (season of year), interarrival time between events, depth of precipitation per event, duration of precipitation, and maximum fifteen-minute intensity of rainfall. Utilizing event-based data yields more data points for frequency analysis than when using monthly averages.

Winter storms do not show the same degree of independence as summer storms do. Winter storms tend to come in sequence in which one storm follows another in a short time interval. Under certain climatic conditions, however, individual storms appear to be independent of other ones. A more complicated, mixed model is necessary to describe winter storms.

Such stochastic models have been useful when coupled to a deterministic model of rainfall runoff in the design of engineering structures. Research on desert precipitation has been limited compared to that for more humid regions, and further research on models and statistical techniques is needed to gain a better understanding of this important input to desert ecosystems.

Precipitation interception by desert plant canopies, although small in magnitude, can markedly affect the spatial distribution of water reaching the soil surface, which in turn affects depth of water penetration into the soil. Many desert plants have morphological features that are affective in concentrating precipitation at the plant base or at drip locations. Although interception may be less than 5 percent of precipitation, concentration effects may amplify the amount of water reaching certain areas of the soil surface by a hundred times. The greater depth of wetting alters the evaporation rate and thus yields more opportunity time for water uptake by plants. Interception of not only rainfall but snow and fog can be a significant factor in desert ecosystems.

Measurement of interception by desert vegetation requires numerous samples because of the large coefficient of variation and small amounts. Evans, Sammis, and Asher (1976) measured throughfall for creosote bush and bursage using miniature rain gauges. With three gauges under each of the two plant types and ten gauges in the open, an average of 90 percent of total rainfall occurred as throughfall for creosote bush and 68 percent for bursage. However, the percentage for different storms ranged from 67 to greater than 100 and from 26 to 100 for creosote bush and bursage, respectively. Some measurements showed greater throughfall than rainfall due to the confounding drip phenomenon. Even though interception and its effects on spatial distribution of applied water at the surface may be difficult to assess, its recognition as a significant phenomenon is important in analyzing desert ecosystems.

The microrelief of desert soil surfaces usually exhibits roughness sufficient to retain water in depressions, thus reducing surface runoff. It also increases the spatial variability of soil moisture following a precipitation event. Although the soil surface elevation is commonly greater under plants than between plants, infiltration rates are usually higher under the plants because of soil characteristics and, therefore, ponding of water there is not as frequent as between plants. Ponding in depressions may also greatly affect erosion and sediment deposition as well as seed distribution, which in turn affects plant dispersal. Surface water retention and detention on the soil surface allows more time for infiltration and also affects soil moisture variability.

The infiltration rate of a desert soil depends on many factors, including initial water content, soil texture, plant cover and litter, and rainfall intensity and duration. When rainfall intensity exceeds the infiltration capacity and ponding on the surface occurs, the infiltration rate may be described by an equation such as (Philips, 1957):

$$i = at^{-\frac{1}{2}} + b \qquad\qquad (13.1)$$

where a and b are constant soil parameters and t is time from initial infiltration. Parameter a is referred to as sorptivity, while b approaches the saturated hydraulic conductivity of the soil. At small times the first term on the right is dominant, but as time increases a constant rate equal to b is approached. In the derivation of the equation from a theoretical basis, the following assumptions are made: (1) soil properties are uniform at all depths, (2) soil depth is infinite in the vertical direction, (3) initial water content is uniform with depth, and (4) water ponding is continual on the soil surface. Under natural desert conditions, these assumptions are not completely met, but to simplify analyses, they are usually assumed valid.

Time required to reach a nearly constant infiltration rate depends on soil and rainfall characteristics. Nnaji, Sammis, and Evans (1975), using a rainfall simulator on the Silverbell desert site near Tucson, Arizona, found that a nearly constant rate was established after about fifteen minutes of water application. During their study, a and b of equation 13.1 were determined at seventy-five sites, representing four soil series and nonvegetated and vegetated areas. Although the magnitude of the variability and the limited number of samples for each condition contributed to the result of nonsignificant differences among soil series or plant cover, results did show an average initial infiltration rate of 90 cm/hr and a final rate of 4.8 cm/hr. With these high infiltration rates, it is not surprising that runoff occurs only for extremely high-intensity storms. All of the soils included in the study had a surface texture of gravelly-sandy loam, with up to 70 percent of the surface covered by gravel. However, infiltration rates for desert soils in general would be expected to be highly variable depending on soil texture, structure, salinity, and exchangeable sodium percentage.

After it enters the soil and surface infiltration ceases, water continues to move due to potential gradients. The rate of movement is relatively rapid at first, then decreases with time as the potential gradient and soil moisture related hydraulic conductivity decrease. The commonly used concept of field capacity may not be useful for desert conditions because of the normally shallow depth of wetting. The vertical potential gradient would be expected to be greater for shallow wettings than when a deep soil zone is wetted, as may exist in irrigated areas or in higher rainfall regions. Also, evaporation at the soil surface usually commences immediately after a rainfall event, and the moisture content in the wetted zone decreases as a result of both evaporation and downward redistribution.

A sound theoretical basis exists for predicting water movement through unsaturated soils, especially for isothermal conditions. Theory is based on the equation on continuity coupled to a set of initial and boundary conditions. Several analytical and numerical approaches are available for predicting moisture content as a function of time and depth for selected conditions, provided that realistic soil parameters are available. The necessary parameters, soil moisture diffusivity and conductivity, depend on soil characteristics and moisture content, and adequate methods are not available for simply estimating them in the undisturbed field state. This is particularly true under the variable conditions found in deserts. Also, boundary conditions are likely to change with time because of variable meteorological factors.

Under isothermal conditions, water vapor movement can be considered negligible. The narrow range of relative humidity is from 100 percent at saturation to 98.8 percent at -15 bars potential (corresponding to the permanent wilting point). This small difference coupled with the small diffusion coefficient for even dry soil results in a relatively low net mass transfer of water vapor compared to liquid transfer under isothermal conditions. Under desert conditions, isothermal conditions can seldom be realistically assumed. If a significant temperature gradient exists, vapor transfer may exceed liquid transfer, particularly at low soil moisture contents. Modeling techniques must then involve simultaneous energy and water transport equations. The analysis requires additional soil parameters and becomes quite complex. As a result, most analyses are made assuming isothermal conditions. These analyses, even with several tentative assumptions, help in gaining an improved perception of soil moisture behavior under complex field conditions. To gain an improved understanding, more sophisticated models are required, and more suitable methods of estimating soil parameters must be developed.

Evaporation from the soil is a major component of the hydrologic balance of a desert region. Under isothermal conditions, the evaporation process is limited to very near the soil surface, but where strong temperature gradients exist, evaporation may occur from several centimeters of depth. The large amplitude of the diurnal cycle of soil surface temperature common to hot deserts causes evaporation sometimes to occur well below the soil surface. The change in temperature between night and day causes a reversal in vapor movement. However, there appears to be a net daily movement upward to the soil surface for at least portions of the year. The consistent flow of geothermal energy to the surface may contribute to this net flux of vapor.

From studies previously discussed, there were no measurable differences in soil moisture for vegetated and nonvegetated desert plots, indicating that direct evaporation from the soil was as effective as evapotranspiration in reducing soil moisture content during the periods of measurement. If more precise and numerous measurements were made in a replicated experiment, perhaps a difference could be measured. Under bare soil conditions, annual evaporation was found to be essentially equal to annual precipitation minus runoff.

Evaporation at or near the soil surface is governed by climatic and soil factors. Climatic factors at the soil surface, such as net radiation, relative humidity, and wind speed, are influenced by plant morphology and density. Sparse desert vegetation certainly does not alter climatic variables as much as a more dense canopy would. Therefore, the evaporative demand of the surface atmosphere is greater for the desert than for most other agricultural conditions.

The evaporation rate may approach that of a free water surface for short periods of time following rainfall events. With time after a rainfall event, the evaporation rate will normally decrease rapidly to a value less than 1 mm/day. Although the rate may approach zero, the finite rate may continue to be significant in reducing the soil moisture content during long periods without rain, and the effect appears to extend to a greater depth than is usually associated with evaporation losses.

The presence of desert plants does not appear to significantly alter the rate of flow of vapor to the atmosphere under a range of conditions. Actual transpiration per unit area by desert plants during extended periods without rain is low because of the sparse plant cover and the transpiration control mechanisms of many types of desert plants, such as stomatal closing, impervious cuticle, and leaf surface reduction. Caldwell et al. (1977) estimated that no more than 50 percent of effective rainfall was directly transpired by two cold desert plant communities. The remainder was assumed lost by direct evaporation. The percentage would be expected to be even lower in hot deserts. Precise measurements would be required to differentiate between direct soil evaporation and transpiration, especially under highly stressed conditions.

As with evaporation alone, evapotranspiration may be near potential rates immediately following rainfall and similarly decreases to values less than 1 mm/day during extended periods without precipitation. Evapotranspiration may remain high along permanent water courses or where the water table remains close to the surface. Such areas are common and important to desert regions.

A potential flow model appears to describe satisfactorily the flow of water through the soil-plant atmosphere continuum. Water flows due to the continually decreasing moisture potential from the soil, through the plant, and to the atmosphere with the rate in each segment governed by the product of the potential gradient and a conductance parameter. Potential theory has allowed a unified approach to soil moisture flow, plant moisture flow, and vapor flow into the atmosphere. Models have been developed to examine flow through the entire soil-plant-atmosphere system, but realistic values of the variable, and often transient, parameters of the models are most often a constraining factor in their use. However, model studies have improved the understanding of the moisture transport phenomenon even if idealized systems must be employed.

Although surface water runoff is infrequent in deserts, it may be important to many considerations. Also, water entering a desert region from a higher elevation may greatly affect water availability to desert plants and soil surface morphology. Numerous rainfall runoff models have been proposed for predicting runoff and sediment behavior. Obviously a realistic, complete model would represent a segment of the hydrologic cycle and, if developed, would provide a quantitative method for complete analysis of desert water systems. Such a complete model would need to incorporate the rainfall input, overland flow, stream flow, infiltration into the soil and channel bottoms, evaporation from free water surfaces, and soil moisture depletion through evapotranspiration and, possibly, deep seepage. The hydrologic processes could not be described completely unless the hydrologic model had an interface with an energy model and a sediment transport model.

Because of the many stochastic processes and parameters involved, simplifications are essential for pragmatic reasons. Adequate simplified computer models do exist for restricted purposes, but they require site specific adaptations and calibration.

An important aspect of desert hydrology is associated with the lineal strips along stream channels that commonly traverse deserts. These areas can differ markedly in water availability and vegetation from the surrounding desert. Soil moisture and possibily a relatively shallow aquifer are recharged during stream-flow events, thus amplifying the water supply to plants to such an extent that phreatophytic plants are common. The areal coverage of phreatophytes in the fourteen western U.S. states has been estimated to be 11,090,000 acres, with an annual water use of 16,750,000 acre-feet (Todd, 1970). Essentially all of the acreage is located in arid and semiarid regions. An annual rate of evapotranspiration of up to nine acre-feet per acre has been measured. The high water usage and the excellent wildlife habitat make these areas important considerations in analyzing desert ecosystems.

The hydrology of the stream-influenced areas is significantly different from that of the surrounding desert. Evapotranspiration rates may be near potential rates for most of the year. A shallow aquifer may provide an ample water supply for perennial plants that is independent of local precipitation characteristics. During periods of stream flow and potential recharge of the aquifer, the diurnal cycle of evapotranspiration causes a similar cycle in stream-flow and water table elevation. The magnitude of the oscillation in the water table depth is dependent on evapotranspiration rates, as well as the transmissivity of the aquifer and distance from the stream source. Bouwer (1975), for example, presented a simplified mathematical treatment of groundwater recharge in the presence of phreatophytes.

Another hydrologic aspect of many desert regions is a relatively deep underlying aquifer, which may be exploited as a water supply. Groundwater exists at variable depths under large portions of the deserts of the world, and its development has played an important role in desert transformations, such as those associated with irrigated agriculture and urbanization. As an example, nearly half of the water depletion for all uses in Arizona comes from aquifers beneath the arid and semiarid regions of the state. For large desert regions, withdrawal of groundwater greatly exceeds recharge, resulting in a gradual decline in water table elevation. This lowering of the water table has had a direct ecological effect in certain areas through the disappearance of phreatophytic plants and their replacement by typical desert vegetation. Also, in certain areas irrigated agriculture has been abandoned because of the cost of increased pumping lift, resulting in a drastic change in vegetation.

Playas are also important features of arid regions that influence desert hydrology. Playas are undrained desert basins that become shallow lakes during periods of surface runoff. They provide a sink for water, sediments, and salts. Water entering a playa either evaporates or percolates downward, providing a possible recharge source to an underlying aquifer.

Human-related activities have greatly influenced the hydrologic characteristics of deserts. Probably the most significant are those associated with irrigation development. Currently about 20 million acres, which were originally desert, are under irrigation in the United States west of the Rocky Mountains. Obviously irrigation development has significantly altered hydrologic conditions within irrigated boundaries, but there are effects beyond the boundaries. Side effects include increased population in the surrounding areas with all of its ramifications, changes in drainage patterns due to land shaping, changes ensuing from excess irrigation water disposal, changes due to possible subsidence and vegetation as a result of lowering of the water table, and possible changes in climatic conditions resulting from increased regional evapotranspiration rates.

Other agricultural effects on desert hydrology include livestock grazing, water harvesting techniques, and desert farming. Overgrazing has long been recognized as a contributing factor to desertification in many areas through its impact on such soil characteristics as compaction, water infiltration rate, and erodibility. Development of groundwater for stock watering in water-scarce areas has tended to cause an increase in livestock population beyond the carrying capacity of the land, thus accelerating the desertification process in many regions. Water harvesting techniques involving practices that reduce the soil infiltration capacity and increase runoff from a catchment area obviously have a pronounced effect on the hydrologic properties of the treated area. Also, practices employed to enhance and concentrate surface runoff for crop production in arid regions have hydrologic consequences.

Urbanization of desert regions has an inescapable pronounced effect of hydrologic properties of the region. Through the removal of vegetation, construction of buildings and the paving of streets, and other changes, surface runoff characteristics are greatly altered. A sixfold increase in total runoff has been measured for a section of Tucson, Arizona, upon urbanization. In addition to changes in total runoff, peak flows are increased and contaminants in the runoff water are increased as deserts become urbanized. Other possible hydraulic effects of urbanization may include those associated with water supply development, sewage water disposal, transportation and communication systems, flood control measures, energy development, and recreation. Many of these impacts are felt at a distance beyond the urbanized area. As an example, recreational impacts may be through the development of water-based recreational facilities and off-road vehicle traffic at some distance from a population center. Another far-reaching effect of urbanization and industrialization in general is the possibility of changes being induced in global air mass movements due to increased carbon dioxide and particulate matter emitted to the atmosphere. Although not documented, this effect has been proposed as a major cause of shifting rainfall patterns and, thus, a major contributing factor to the desertification process.

The hydrologic aspects of deserts point to the need for a much better understanding of water in desert systems than exists at present. Studies to date have given only a meager insight into the complex properties and processes of the spatially and temporally variable deserts. Much additional research is needed to understand and manage these fascinating regions of the earth.

REFERENCES

Bouwer, H. 1975. Predicting reduction in water losses from open channels by phreatophyte control. *Water Resour. Res.* **11**:96–101.

Caldwell, M. M., R. S. White, R. T. Moore, and L. B. Camp. 1977. Carbon balance, productivity, and water use of cold-winter desert shrub communities dominated by C_3 and C_4 species. *Oecologia* **29**:275–300.

Evans, D. D., T. W. Sammis, and J. Ben Asher. 1976. *Plant Growth and Water Transfer Interactive Processes under Desert Conditions.* US/IBP Desert Biome Res. Memo. 76-33, Utah State Univ., Logan, Utah, 14 pp.

Nnaji, S., T. W. Sammis, and D. D. Evans. 1975. Variability of infiltration characteristics and water yield of a semi-arid catchment. In *Hydrology and Water Resources in Arizona and the Southwest.* Proc. 1975 Mtg. Ariz. Sec. Am. Water Res. Assoc., Hydrol. Sec. Ariz. Acad. Sci., 11–12 April 1975, Tempe, Ariz.

Philips, J. R. 1957. The theory of infiltration: 1: The infiltration equation and its solution. *Soil Sci.* **83**:345–357.

Todd, D. K., ed. 1970. *The Water Encyclopedia.* Water Information Center, Port Washington, New York.

Plant Species Index

Subject Index

CKKD